THE
SOULFUL CHILD

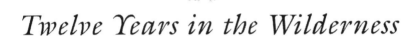

Twelve Years in the Wilderness

THE
SOULFUL CHILD

Twelve Years in the Wilderness

CHLOE RACHEL GALLAWAY

Disclaimer: In this memoir, the author told the story that she needed to tell, listened to her inner voice for guidance, and relied on emotional memory, as well as rote memory, to access her story. She also relied on her mother's stories and her brother's memory for accuracy of details.

Editing by Penelope Love and Heloise Jones
Copyediting and proofreading by Jeanne Shannon
Cover design by Rolf Busch
With editorial assistance from Kathryn de Grasse
Front cover photo by Mady Maraia
Back cover photo by Christian Diaz de Bedoya

Library of Congress Cataloging-in-Publication Data

Gallaway, Chloe Rachel
The Soulful Child: Twelve Years in the Wilderness

p. cm.
Paperback ISBN: 978-0-9975470-8-5
Ebook ISBN: 978-0-9975470-9-2
Library of Congress Control Number: 2017949774

10 9 8 7 6 5 4 3 2
Second Edition, June 2019

CITRINE PUBLISHING
Murphy, NC, U.S.A.
828.585.7030
Publisher@CitrinePublishing.com
www.CitrinePublishing.com

To my mother and father
and my Ida

Prologue

On the side of the mountain, I stood a pillar of strength against the forcing winds, an inner knowing grounding my feet in the midst of a storm. Bundled in a brown corduroy jacket with an orange sweater underneath, I was one with nature. Long, thick locks of brownish-blond curls fell around my shoulders. Dimples had been etched in my cheeks at birth, but my face was solemn. No smile for the camera about to capture my photograph. I didn't even know what a camera was. The flash went off. My light brown eyes were still, glazed over, peering deeply ahead. I did not blink.

No blinking, not in this life where winter meets the bones under the skin. The blizzards come fast and hard in the woods. No time for blinking in this realm. One must gather firewood, milk goats, grow food, and prepare for whatever comes. Winter is long, the days darker even as the sun peeks through a benevolent sky with grace when the clouds part. The clouds part like the sea did when Moses from the Bible parted the sea for his people.

I was one of his people too, my father had said, only thousands of years later when the world was buzzing with society, evolved. Machine pressed against machine, cars roared, towers stood, buses moved amidst oil burning into the air. All this buzzing with no direction, that's what my father taught me.

Thousands of years after Moses parted the sea, I was born and lived, but I was not of the world like everyone else. I had never seen a bus or a tower. I wasn't buzzing without direction. I was running up a hillside, across a mountaintop, where trees streamed for miles, and red and orange cliff sides peeked top over top. I lived as one of God's children. I only knew this life existed.

I was a peaceful child in the woods. I was connected, grounded to the earth. Work and play meshed together like a woven blanket. All the colors of life blended into one.

The woods cannot calm every human mind, and my father's mind was not always calm. He ran to the woods to slow it down, but it caught up to him no matter where he went. He, too, was a child of God yet had demons raging inside. He couldn't always connect to the peaceful place deep within himself. He was a boy born of the world, where machine pressed upon machine, man pressed upon man, and father upon son. He could not escape this pressing. It pushed at his insides and breathed fire into his heart, his lungs, his sternum, and right out of his fist.

Yet I also knew him to be a completely different man, from one rising sun to the next. When he would gather wood at 4 a.m. to build a fire in the cabin, kind and gentle were his eyes, soft his hands upon the guitar strings. He played the chords of my life and the rhythm was flowing and smooth. He was one with nature, wise in his actions and footsteps as he cleared a path to build a strong foundation for our lives. Though he wanted the woods to be our place of refuge it was not always so, because he was both of these men.

My mother fell in love with my father in another time, another place, far removed from the woods of my father's dreams. She like so many was moved by his hands upon the guitar strings, his voice piercing the air when he sang, his strength and love one powerful force igniting a religious movement within her. She would follow him without question, and that she did, leaving behind a life of privilege and possibility. My mother became a rebel, refusing to become a teacher or a nurse, the two most respectable careers for a woman in her time. She pursued art modeling and a rebellious social life, which went so far as to throw a party for Bob Dylan in her apartment one night. She traveled to and from Mexico exploring ideas of a new and enchanting world. She had friends who had gone to San Francisco. She had heard it was the place to be.

My mother had been a ballet dancer for fifteen years. She wore the most delicate dresses and fitted her body into everything princess-like. Her rebel attitude led her to buy a motorcycle. She rode her Honda 350 from Austin, Texas, several hundred miles to Dallas to Houston, her red hair flying in the wind, white scarf tied around her neck, the open road before her. She was unstoppable. When it came time to drop her life of going to class, making good grades and upholding the dream her mother had for her, she had enough wind in her hair to let it all go.

My mother met my father on the streets of Haight-Ashbury in San Francisco. She sat across from him in a circle of musicians, Janis Joplin being among them. It was a group jam and my father was the only man that played the twelve-string guitar. Life was in motion, present, real. The times, they were a-changing, as Bob Dylan had sung only a few days before on stage. My mother was surrounded by what she called "true talents in the flesh" and my father was the best of them all, she said.

Two years later, she was giving birth to her first son on a dirt floor inside a teepee, the pressing and pushing of each contraction bringing her to her knees. She was a young woman with little knowledge of childbirth. She learned quickly of the searing pain that only God can help one understand. My brother's little body came through, the gushing blood spread onto the dirt floor and cries of a newborn sounded over the hilltop in the early morning hours; my mother's faith was transformed.

For all that my parents were and were not, they gave me life. Gave me a life most unpredictable. My father had been voted most likely to be the next President of the United States of America in his high school yearbook. He was the all-American kid, the quarterback of the football team. He got straight A's in school, was accomplished in Latin and had a benefactor who paid his way to an elite private school on the east coast. My father was pure charisma. In 1968, he stood on the verge of fame as the lead singer for a band called "The Human Factor." He chose anything but fame and left the world behind to raise a family in the wilderness. He would say this life chose him. I can't confirm this to be true, but I can say he gave me a life worth living, full of the realness of every tree branch, every barefoot moment in the dirt, every warm summer sunbeam melting on my child face, fall's fresh air, winter's harsh blows, and spring's soft smiles. I was given the gift of living in nature right from the womb and learned from the truest part of myself.

THE
SOULFUL CHILD

The sun lit the earth, its yellow haze a filter to the eye. Where, Mommy, where, Daddy, should I go today? I can pick the berries from the bush, pick the flower from the plant, touch the bee's wings as she flies to me.

Child, you shall not fear. You shall not be stung by the bee nor by the pain of mankind upon your chest, upon your brow. No, child, the world is not for you. There suffering comes from the dulling down of the truth, from lies spread wide. There is no place to hide and you will desire to go back to the womb. We shall meet in this world someday, eye to eye, but for now, while you grow, keep your eye steady, keep your face lit by the rays of the sun, your hand upon the fresh berries, ripe and red with the brightness of love shining through them. Keep your eye, too, upon the cross, the blood red of Christ, for like juice through the berries, the fruit of life comes through his blood. Take up arms and feel the earth between your bare toes. You were born to this foreign land for a purpose, for many reasons yet to be revealed to you. Keep your eyes upon the light of the sun, your hand upon the fruit, your heart upon each beat, thump, thump, thump inside your chest. Beat, beat, beat, the drum of life drums, God has printed his mark upon you. Feel it now, breathe it now, hold it now, and keep your eyes upon the sun.

The Soul Answers the Call

I sat in the back cab of a four-wheel drive, dark blue pick-up. The smell of new was everywhere. It felt like a box of armor. Slightly tinted windows filtered a hazy rain that drizzled outside. I pushed my feet against the plush new floorboards and braced my back against the cushioned seat. There I felt the heaviness of my newborn baby in my arms. I lifted the weight to feel her resistance. My firstborn, a daughter, lay stretched across me, her three-month-old pale, little legs and feet dangling off my lap, her perfectly round head covered with wisps of red hair brushed to the left. Holding her, I looked down at her perfection: her big, blue eyes with soft, golden eyelashes, her tiny fingers tucked at her chest, her pink, round mouth on my breast.

My first child had sprung from the womb—the earth shifted and I shifted with it, a mighty force that brought me to my knees and awoke me at the same time. My arms fought tiredness as she nursed, the life-giving force of love pouring into her. Her eyes danced slowly open, then closed, open then closed as she drifted into a soft sleep. The rain fell. It was late afternoon on a fall day. I let her body rest onto my lap, my hands still cupping her on each side. My heart was heavy as I looked out the window of the truck. Just to the right of me was my childhood home. I had brought my daughter to meet my father, the man who had given me a life, one I still could not wrap my heart around. But on this day, unlike so many days of my childhood, I was no longer running away from my father. On this day, I was coming home.

The two-room, cedarwood-and-pine-board shack tilted to the side, looking as though it might fall over at any time. A piece of stained glass hung in the window, a small cross about four inches long, the center of the cross red and the T of the cross blue. The rain stopped. A stream of yellow sunlight streaked the acres of piñon and cedar forest, the light making its mark right on the cross hanging in the window. God was in me, outside of me, all around me. My daughter slept, no movement in her body, her chest breathing in and out. I watched her breathe and wondered how I had survived the childhood I'd had. How delicate we are coming into this world, how fragile our bodies, our minds, our little hearts to be molded by fear or by love. But oh how resilient. How tough, how strong, how unbreakable we are when we don't even know it. My father must have known it, and so he thought raising me on three hundred acres on a mountain range, and letting me run wild like a mountain goat, would instill in me a realness of faith and heart that the outside world could not give me. He followed this dream. So it was, that I would learn so many lessons by being broken apart and molded back together, time and time again.

I was ready to take Sofia, my Little Wisdom, inside the cabin, when I looked back at the cabin window and there an old man appeared. He was tall, and slightly hunched forward. A gray and white mixed beard covered most of his face. His weepy eyes looked with longing past the cross in the window. This was my father. He had made it to sixty-seven years, an old man for the life he had lived. My eyes rested softly on him, my heart sank inside my chest, the weight of my daughter in my arms lifted, and for a moment I was a child holding a child.

It was from that very moment that my book would be born.

My heart stretched across an unwritten page and a voice called out to me.

"You know your father is going to die."

With a deep-seated need to understand the man who gave me life, and an internal voice like a herd of wild horses stampeding across my chest, I knew I had to write this story.

I will no longer be afraid to find out who I really am.

The Singing Heart

There was no radio, no TV, no outside source to entertain. My father's music kept us alive through many winter days and lulled me to sleep in spring, summer, and fall. He was a man who sang of the earth and the sky, the world and the heart of man, the dark and the light, the love of God, and the hope of mankind. His songs taught me all about photosynthesis, and how the rain watered the trees, how the trees needed the sunlight to grow and produce oxygen, giving us air to breathe. His words wove a magical tale of how everything and everybody was needed.

When he told his stories with song, it was an even bigger magic. He sat in front of the fire, his feet with wool socks tapping the wood floor, his strong hands a soft whisper on the guitar strings. He sang of the moon and the sun dancing in circles together. The sun was like the father pouring out his bright light and strength to better the world; the moon was like the mother, graceful, mysterious, with a strong pull upon the earth. The earth was like the children who danced between the sun and the moon, the moon pulling the earth along with her, making the ocean waters glide back and forth from sea to shore. The sun tugged at the earth and the moon, making a life circle of up and down, round and round.

I could see the dance in my mind, feel the dance in my body—I was living the dance in the woods. We woke when the sun came up, and we crawled into bed just after the sun went down. We planted by the seasons and knew time by the sun's location in the sky. At night the moon was my only guide; there was no true darkness. Life had a rhythm and we lived within that rhythm.

God's Country

The September morning sun cast slanting rays across the yellow and brown dirt. I skipped through the front yard twirling in circles, my peach faded dress covering over my brown pants and flapping to the sides as I spun. My multicolored knit hat was tucked tight around my ears, and my orange sweater was buttoned taut over my dress. My father loaded the truck with small brown burlap sacks once filled with beans. His black cowboy hat was tilted slightly down. I could not see his eyes, only his thick, untamed beard.

In five-ten-fifteen minutes, we would load into the truck and drive away.

There was no clock to show the passing of time, only the pounding of my heart that raced through my chest, past my legs and right out my feet. All I could do was dance. It had been six months since I had been off the mountain. We piled into the back of my father's red '57 Chevy.

There were six of us children, and we were all about two and a half years apart. Except John, the eldest, and Carey, who were fifteen months apart. Then came Nye, me, Rose and Jacinth.

John's body resembled my father's, tall with broad shoulders and soldier-like straight lines in his back.

Carey was muscular, but shorter than John. He was witty and moved his body swiftly, like an arrow through the woods.

Nye was still small. His frame was athletic, his arms and legs still trying to reach their muscular potential. Nye was shy and held back his voice until he had something really important to say. Every so often, he would make a joke that seemed like it came out of nowhere.

I was a mixture of my brothers, strong and quiet, and observant, too. On this day I was six, grown up enough to notice that Rose was barely old enough to make this trip. She was walking but still needed to hold someone's hand. She too was shy and clung to Mom, Dad, or John, depending on who was there for her to grab onto. Her blond ringlets of hair naturally flowed around her neck and down her chest. Her skin was porcelain, her hands little, but her walk sturdy. She always looked as though she was taking it all in, but she never spoke.

I sat squeezed in between my brothers, John on one side and Nye and Carey on the other. Rose sat on John's lap; his long arms reached all the way around her, holding her tight like a seat belt. We were a collage of colors—orange, purple, green, and red—in our hand-me-down sweaters, corduroy pants and knitted hats that my mother had made for us. Our skin was slightly darkened by patches of brown dirt from weeks past.

The smoke from the two-room cabin rose slowly from the chimney into the cloudless air. I watched my mother standing in the doorway, holding baby Jacinth in her arms. His tiny feet stuck out from the edge of the blue knit blanket. She had worn the same long, brown wool skirt for a week. Her auburn hair was pulled back from her face and wrapped loosely in a bun.

Poor mama, I thought. *She has to stay behind with the baby.*

But as we pulled away, I noticed the lines in her face relax and a glimpse of a smile appeared.

No seat belts, hands free swaying in the wind, we traveled up the long canyon road. We climbed higher and higher. The air felt cool and thick. The truck etched its way through a tunneling, bumpy road, spruce and aspen trees brushing against the sides of the pickup bed. I could feel my body vibrating until the truck jolted to a stop. All at once, my brothers and I hopped over the side of the pickup. My brothers were strong and fearless. I saw no reason I couldn't keep up with them. My father handed each of us a bag.

"Let's meet back here once you have a full bag of raspberries," he said. Taking my little sister by the hand, he set off. My brothers shoved one another back and forth, making small talk as they walked away. To prove my independence, I marched in the opposite direction.

I walked alone up a slight hill and through a grove of aspen trees, the leaves a delicate shade of yellow. I stopped and listened to the whispering of the leaves brushing back and forth, surrounded by a blanket of wild oregano plants, the tops beaming with deep purple flowers, the aspen leaves overhead glowing in the sunlight. Whoosh, whoosh, back and forth, the leaves danced.

These woods had a secret message, and that day they whispered it to me. I felt it with all my body seeping through me like a cool drink of water.

As I started through the field of oregano, the green leaves slipped against my pant legs, the minty thyme-like smell awakened my body, as a field of purple stretched out before me. I bent down and picked a handful of flowers to save for my mother. I held them tight in my hand.

I looked back and couldn't see my father or brothers anywhere. *I'll go a little ways further,* I thought, as I spotted a thick raspberry bush in the distance.

Fuchsia-red berries dangled heavily from the bush. I grabbed a handful. Bitter, sweet, soft, and moist—the colors of rain mixed with sun melted onto my tongue. I dropped the bag and shoved a handful into my mouth. Juice ran down the sides of my lips. After several handfuls, I realized that I had eaten away at the goods while my bag lay empty. I began to pluck away, hurrying to fill my bag, when I was interrupted by a loud crunching sound.

I peeked over the raspberry bush, and there, not far off, was a black bear. She looked stocky and round with thick fur covering her body. She was grounded on all four paws, sturdy and balanced; she was in her element. I clutched my bag tightly and pressed my feet into the solid earth.

My mind raced. *Should I hide…or run?*

My legs were heavy and I couldn't move. Then, a few seconds before my panic set in, I remembered what my father had told me about wild animals.

"Animals are only afraid when we are afraid," he had said.

My father's voice came through clearly to me now. I watched the bear intently.

"Don't run. Be calm. Stand up tall, and state your intentions to the animal."

The bear stood on all four legs, its nose twitching, its eyes bearing down at me. I gulped, my mouth dry as I pressed my lips together. I could see that there were no cubs around, and this gave me confidence to speak.

"I am here to pick the berries—I don't want to bother you."

The bear wobbled a few steps forward. I stood my ground with my feet planted firmly, my body facing the bear.

"Now you go on your way, and I'll go on mine."

We stood there for a moment, each of us taking in the other. She was beautiful. I had never used that word in a sentence of my own, but now I knew what it meant. Her light black fur was soft and fluffy, her eyes looked with longing. I waited, my body now calm, my mind still. She turned her head and started up the hillside away from me. I clung to my bag of berries until she made her way over the hill, her butt bobbing back and forth as she disappeared into the aspen trees.

As the sun sank low, lines of soft light stretched out from the aspen grove to the meadow of oregano—purple, green, yellow— the earth spun around me with color. I felt the chill of evening come over my body. I grabbed my bag and ran, tumbling over my footsteps all the way back to the truck. Out of breath, I yelled as I neared the pickup bed, "I saw a bear! I saw a bear!"

I came to a sudden stop in the dirt and leaned forward with my hands on my knees. My father was on the left side of the pickup bed loading a bag of oregano, the purple stems sticking out the top of the burlap sack.

He approached me, "You saw one, did you?"

He knelt down and looked at me. His face was soft in the evening light, tanned by the summer's sun. He wore a red handkerchief around his neck and his brownish red beard glistened in the light.

"Dad, Dad! She was right there when I looked up from the bush!" I breathed out all the words in one breath.

"Well, this is bear country. How big was she?"

Nye, Carey, and John came running from the hillside with bags full of raspberries.

"Look at my bag!" Carey shouted as he propelled his body forward, still running.

John and Nye walked behind him.

"She was big, Dad." I got out before the boys swarmed the truck. Dad stood up and announced it to my brothers.

"Chloe saw a bear."

"I did! I did!" I echoed.

"Cool!" Carey said. "Where is she?" he asked, looking off into the forest, his body ready to charge after her.

"She is already gone. I watched her climb over the hill through the trees," I said.

Dad went around and finished loading the truck. John and Nye asked about how big the bear was. I told them what she looked like, and how I wasn't afraid.

They both looked at me as though it was not a surprise that I wasn't scared.

"Good thing she didn't eat you," Nye said and poked me in the belly before climbing into the truck.

Rose looked tired. She sat in the back of the pickup bed, her head drooping down, her arms wrapped snug in her sweater. John climbed in and scooped her up onto his lap. I followed and curled up next to him and Rose, then Nye and Carey climbed in and smashed against us. The truck started, and we pulled away. I looked back down the long, bumpy road, the aspens glowing in the evening sunlight, the purple oregano fading into the distance. Dusk enveloped us as we drove. I leaned my head over onto Nye. The soft wind blew across our faces as we made our way down the mountain.

That day I came to know the woods and what my father saw in them. Secret messages encoded from God—a passage to an unknown place.

There is a place
Filled with grace
Where beauty abounds
I can be found
Traveling along
A canyon road
Carrying a
Delightful load
Of raspberries

Small Towns

Small towns are all across the lands of North America. Down in the Bible Belt, across the Mississippi River, or far to the western regions of the United States. In the dry deserts of Arizona and stark flatlands of California, with cacti popping up everywhere like parched townspeople, waiting for rain that may only come once a month. Keep going past all that dryness into the far west of the Oregon Mountains, where tall trees cascade overhead and thick, green blackberry bushes creep alongside the road. There off every highway, on every small dirt road winding through the backwoods, there is some small child putting their bare toes into the dirt.

There may never have been a town as small as mine, a place which drifted so far off the map that the actor Dennis Hopper himself could barely find it. After Dennis completed the movie *Easy Rider* in 1969, the picture of Peter Fonda riding his motorcycle across wide-open space symbolized the idea of freedom to many. Freedom was a big lump in the throat and on the minds of thousands of baby boomers rising from the underbelly of cultural norms and political ideals they couldn't agree with. For some, like my parents, fixed ideas embodied the oppression of the '50s still clinging, gnawing at the core of the American culture. Just as the battles were being fought on the open grass fields of Vietnam, so were there battles on American soil. The ropes of history were sure to be cut, a knife straight through the center of the rising social and political warfare bringing the questions that would be asked for generations to come: *Who are we? What does it mean to be free in a society? What is freedom of expression when it comes to our sexuality, our religion, and our ideas about war and peace?*

Ideals of the baby boomer generation were awakening as a movement among the hippies, a movement that would change the course of American history that became known as the "counterculture." The music of the sixties was alive and pumping through the veins of every young person. But for those labeled as hippies it was about questioning the status quo, and bringing peace through connection, community, and acceptance of one's ideals and desires to live a free life. One in which the government didn't print its mark on everything and every decision you made. Inside of the counterculture movement, every person was an individual gaining new awareness around what it meant to be a part of a group, a part of the movement. As the oldest daughter of a counterculture figure, this is how I experienced the story of the '60s through my parents' constant reconstruction of it.

They told me that their friend Dennis Hopper had broken a chain bound by fame and was looking for a hidden sacred-space to crash on whenever Hollywood rubbed him or dubbed him the wrong way. A place to escape should the world come to an end amid the chaos of the times. He found the small town of Lindrith, New Mexico, tucked in the far northern part of the state, not far from the Colorado border. Land near the Jicarilla Apache reservation, untouched soil, where wild horses ran with gusto and southern winds blew old windmills late into the day. You could drive for miles with little civilization to be seen. Beyond all that was civilized was a 320-acre piece of land at the end of the last dirt road that curved its way up a vast rocky hillside and tree-covered mountain range. Acres of pine, piñon, cedar, juniper, and wild sagebrush outlined by a two-mile ridge of cliffside—Native American land. The past of hundreds of years was right under you as you set foot on the red, brown, and yellow clay. Dennis laid claim to this spot, buying it up from a young heiress named Rebecca. The property had been gifted to Rebecca from an uncle who homesteaded the property in the early 1900s and nothing had changed since then. The sagebrush glistened in the afternoon rain, the piñon tree branches fell heavy with piñon nuts, silence fell through the cracks of the wind—nature was untouched and alive. Years later on that very land, my parents would tell me of a world outside of this pristine land, a place that seemed to be running rampant with war, violence, racism, and a counterculture movement that swept across the country and captured my father's heart. He would become a huge part of that movement.

A young boy straight out of Dallas, Texas, he was the quarterback of the football team in Irving. His name was often in the paper. Jerry Gallaway—"Galloping Gallaway" they called him—was headed for greatness. A straight-A student with high scholastic achievement. His father had his son's IQ tested. Final reports came in: Galloping Gallaway was a certified genius. Jerry came from a family of six. His father, Ira Gallaway, was a judge in Coleman County, Texas, and later ran for Congress. His mother, Sally, was a sweet country girl who grew up in the west, in Clovis, New Mexico, where she rode horses and helped her father on his ranch. Jerry had three younger siblings, Cynthia, Timothy Harold, and Craig.

Not far from Dallas was my mother, a blue-eyed, red-haired ballet dancer, the apple of her daddy's eye. Raised by a Russian immigrant who married my grandmother, a Scottish redhead from Oklahoma, my mother had a seemingly perfect childhood, an only child for the first ten years of her life. At age five, she immersed herself in ballet with a known Russian instructor, she went to temple with her Jewish father, and on Sundays watched him smoke his cigar, the smoke fuming in the air as they sat and ate a traditional pancake breakfast with eggs and maple syrup. She watched her mother play badminton with the world's badminton champion from Indonesia, Tom Joe Hok. She played dress-up with her friends and had a French African-American nanny and housekeeper named Blanche.

At eighteen my mother, Reva Lynn, left her fine nest of a home on Tampa Street in Houston. My grandfather, Oscar, and my grandmother, Ogreta, loaded the green Oldsmobile with all of their daughter's belongings and set out to drive her the short distance to Austin, where she would attend the University of Texas. Her little brother, Victor, a surprise that came along ten years after my mother was born, sat next to his big sister in the back seat. The family of four rolled down the stretch of highway, not knowing what the future would bring. My mother was headed toward her dreams, and her parents had no doubt she would achieve them all. My grandmother looked in the rearview mirror and adored her daughter's blue eyes, round face, high cheekbones, and pouty red lips. She wore a cream-colored dress with red polka dots scattered about, a red belt showing off her slim waistline.

Living in the wilderness was nowhere on my parents' life map. My father had received an offer from a big-time oil tycoon from Dallas who agreed to pay for his full ride to "The Hill School," a private school in the East. The boys who attended the Hill School were typically born into families of power and great wealth. As my father reluctantly packed his bags for The Hill, he was still forming his identity inside the thick branches of the nest his father had built for him. Jerry arrived at The Hill School in Pottstown, Pennsylvania, tall and lanky with a solid arm that would again position him as quarterback of the football team. He spent his days in the deep, thick walls of the old stone building, breathing its history through the back of his neck. There was much to offer his young mind, and he took time to breathe his own breath and consider what he had never considered before: what did he want? He joined the glee club and the folk music club. Music set him free and brought him back to a piece of himself that had been missing.

Galloping Gallaway studied Latin and learned the original meaning of much of the English language. He also studied Ralph Waldo Emerson and Henry David Thoreau. My father may have seemed free while carrying a football downfield over the goal line, but he was not free in his will and in his mind. Reading Emerson and Thoreau gave his soul hope that man was more than the sum of the world they lived in, and more than the actions they took to be obedient with respect to the law. My father particularly loved Emerson's ideas of nature and started to write his own music about the human struggle and natural order of things. "Do not go where the path may lead you, go instead where there is no path and leave a trail." Emerson's words became a blueprint for his uncharted life.

In those formative years, the Transcendentalists would become mentors to my father, leaving him to question the cultural norms of the time, and yet he was very social and had a tight brotherhood of young men by his side. He had two roommates, Peter Bassett and Fredrick Bingham. My father considered himself to be an outsider compared with these young men and at the same time he adored and befriended them, taking them into his world just enough to know that true friendship was the path of a great character. My father had quoted Emerson in his high school yearbook saying, "The only way to have a friend is to be one."

Social life at the Hill School in Pottstown, Pennsylvania, for my father, was like walking a tightrope high off the ground, trying to fit in while trying to become an individual. The stakes in becoming an individual, in becoming a man who stood for something greater than what the world saw in him, were too high and no band of brotherhood or fear he had in letting down his own father would stop him from choosing his own path in life. My father would find his way and his voice in his music.

The Door to the Future Is Inviting

In 1967, my father arrived in San Francisco with his guitar strapped across his back. He had learned to play with some of the best, and was now the lead singer in his own band called The Human Factor. They were a folk band, the sort popular at the time, that made music about life's challenges and the human condition. My father played the guitar like he played everything else—strong, capable, and with pure confidence. The strings moved between his fingers and love poured out into the crowd.

My parents felt the flow of life in San Francisco, a center for the massive explosion of those rebelling against the status quo, those against the war, those against the bloodshed and racism of the times. "Let freedom reign, let the wind sing, let today be a day of reckoning, let the souls march free." Young women and men shouted it from the street corners and smoked it in their pipes. "Let freedom reign." My father played in bars late into the dark hours, smoky rooms with alcohol pouring and joints being passed from person to person. On late mornings while crawling into bed, with tired red eyes, he thought of his mother's face. Sweet her blue eyes, sweet her touch, the woman who brought him true to Christ was still in there. He would push aside these feelings, for going home was too much a thought, and too heavy a bag to pack, and too many people to leave. And so he went to sleep and woke up the next day surrounded by crowds of seekers.

He was a known face in the Haight-Ashbury District, but fame was not his goal. He wanted to play the music that inspired a life-changing movement, and it didn't matter if his face was on the hearts of the changed or not—he just wanted to play, and so he did.

My mother had embraced dancing for two years in Austin and had worked as an art model, traveling between Austin and New York. She was known for her classy red hair piled high atop her head, and her rebel attitude, a free spirit flittering among the society moving toward complete change. She frequented Mexico with friends and alone. My mother was fiercely independent even though she had a relationship with a young man in Austin, Texas. She was not able to stay in one place, or live out a life the world expected of her: to be a teacher or a nurse, get married, and stay home while raising children. Even though she found herself in a relationship with a man who adored her and gave her a lot of space, she had the need to run, to be on her own. She would travel down to Puerto Vallarta and lie on the beach for days taking in the sun and sea, her mother's voice now far in the background, her future outlined by her parents receding like the ocean waves that washed in and out. She was still in school at The University of Texas, but had not yet found her calling. While lying on the beach in Mexico one afternoon, she tuned into an American radio station as the announcer came on and spoke of the movement taking place in the Haight-Ashbury District of San Francisco. She lay there, her wet hair full with salt, the sun blocking her sight, her mind struck with inquiry. Might San Francisco be her next destination? Her thoughts swirled around in her head. That afternoon she packed up her beach towel, dusted the sand off her feet, and caught a ride to the airport. She was headed back to Texas, and then California.

She left behind a man she once loved and the dream of an education, and flung herself into the open wind, knowing that the force of the movement would catch her. She had practiced yoga for a year now and was feeling confident in her spiritual strength and in her body; with this she knew she could take on the Haight. Yoga was not a booming sensation at that time and my mother, being the rebel she was, went right into it, finding it bringing her inward in a way she had never experienced; holding tree pose she found her strength and beauty and she was able to let go of her old ideas. She had known Janis Joplin, as they both attended UT together, and had traveled in the same circles, along with my father's sister, Cyndi, whom she also knew. Janis had already left Texas for the west coast and my mother decided it was her time.

My mother arrived in San Francisco, the night lights streaming down the sidewalks, the bars open to the many faces who passed, street singers and dancers swaying in movement, no one person seeming subject to another's views on life. Just life it was—full, rich, warm, and inviting like the warm sidewalks that keep the traveling feet moving. Bare feet, feet with shoes, feet with direction, feet with no direction, it didn't matter. The world at large was loaded with judgment; but my mother only saw through the eyes of the seeker and the many doors that were opening before her. This was the place and no face was to be judged by its color, its lines. There were good-looking people, bad looking people, people of all sizes, women in dresses and heels, women in flowered pants, men with long hair and bare chests peeking through white, flowery shirts. The music was everywhere, and the movement was one song in motion. Day and night, the earth was spinning and those on hallucinogens were spinning with it.

My mother had dabbled in pot, LSD, and mushrooms. She had experienced spiritual transformations while she traveled in Mexico, from taking mushrooms. A few days after her arrival to San Francisco she sat in the great Avalon Ballroom, a dance hall with wood floors and psychedelic lighting. She listened to the B-3 organ play. This was no keyboard organ. The sound filled the entire hall and the music rose up in her, taking over her whole body. This is my religion, she thought to herself.

A few days later, she met my father. Tall, lean, with a muscular build, he had come into his manhood with full force. He knew himself well and it showed as he strutted down the street, women gathering around him, reaching for him, wanting and wishing for connection. He seemed unimpressed and would step onto the stage at night to play his music, his voice ringing in the air, the crowd gathered and shouting his name, "Jerry, Jerry, Jerry." My mother was part of the crowd and watched with a wishful heart the man that every woman dreamed of.

The Law and the Heart of Man

In 1967 and 1968, my parents lived in an apartment in The Upper Haight district of San Francisco. They were rarely alone, as people flocked in droves to the apartment and hung out to smoke a joint, drink some drinks, and join in a music jam. My father was open-hearted and gave away much of what he had, never keeping his food, or drugs, to himself. Jerry and Reva were welcomed by everyone, seen by everyone, my father loved by everyone—never skipping a beat of the heart that reminded him that he was running from his past and the life his father wanted for him, traditional schooling and a traditional career with riches and wealth. He constantly wrestled with the Fifth Commandment, honoring his mother and father, versus choosing his own life, so vastly different from what they had hoped for. His father was the man who had put structure under his feet, who had shown up as the law of the world, the iron fist of a soldier, and the heart of a lion. My grandfather had to let go of his son's hand. Weeks would turn into months and months into years; my father would once and for all march to his own music.

The days came and went, the nights' long hours fading into sunrise over the Golden Gate Park oak trees that swayed in the breeze. My father did not speak of God or live by God's rules at this time. His father had gone from being a judge to becoming a Methodist minister, so my father had many teachings from the church on religion and worldviews. My father was blazing a new path in life and to do this he had to let a new self rise to the surface. He was defining himself by new rules.

He was a man with many friends and befriended not just those to whom he felt a moral obligation. My father was storing fifty kilos of marijuana for a Mexican cartel group that he had met one evening through a connection. The deal was simple: "Jerry, share with whoever you like, and at the end of a few weeks we will pick up the shipment and move it elsewhere." My father, the clean-cut football player from Austin, Texas, had grown his hair long and become a rebel.

In October of 1968 the streets of San Francisco were rampant with pot-smoking hippies, flower children, rebels with a cause. The lawmakers were struggling to maintain order in the midst of the uprising of music, free love, drug use, and antiestablishment idealism. It was a weekday at three o'clock in the afternoon when six policemen raided my father's apartment. My mother sat on the couch, her feet up on the coffee table, her boots still on. My father was asleep in the next room. A bang, bang at the door grew louder and louder. My mother jumped to her feet. "Jerry," she called to him from the other room. "Jerry, there's trouble," she warned him in a calm voice.

"San Francisco Police!" a voice carried loud from the outside. "Open up now."

My father came from the back room and slipped his boots on, ready for war, ready to negotiate. He unlocked the door, and let them in.

Six officers bolted into the room. "Stand back, sir!" one shouted and shoved him against the wall.

My mother stood up and moved over next to my father, no words spoken.

"License," the officer demanded of my father. "License, sir."

My father reached into his back pocket and pulled his wallet out, handed the officer his license. The other five officers raided the house with guns drawn, and flashlights looking in every corner. The third bedroom was full of bales of marijuana. The officers gathered round the room, and then marched out together.

"Mr. Gallaway, is it?" a tall officer questioned him.

"Yes, sir," my father said.

"Mr. Gallaway, does the marijuana in that room belong to you?"

My father looked the officer dead in the eyes. "No, sir, just holding it for a friend."

"Is that right," the officer poked my father in the chest. "Well, who's the friend?"

My father refused to answer. "Alright, let's go, Gallaway." An officer handcuffed my mother and my father and marched them off to the police station.

A few days later, an photograph of my mother came out in *Newsweek*. She was dressed in her favorite multicolored poncho, her hair let down around her shoulders. The caption read something like, "Flower Children: The Great Believers or the Great Sinners?" My mother had long let go of her dream of being a ballet dancer, of making her parents proud. She was released from jail within a day, but my father was held on a ten-thousand-dollar bond.

My mother went to a wealthy friend of my father's and asked for help. Phil, who had plenty of cash, was a big supporter of my father's music and believed my father had it in him to make it big in the world. He told her they were going to make a case out of my father to prove a point about the ramifications of pot smoking. He handed my mother the ten grand and said, "Get Jerry and run." My parents left San Francisco with the shirts on their backs and no shoes on their feet.

Refugees

My parents caught a flight to New York, where my father had a connection. From the airport, they took a cab to a nice hotel in downtown Manhattan. My father was wearing his white peasant shirt. His hair was long, brown and flowing over his shoulders; his beard was trimmed and it outlined his jaw. My mother was wearing her wool poncho with a pair of slacks and her hair was loose and draping around her face. They entered the hotel with some strangers staring at them. My father approached the front desk, where a young, clean-cut receptionist in a suit and tie looked at my parents like they were out of place.

"May I help you?"

My father asked to speak to his friend Richard, who owned an art studio in San Francisco and was a respected artist in New York. The receptionist paused for a moment, and then picked up the phone. "There is a Mr. Gallaway, here to see you." He waited for a response on the other end to see if my father was legit. A few minutes passed.

"Jerry Gallaway," a man's voice pierced the thin walls of the hotel. Richard greeted my father with open arms and the two men hugged. He then escorted my mother and father to a room. That night they went to a party with Richard, in the Village, where she and my father were announced as "the beautiful people," from California. My mother realized that, on the East Coast, the flower children of California were highly admired and highly attractive.

The counterculture movement was finding its way into the hearts of many. At the core of the movement was the idea that we the people had power through our connections to each other and through our connection to music. Music would become the heartbeat of the movement along with the use of drugs to change a known reality. In this there was the good and bad of interrupting a reality to create change. If we opened our hearts to diversity and to nature, we could build community and live freely without money being the main source of power for our lives; this meant growing and sharing our food, and sharing ideas, music and even drugs. My parents were cultivating their ideals around this along with many others, and in doing so they found support wherever they went. Much of the country saw the counterculture as naive and irresponsible, but the movement was gaining momentum and disrupting the status quo.

The time in New York was a cold few weeks in passing. It was early December when my mother looked down at her belly one morning and saw a round bump. She noticed this bump in the midst of a crowd of people, and paused for a minute, knowing there must be a baby. She hadn't noticed she had missed her cycle, but life had been full of chaos. In the middle of the crowd, with my father talking up a storm, she softly relayed the message to him, with a whisper in his ear, "I'm pregnant." Immediately his face was transformed; he sobered up and stopped laughing with everyone. That evening he committed to my mother his protection, planning, and desires to be a father. She and my father agreed to take a train to New Hampshire, where they had other friends, and this would keep my father off the grid, as he now had a warrant out for his arrest. He had missed his court hearing in San Francisco nearly a week earlier.

Vermont was cold too, as it was deep in the heart of winter. My mother dragged her feet through a foot of snow just outside the cabin where they had been staying for a month. It was already March and the snow had not let up. As her belly grew bigger and bigger, she could no longer see her feet. This was her first child, her first time experiencing motherhood. My parents were spontaneous people who made quick decisions and followed their instincts about what felt right. For a few weeks they moved to Boston to get out of Vermont. Late one night, she and my father lay cold inside a hotel room with little money left to their names. The place was run down and the damp walls were caving in on them. At dusk they awoke to a shroud of police officers with pointed rifles coming down the stairs just outside their doorway. My mother rolled over and looked at my father, and in that moment they both realized this was not the place to raise children. My father had not shared much about his feelings on Emerson and the idea that you could get everything you needed from nature. He was simply going with the flow and connecting to the people.

Two nights later, my father played three songs as trade for a run-down VW bus and they drove across the country to the state of New Mexico. A friend told them of a community farm in a small town called Placitas where they could live with others and grow their own food.

They arrived at midnight in the South Valley of Albuquerque, New Mexico. The South Valley was the poor part of town in the southern outstretch of the city. My father followed his heart into the core of a small village, where he spoke to an old Mexican cowboy in Spanish. My father traded him the VW bug for a horse. With no saddle, he helped my mother on the back of the horse and they rode from midnight till four o'clock in the morning. The morning star guiding them, the brightest they had ever seen, my father said. It lit up the sky as my mother's round belly was pronounced in the light.

At dusk they came to the sleepy little village of Tawapa outside of Placitas, New Mexico, where they found a mix of intelligent college dropouts, people dodging the draft and people who had just dropped out of the establishment altogether. The village was a peaceful land that sat on a hill just above a creek. There were trees that gave shade in the afternoon, with huts, teepees, and small adobe houses all tucked in close together on several acres of land. It was here that they would make their attempt at living peacefully while sharing the responsibilities of building a self-sufficient community. The people of Tawapa all had a story and were running from the world, from the establishment, the law, family, and anything that would keep them from their freedom. It was May and by June my mother's belly was about to pop. On June 20, 1969, my mother fell to her knees in the middle of the night, grabbing at her belly. She was delusional with no sleep, and never having been in labor, she thought she was sick. She was buckled over on the dirt floor inside a teepee while my father slept, his head resting on a handmade straw pillow. Finally after much pushing and breathing, moaning and groaning, my mother called out, "The baby is coming, the baby is coming!"

My mother fought through her pain, her knees shaking, her body convulsing, sweat pouring from her skin—she was sure she was going to die. But the body knows how to give birth, and at the final stretch of the crowning head she gave it all to God. My father caught my brother's head and then his body. He held his wet little body with two hands, keeping his butt from touching the dirt floor.

My mother moved over to the cot and collapsed. My father held the new baby in a gallon pail of water that he had warmed in a fire pit on the ground and bathed him. There were two candles giving light to the interior of the teepee. The baby had a perfect, round head, stout arms and legs for a newborn. My father watched his son's gleaming body in the candlelight. The baby made no sound, no crying, nothing of fear. He was here brought to earth on the twenty-first of June as the summer solstice about to begin. My mother slept till the sun came up and awoke to her first child tucked at her chest; my father was stoking the flames of the fire pit at the center of the teepee.

"I think you may need to nurse him," he requested of my mother.

My mother rubbed her eyes and looked down at the round, little head tucked against her chest. She had passed out in exhaustion after giving birth. "Well, what's the sex?" she gave my father a look.

"That's your son, a strong boy," my father responded.

My mother, who grew up attending Jewish synagogue, had never felt a true confirmation of faith and now it was in her hands. She cupped the baby's head to her nipple. "Come on, little guy," she said as she pressed his mouth to open and within seconds he was nursing. My mother felt the tugging and suckling from her breast, the pulling of her insides back together, and she knew the natural order of things had its purpose. She knew how to birth a baby, how to face her own death, how to breathe through it and come out the other side. There was no storm that would take her down, not now, not ever.

A year and a half passed with the arrival of a second son and my parents living on the farm. Family, community, and faith-inspired days were all in the music my father sang around the campfire every night. My mother now had a second child, my brother Carey, known as the Rising Sun, born as the sun was coming up. My mother and father were learning new rituals to mark their life outside of society, a way to help them embrace nature and surrender to the natural order of things. Each child born would be given a world name and a nature name. John was known as "Little Thunder," Carey, "Balancing Scales-Rising Sun." Nye, "Many Waters," myself, "Flowing Spring River," Abigail Rose, "Flower," and Jacinth, "Strong Horse." The names came from something that happened at our birth, a vision or natural force that occurred. The names were meant to help us live out our life purpose.

There were about forty people who lived at the farm known as The Lower Farm. It sat on a hill, and down below there was a creek that ran though a thicket of trees.

My father had a way with words and knew how to befriend just about anyone. He was becoming a man of spiritual law, a hippie, the old cowboy of the land, who came to this part of the country for solace. My father's time in Mexico a few years earlier was now helpful with his speaking Spanish to the locals. He had spoken to a sheriff friend of his earlier that week in town. The sheriff had warned him that there was going to be a drug bust. "They are coming in for you all," he said.

My father had warned the others and asked them to pull up their marijuana plants but no one believed him. They all shrugged him off. "Ugh, Jerry leave us alone, you've told us this before." It's true he had told them before and then nothing had happened, but he was sure this was time it would happen.

It was a brilliant New Mexico afternoon and my father was standing in the middle of the garden surrounded by squash, snap peas, carrots, lettuce, and stalks of green beans dangling. At the center of the garden were ten large marijuana plants growing tall. My father was taking in the afternoon sun when he saw a line of white FBI cars trailing the long drive of dirt road toward the village. He had been running since San Francisco.

He looked back toward the teepee, where my mother was with the boys. There was no time to get her; the white cars were getting close.

He yelled out as loud as he could. "It's a bust!" He yelled again, "It's a bust!" and bolted for the hills in a full-speed run. He made it over the top of a hill and hid between two large boulders, peeking out to see the white cars stop in the village down below. He watched as they gathered up all forty of the men, women, and children. My mother was among them, holding John on one arm and Carey on the other.

The agents, who were wearing all dark blue, gathered the crowd in one large circle. My father watched as my mother silently walked away from the crowd and the agents. She slipped anonymously from the group and walked down the hill and toward the creek below the village, where she would be out of sight. It's questionable whether the agents saw her or not. They either let her go because she held two infants or they just didn't see her. My mother was a risk taker, a rebel. She always pushed the limits to see how far she could go. It was part of her following my father into the wilderness.

The agents loaded the rest of the folks into the cars and drove away. The entire group of revolutionary freedom seekers were jailed.

My father rode his horse into town and called the one lawyer he knew to get them support. There was only one man in the group who had no previous record. Jane and Eli Rivers had partnered together at the community farm and had become close friends of my parents. Jane helped my mother with being a mother, growing and cooking food and cultivating connection to the community. Jane had a son named Luke, and had left her first marriage that was falling apart. She and Eli had been going together for over a year now. Eli was both kind-hearted and sensitive to Jane and the others.

When it came time for the group to face charges, Eli stepped up and took the rap for everyone. He pleaded a deal with the lawyer, who got him two years of probation and a sentence to run a drug rehab organization to fight the war on drugs in Albuquerque, not far from Placitas. People were greatly relieved and some of them returned to the farm. Others were scared and thought it might be time to go back to a normal life; maybe going home wasn't such a bad idea. My father felt uncomfortable with the whole scene, the number of folks that were there, the drugs being used, and the law not far off. My father didn't want his children in school, nor did he want them to be surrounded by a lot of drug use. He was coming into his independence, into fatherhood, which meant standing behind his beliefs as they surfaced. The line between my father and the rest of the world was growing thinner and thinner.

The Long Trek into the Woods

"Nature always wears the colors of the spirit."
—Ralph Waldo Emerson

My parents left the farm in Tawapa with John and Carey on two donkeys. They didn't have a place to go, but my father knew when it was time to leave. In this rebel life, you were led by instinct. All of their belongings were strapped on the back of Cedar and Rosemary, two furry gray donkeys. Carey and John got to ride together in one saddle while my mother rode on the other donkey, and my father walked on foot, leading his family.

Like Moses from the Bible, my father was moving further into the wilderness, leaving behind everything he had known, including the community at Tawapa. Moses stayed forty years in the desert when seeking guidance from God. My father would now trek on foot forty miles from Tawapa to the mountain of Jemez. From Placitas, New Mexico, where the community of Tawapa was, to the west where Native American land stretches across flat grasslands that turn into red and white vistas and then onward into the Jemez Mountains. Jemez Valley is within the Santa Fe National Forest, smaller than the Grand Canyon, but massive in its beauty and spiritual feel, a feeling of God and universe as one coming together under the healing waters that flowed from the natural springs of Jemez as one walks the red roads with ten-thousand-foot mountain ranges caving in on all sides. At the center of the valley, just below the rising mountains is a small village and then the mountain range gets higher and goes on for miles and miles, with steep cliffs and natural hot springs flowing in all seasons.

They left the village of Tawapa in the spring, the warm sun glowing above their heads as they trekked by day, and camped by night underneath large trees for shelter. When they arrived in Jemez, they were low on food and weakened by the journey. Much of Jemez at that time was still occupied by the Native Americans, with whom my father was attempting to make an authentic connection by building a bridge between the past and the present, leading with the idea that we are all children of God, and no man should be judged by the color of his skin. My father was and had been a privileged white man for much of his life. He was now humbling himself to the natives of the land, asking for their wisdom and support to forge a new way of life for his family. In this exchange, my father brought his music, his heart and his working hands to return support to any who were needing it.

When they arrived at the village of Jemez, a tribal feast was underway. My father was becoming accustomed to the rituals and etiquette everywhere they went; his wisdom and his sense of humility brought grace to many situations. My father always knew someone and on that day he knew someone from the village. They rode the burros into the town square, where a few adobe buildings flanked the banks of the river, with large cottonwood trees blowing in the wind. You could hear the music and dancing coming from inside the walls of a closed-in area down by the river. My father asked my mother to stay with the boys and the donkeys. A few minutes later, he returned with a man all dressed in costume, wrapped in many colors with feathers on his head and moccasins on his feet. The man welcomed the family to join them in the feast. The boys were hungry and went straight to the food with my mother, who was watched by native women for a few minutes before they offered her a hand.

That day in the village, my father had learned what it meant to play his music with a new group of people. Listening with his heart, he felt a kindred spirit in all the men, women and children running in circles to drumming sounds echoed by the cliffside. My mother rested in one of the teepees while John and Carey chased boys and girls around a fire into the late evening.

John asked my mother, "Are we Indians, Mom?" My mother had read them stories and my father had talked about the Native

Americans and how much wisdom they bestowed in their
connection to nature. John was unsure as to what he and Carey
were and asked the question. My mother responded, "You are
just like them, but your skin is white." John took favor to this and
jumped right into to play with the others. By dusk, my father got
out his guitar and played his soulful music, bringing his message
of faith and hope by loving the earth and loving God.

They stayed the night in the village and left the next morning
to continue on into the mountains of Jemez. Their trek would
land them deep into the woods, high on top of the world, with
only the sounds of the wild echoing in their midst, again camping
under large trees, with the stars, a giant dazzling light show above.
They camped for weeks like this, and one afternoon a bear came
through the woods and Rosemary and Cedar got spooked. The
two donkeys bolted from the campsite in a full run, not being
tethered by rope. My father went after them, but they were too
spooked and ran through the woods until they were gone. The
only hope was to wait for them to come back. When they didn't
return a day later, my father made plans to go into the village and
get support to move his family someplace safe.

It was the middle of summer now and once summer was
over, you could not survive the Jemez. They had to leave behind
many of their belongings and were quite hungry at this time.
Hiking down through the Jemez they came across an abandoned
trailer house sitting at the edge of the forest. They went inside and
rummaged for food, finding a can of corn and instant mashed
potatoes. They ate the corn and continued on their trek. They
were able to get support in the village from my father's friend,
who took them by vehicle to La Ventana, an even smaller village
way outside of the Jemez on the way to Cuba, New Mexico.

For the few years my father had spent in New Mexico, he
somehow had made connections by riding on horseback all over
the small towns of this land of enchantment. La Ventana only
had two adobe houses and one church with the population of
about ten people. My father knew one of those ten people. This
fella would welcome them into the adobe home and feed them.
They spent a few days there, during which John had a birthday
on June 21st. My mother was able to make him a cake. Carey

was so excited about the cake that when my mother left the room for a minute, he climbed on top of the kitchen counter to look for the cake. The cake was disguised in a round pan covered with a towel, and while looking, Carey stepped in it. It was not ruined by any means, because when you had nothing and you got something special, it was special even with a footprint in it. John and Carey spent the afternoon running in circles around the yard with their mouths full of cake.

The next day they discovered dog food for the first time and decided to try it out of curiosity. They put handfuls of dog food into their mouths and chewed down on the crunchy dry goods. It was pretty tasty, they thought. My father had left for the day with the friend to negotiate a new place for the family to stay. When my mother found her sons eating dog food, she gasped, "Boys, that's for a dog, don't eat that!" She pleaded with them, thinking maybe they were still starving and it was her fault. "Mom we were only curious," John replied to her. "We wanted to know what it felt like to be a dog." My mother laughed and they agreed not to eat more dog food. But deep inside, past my mother's laugh, was the concern for the first time on how they were going to make it.

By sunset my father had returned and let them know he had arranged a new place for them to live. They would head northeast toward another mountain range, called the San Pedro Mountains.

The Peacemaker and the Natives of the Land

My father had many debates in his formal years of schooling, but this is not what gave him his negotiating skills. He was raised in the home of a World War II veteran who was a judge and then became a preacher. His acquisition of language, from the years of studying Latin, and then learning Spanish while spending some time in Mexico, gave him much to work with in conversation. But underneath all of that were the years he spent in his father's home observing in silence, taking notes on power, submission, religion, war, and love. All of who he had been and who he was becoming, he was now able to release.

My father's friend drove them from La Ventana to the northeast in Northern New Mexico. North was past Abiquiú, Georgia O'Keeffe land, up the mountain ranges of the west, past the red cliffs standing against the blue waters of Abiquiú Lake and onward into the San Pedro Mountains. Inside the San Pedro Mountains was a tiny tinker village, known as Mesa Paleo. The characters of the land were a mix of the young rebels running from inner city life, from the establishment, and their upbringing, and some who were simply looking for adventure. There were families like Michael and Mady Maraia, a young couple from Brooklyn, New York, who got married one afternoon on a cloudy day in a courthouse with a few friends gathered around them, leaving for the Wild West. They came to northern New Mexico with a dream of living independently, surviving off the grid, and connecting to nature. Michael and Mady had two children, Madea and Micha. Michael and Mady knew what it took to live off the grid: hard work and a solid soul purpose. Mady would be a friend to my mother and later a rock for me to lean on, with her candid heart and straight-shooter personality. When I was thirty-five years old, she would give me the picture on the cover of this book, and say to me, "I knew you were going to be great someday." She had taken this picture on a cold November day, while she watched as Nye, Carey, John, and I played with Madea and Micah on the hillside next to their log cabin.

Five young souls
Running free
Five young souls
Who will you be?
The catcher of truths
The lion who roars
The yielded solider
The broken swan
The wizard's magic
You'll it carry on!

There were small towns like Gallina, Coyote, and Mesa Paleo. The word *coyote* is Mexican Spanish, from an Aztec root, *coyotl,* or trickster. Another informal meaning of the word, used mainly in the U.S. Southwest and Mexico, is one who smuggles immigrants. Gallina literally means chicken in Spanish, but also refers to ancient culture in New Mexico. Mesa Paleo means an ancient isolated flat-top hill with steep sides. There among the real coyotes and the real chickens were the Spanish locals, and many of them had a long-standing family history of living in this part of the West. My father was blending himself between the White Man and the Spanish, the Native American and the Hippie Cowboy. Everyone had a place and my father would use all of his life experience to find his place in these communities.

My father's trust was in the village people, the poor man, the man who was not a part of the system. He spoke in Spanish to the elders on the Mesa Paleo with respect and kindness. He negotiated for food, cattle, land, horses, goats, and chickens. He negotiated with words and with music, with wisdom and with fierce charisma. It was from the Spanish and the Native Indians that my father would learn which plants to use for healing illness. At this point my father had denounced the medical system altogether. We moved from clay hills to grasslands to high ridges to low plains, all within a four-year span of time. My father was always navigating and building trust with the locals while standing in his principles that God and nature were the two needed elements for a healthy life.

My father's past had many layers, as I would find out in stories though his music or his venting about why we didn't live in the world. My father had lived in Guadalajara, Mexico, ten years earlier, during his early twenties. He and his girlfriend at the time, Jane, had traveled to Mexico seeking adventure. They spent a full year south of the border. Jane was a weaver and spun beautifully crafted rugs that they were able to sell. My father played music and socialized with the locals.

When Jane found out she was with child, they decided to stay and have the baby in Mexico. My father had been negotiating using his newly learned Spanish language skills, and now he would need to negotiate with doctors to bring his child into the world. They visited a village hospital in the region, in which my father agreed with the head doctor on a price for the delivery. Jane went into labor on a dirt floor inside the casita they had been renting and within minutes, my father drove her to the small medical center in town. My father was asked to stay out of the delivery room, an order he was not pleased with. After some time had passed, he pushed his way through the door, nearby which he was met by two large female nurses.

"No puede entrar, señor." "You cannot come in, sir."

He was pushed back outside the door. The head doctor then came out and informed my father that the baby was not coming out by vaginal birth and they would need to do a C-section. My father felt helpless and waited. Hours later the doctor met my father in the hallway.

"Tiene un hijo, señor." "You have a son, sir."

My father rushed to Jane, who held their newborn son wrapped in a thin, yellow cloth against her chest. The two of them sat stunned looking at the white walls. They went through a list of names they had both been fond of and within minutes they came to the name Mateo or Matthew.

"I will have to pay so we can get out of here," my father said.

He left Jane and went down the hall to where the head doctor was sitting in his office. "*Señor Gallaway,*" the man greeted him.

They had originally agreed that the delivery would be 1,200 pesos. That was all my father had and when he tried to pay him, the doctor refused and said the price had doubled because there had been a C-section.

My father negotiated with the doctor in Spanish. "*Señor,* this is all I have. We agreed on this price and this is what I have."

"You will have to come up with the rest," the doctor said. "You can go but you must leave the baby with us and come back with the rest of the money."

My father stood up from his chair, looked at the man, and left the room. He went to Jane. "Can you walk?" he asked.

"Yes," she responded. "What's going on?" She was tired and scared, holding Matthew pressed against her chest.

"They are not going to let us take the baby." My father lifted Jane to her feet. "We have got to make a run for it." He said and grabbed up Matthew from her. My father advised Jane to walk down the hall and out the front door; he would then follow her a few minutes later with Matthew.

Jane gathered herself, holding onto her stomach that was wrapped with white gauze, her wound still pulsing at her insides. She moved quickly with little notice from any of the nurses. When she got to the door, my father grabbed Matthew and started down the hall. A nurse yelled out from behind him. "*¡Señor,* you must leave the baby here!"

The nurse ran after him down the hall. My father grabbed Matthew against his chest like he had done with a football years before and ran full speed to the front door. "*¡Señor, señor!*" the head doctor stepped into the hallway and yelled after him. "*¡Alto, alto!* The *federales* will come after you, *señor,*" the doctor's voice trailed behind my father as the hospital doors slammed in his wake. Jane was waiting in the car, my father handed her the baby, and they sped away.

In those days it was unlikely that the Mexican police would come looking for you for such a little amount of money. They took a chance and stayed a while longer in the casita with Matthew before returning to the United States. Sometime after returning to the States, heading back to San Francisco, my father and Jane split. Jane took Matthew with her and my father went on to play music and later met my mother.

My father had learned how to negotiate in life and death circumstances. This event was partially what solidified his belief that the natural way of life was the only truthful way to live. He never wanted to have a child inside a hospital again. He didn't believe the C-section was necessary and feared that greed, when getting the best of men, would destroy their honor and their word.

Throughout my childhood, he spoke of his first son, Matthew. Every time he played the flute, he would repeat the same story over and over about how he played the flute for Matthew when he was a baby. Matthew would be crying and as soon as my father played the flute, he would stop. My father never talked about why Matthew was not with us, and I didn't ask. It was almost obvious that life was just too difficult. We could just barely get through our days there on the mountain. My parents, along with John, Nye, and Carey lived on Mesa Paleo—what locals called the Mesa. They lived in a two-room adobe house that was right in the middle of a wide-open field where wild grasses and red berry bushes popped up everywhere with a thick forest of pine trees bordering all of the land. It was a fairytale of a place, with a creek running through the middle of the field, the San Pedro Mountains just to the northeast rising up to meet the clouds. It was not a place you would ever want to leave. But leave they did, when neighbors on the Mesa started to question why my father didn't have his children in school. He knew he would have to move or get into battles around his beliefs. Explaining that he didn't want his children vaccinated with toxic poisons, or indoctrinated by a school system that believed in Darwin's theory of evolution, was not a battle my father wanted to engage.

Birth Is a Natural Part of Life

After my father's first experience with Matthew's birth, he would never again have a child in a hospital. My mother agreed that natural childbirth would give a child the best start in life. We would all be born in nature, but in different parts of the land, nature being home to my parents wherever they went, always seeking a sacred place to rest. Sometimes during birth my mother had a midwife, which really just meant a friend who came during the birth. My mother's labors were never easy but had no major complications, with the exception of Carey, who was born premature and unable to nurse for several days, putting his life at risk. On the fifth day after his birth, my mother got him to nurse; it was a close call, as his body was already small and had some catching up to do. Later in life he would become a focused hunter of the land with a sculpted, strong body and unflinching heart when in the wild.

My parents left the Mesa after they had John, Nye, and Carey. They moved further north and west. They kept moving north in New Mexico as my father's ideals kept growing bigger and wider. My father loved people, but the constraints of society always found their way into the conversation. Both my parents agreed that raising free-thinkers spiritually connected to God and nature meant keeping us out of public school. They continued to seek new places to live in an effort to maintain the principles and values they were building a new foundation upon.

Stone Mountain was a one-room stone house with a loft that had a balcony overlooking the one room down below. The house was perched high atop a hillside in the middle of the woods in the small town of Lindrith, New Mexico, where few traveled and even fewer lived. As usual, my father had a friend and this friend owned the property called Stone Mountain. Mel was a kind, laid-back fella who drove a motorcycle, a free spirit who loved to share, and when my father asked for a place to stay for a while, Mel offered up this remote place far from civilization.

You traveled by dirt road, to more dirt roads, and finally up hills and around corners and rocks and small ponds, on dirt roads, till you reached a flat space to park your car. There were hundreds of feet to walk by foot, plus lots of space for keeping animals and for planting food. This was down at the bottom of a grand hill. To get to the stone house, you had to climb the hundred yards of hillside. Once you arrived, you were on top of the world. It was on top of the world that I would be born. My mother would climb that hill in the middle of her contractions to find her safe place to give birth in the loft.

My mother had given birth to three sons—three times she had given it all to God, with no medical intervention, my father the safety net to help her though. My brothers were all healthy, but birth was not easy; there were no words to describe it, as it was always its own thing, facing fear and letting go. Every birth was a chance for something new to be revealed to my mother, about herself and life.

They never knew if they were having a boy or a girl. It didn't matter, they were having a baby. Complete trust and strength was needed to make the journey, to bring a child into the world.

My brother, Nye, was born on March 11th at noon. He was now two years old, it was his birthday and another baby was coming. It was March 11th and that day they ate homemade carrot cake to celebrate his life, and in the middle of the afternoon my mother felt contractions that came and went into evening. My mother climbed the steep steps to the loft where all the beds were laid out in a row for sleeping. She crawled into the bed, rocking back and forth on her knees. Night came quickly as my mother's contractions came even quicker. She was now in full labor, no midwife this time. My father heated water on the stove downstairs and my brothers waited, listening to my mother's cries. Upon my birth, my father was in the loft to help me into the world. He cut my umbilical cord, like he had done for all the others, after letting me lie naked pressed into my mother's chest for a good while. Once he cut the cord, he gave me back to my mother. She was awake. My father left to go outside and stand with the moon. It was a full moon and he ascertained that it was after midnight on March 12th. Just passing the March 11th mark, so as not to be born on the same day as my brother, Nye.

My mother held me in her arms wrapped in a white cloth. I had thick silky black hair that would later fall out and turn strawberry blond. She looked me over, mesmerized by my soft skin and glowing eyes. This time it was a girl. She felt the grandeur of birth and the wonder of life floating in her hands, this precious being had come from somewhere magical, a place far beyond the windows of that loft, far beyond the cosmos. When I was an adult, my mother would tell me the story of my birth, using these exact words to describe that moment when she had her first daughter. She had named me after *Daphnis and Chloe,* the ballet she performed in for many years. I believe that for my mother I was a connection to her past, to the young girl that wore tutus.

I would become one with that land, one with my brothers playing on the hillside of Stone Mountain. The stone house had glass windows that surrounded the entire south portion of the loft. When the light was clear and bright you could see for miles green trees, red cliffs, gray rocks, and the pond to the west, full of ducks.

My first memory is from this place of the heart. I stood on the west side of the stone house, facing the sunset that melted into my three-year-old body. I held a bottle of goat's milk in my hand. I walked a few steps to the south, the sun lighting my way. I dropped my bottle and watched it roll off a huge boulder and then down a steep path that led to the goat pen. I went after my bottle, feet moving quickly, my eyes on the path ahead, but first I had to scale that boulder. I was wearing only a cloth diaper. I balanced myself on top of the boulder and lowered my body off the side, scraping my ribs and my heel. I let go and dropped to the ground. I landed on my butt. My ribs were stinging with pain, but I wanted my bottle and chased after it down the hill. It had rolled all the way down the path and stopped at the gate of the goat pen. I ran to it and grabbed it up. The stinging on my side was subsiding, numbness fading the pain into the evening sunset. I pushed at the gate to the goats' home and it opened for me. We had a large herd of about twenty goats. I walked among them and sat down in the middle of the pen. They gathered around me like earth angels taking me in, wrapping me in love. I drank from my bottle of goat's milk until the sun was gone, the earth turned dark, and my brother John scooped me up into his arms to take me back up the hill.

Our time at Stone Mountain lasted a few years. I was four years old when life brought another change. The world and all its evils could not be kept at bay for some. My father's friend Mel was killed by a hitchhiker he picked up one afternoon while headed to Stone Mountain. Mel had a wife and three-year-old daughter. The three of them were living in California, but Mel had brought them out to Stone Mountain where they planned to stay, until tragedy struck. Young Delana would be without a father and Andrea, her mother, would search to find new meaning in life. We stayed on the property for some time while Andrea went back to California with Delana, but eventually she returned, bringing with her a new man. My father was not much for worldly men and Robert was just that, so after several disagreements with Robert, who offered books to John for reading and wanted to walk around the property in the nude, my parents decided quickly to look for a new home. The place of my birth would be left behind with the evening sunset.

My father's livelihood had become dependent upon every friendship he made. He had met Todd Colombo when he first arrived in the town of Lindrith. Todd was an ex Hollywood film editor who had connections to the actor Dennis Hopper. The order in which my father operated was trust God, nature, then man. When seeking guidance he always waited on God's response for his next steps. He was affirmed in silent prayer that he should connect with Todd around the need to move his family. Todd was not so simple on the inside, years of conflict brewing underneath a simple looking carpenter who gave up his Hollywood life to live in Lindrith and build log cabins. He met my father in the only place he knew how, in directness and confidence that the two of them had a purpose in building things. My father was building a path to spiritual connection through complete immersion in nature. Todd offered to set up a meeting with Dennis Hopper, so my father could discuss living on his property.

Isolation Meets the Heart

The land where isolation meets the heart—this is the story of the land before our time, before we lived and played among the trees and cliffs, before we called it home.

My father told me the story of the land as it came to be, a place of refuge for so many. First the Native Americans whose evidence of life was left formed in the two-mile ridge of cliffside that ranged from the beginning to the end of the property. Among the cliff dwellings, you could find pottery pieces, arrowheads, and fossil bone pieces on any given day. My father referred to the Native Americans as the Indians, like they were a close friend, "my Indian brothers," he would say when commenting about the lives that had passed.

After the Indians came and left, the land opened up to Homesteaders around 1916. During the Depression, known as the "Dustbowl Period" when all the water had dried up around most of Oklahoma, many families left and headed west. Some of them got as far west as our property. One fella by the name of Highsmith was the first one to homestead the property. My father said that, since his name was Highsmith, it was likely that he worked as a blacksmith, as people were often given names after their trade. He was apparently a lonely man who had no children. The land itself could evoke loneliness. When he died he left the land to a niece called Rebecca. Rebecca didn't live on the land and was looking to sell it when Dennis came to her with an offer.

In 1969, Dennis Hopper purchased the land from Rebecca's family right after he finished filming the movie *Easy Rider*. It was a revolutionary time, and Dennis and his posse of friends worried the world might be coming to an end. He became the new steward of the three-hundred and twenty acres of land set at eight-thousand feet. The surrounding area, known as the badlands, was land that was too rocky and rough for having cattle or for growing large crops.

My father relayed to me that anyone who came to the property came to take refuge from the outside world. Some were even running from the law, or "the bankers' world," he called it. If you stood on top of the mountain, you could see anyone and anything coming from thirty miles out. It was unlikely anyone would hike or drive in that far in search of someone, and if they did you could always see them coming. If you hiked half a mile on the property and stood on the edge of the cliff, you could see blue mountain ridges for miles in the distance. At the end of the canyon where the ridge is at its highest point, the land is still—not a sound in range but the wind—and down below a green valley gathers a serene earth known as "the valley of the moon." Under a full moon, you could see the earth hundreds of feet below, with rock edges and shapes of all forms of life shadowing the sides of the cliff. You could hear voices traveling from five miles out carried by the wind and landing softly on the tree branches.

Before our time, the land was infrequently used. Dennis was in "Hollywood" by now, his fame toning the color of his skin, the shape of his eyes, the hunger in his belly for more. He and my father had both resided in California during the same era, during the late sixties, both of them on the verge of fame, my father big in the music scene, and Dennis revolutionizing his acting career. Two men taking different paths; they would land on the same rock someday.

My father entered the room of the cabin where he had been invited to play for Dennis and his pack that traveled with him during the late '70s. They sat with their legs folded on the wooden floor of Dennis Hopper's cabin. My father introduced himself once again to Dennis, as they had only met once prior and now they had arranged a meeting to see about my father being the caretaker of the property. It was a blustery day outside; gray light cracked through the windows. My father pulled his guitar from around his back. The five men sat in a circle, their heads down, their spirit low—they were on some kind of high.

My father had known these faces of his past, he had been down this road. It was a road he left behind when he and my mother fled the world of heavy drug use, rock 'n' roll, and political uprising. My father often played from an intuitive state, creating a song right there on the spot, or he would pull a song he'd already created that fit the moment. Today it was sheer intuition—as he looked around the room, he felt the log cabin walls, the stone fireplace from floor to ceiling, the little house on the prairie-style windows, letting in a natural light, the wind blowing through an open front door, and five men dressed for fame, their bodies sinking through the floorboards, the drug-induced high, taking them so low. My father intended to raise them up from the soul. He lifted his heart to God, pulled his guitar around to the front of his lap, and started to play.

Cowboys and Indians

The land was once ours
And the fighting man came
He busted us with bullets
And took away our name
The fighting man
Then came to live beside us
And asked us for grace
So we gave it back to him
Helped him to his place
Now the cowboy and the Indian
They live with this pride,
They let down their shields
And took up arms side by side
Beside the rivers rushing
Beside the valleys low
Now they ride together
Wherever they may go

The room spun as the five men sat with their heads bowed, the music washed the walls clean, and on my father's last note, Dennis lifted his head, slowly rising from the darkness that lurked beneath his high-priced Hollywood life. He rose to his feet to meet my father, who was now standing in a glow of light. My father showed no judgment toward him. Somewhere inside of him Dennis had a heart of gold, he wasn't about money or drugs, he too was about connection. My father met him right in this place. Dennis understood that my father had a message and this message wasn't meant to come forth on the silver screen. The two men shook hands and Dennis gave him affirmation. "You may stay here till the end of your time, Mr. Gallaway."

The five gentlemen of Hollywood got into a black luxury car and drove away. My father stood at the edge of the cliff, a vast untouched scene before him. God had given him a new chance to raise his family, tucked away in a peaceful land.

A Place Called Home

The sun settled in the sky behind the dual-wheel flatbed truck, red with blue trim around the edges. The back of the flatbed had a large, steel bumper frame that was painted black and in red writing it read, "Jesus Saves." My father had painted the bumper himself. He had known of a certain God in his youth and now he was forced to reconcile his beliefs, finding his true connection to the Holy Spirit though Jesus. He was coming to know Jesus as he was becoming his own man. His mentors were alive and in his presence, Emerson, Thoreau, and Jesus Christ. My father felt as Emerson did when he wrote that "Jesus Christ belonged to the true race of prophets. He saw with open eye the mystery of the soul." My father would not call himself a prophet but, whether he knew it or not, he lived his life this way, too.

We drove over the last hill and the engine revved, the sound vibrating through the truck bed, my small body bouncing up and down. My siblings and I were packed in the back of the truck bed—Nye, Carey, and me on one side, and John on the other. All of our belongings were packed around us, clothes, and bedding in bags, dishes, and a few small furniture pieces. In the middle of all the material things were three goats riding along with us. I climbed up onto my knees to view my mother sitting in the front seat, baby Jacinth was in her lap, my little sister, Rose, was beside her. My father had his hands at the steering wheel.

We pulled into a narrow drive that looked to have once been a road, now covered over with grass and tiny brush-like plants. The pine and piñon trees meshed together—thick, strong, green shades cast light from the sun sinking slowly toward the horizon. I sat up in the back of the bed and peeked over the side. The truck rolled to a stop, the engine cut. My father's door opened and slammed. John, Nye, and Carey jumped over the sides of the truck bed. I stayed on my knees, still looking over the side, before I climbed up to the back window. My mother's thick, luminous hair showed through the thick glass, where she sat in the seat of the truck, her auburn locks glistening in the sunlight.

"Mama," I called to her from the back. "Is this it?"

She turned her head to me, my baby brother, Jacinth, still on her lap and my little sister Rose next to her, with the giant black stick shift of the truck between her legs.

"Are we going to live here?" I yelled at her again.

She turned her head to me and smiled. A hint of her perfect white teeth showed through her thick lips, pale pink in color without any lipstick. I jumped up from the truck bed, threw my legs over the back, and climbed down. I ran around and opened her door.

"Come on, Mom, let's go!" I shouted.

She stepped down, holding Jacinth pressed to her chest. He was wrapped in a white cloth blanket, his blue-green eyes peeking out of the top, a knitted blue hat on his head. He was six months old. Rose climbed toward me and I helped her down.

Together we stood facing an open patch of land surrounded by hundreds of trees. Green-blue sagebrush packed all the way to the front door of a tiny, one-room cabin. As my brothers ran out from the cabin door, they hooted and hollered into the air and ran around from tree to tree. My sister stood next to my mom holding onto her leg. Jacinth made sounds going "ta, ta, ta" and pointed his fingers toward the sky. My mother's wool poncho, covering her shoulders from the sun, was draped around her body.

"This is it, girls," she said. "This is our home."

She took a few steps forward and stopped. My dad unloaded things from the back of the truck, and he hollered for the boys to come and help him. We entered the cabin, a tiny one-room with wood floors, no bed, and a tin-barrel stove. I could walk across the whole place by only measuring a few feet.

"We won't fit, Mom." I picked up my fingers and counted each person in my family. Carey, one, Nye two, John three. I got all the way to eight people.

"We won't fit, Mom."

"It's okay," she replied. "Your father is going to build us a house."

The sun sank below the horizon, darkness grew around us, and silhouettes of the tree branches outlined the land. Dad gathered wood and started a fire in front of the little house. I watched him as he took things inside the cabin. He had to duck to fit in the door, and bending his broad shoulders barely allowed him through the space.

"We won't all fit in here," he said.

"The three boys can sleep in here tonight, and the rest of us will sleep under a tarp outside."

The cabin was so tiny that only the three boys could fit. My mother was nursing Jacinth and Rose and I always slept next to her, so sleeping outside under the tarp made this possible. Nature was home inside the walls of a cabin or lying under a tarp.

My mother was at the fire warming a pot of beans. She handed me a piece of bread she broke off from a loaf. "You want some beans?"

I took a tin cup from the pile of dishes lying out and let her fill it. I sat on a rock and ate the beans and bread. My father laid out a black tarp on the ground. Then he took blankets and rolled them on top of the tarp. It was dark. The boys sat around the fire, everyone was quiet. Mom held Jacinth, his head falling to the side over her arm as he whimpered. She laid her tired body down on the blankets, and told Rose and me to get in with her.

Rose climbed in next to her, and I lay on the outside next to Rose.

"Looks like rain tonight," my dad said.

The sky was dark and smelled of rain. My brothers tended the fire; their voices were low and lulled into the night.

My dad came over with another black tarp and laid it over us.

"Get some sleep, girls."

I watched his feet as he walked away. He came back with a shovel and started to dig around the tarp.

"Help me out, John," he said. "We are going to dig a trench all the way around the tarp so that the rain drains off the sides."

I peeked through the side of the tarp. The firelight was dim, burning red coals twinkled. I saw my father's feet—his boots—

and heard his shovel digging into the dirt. My eyes were weary. I drifted off to sleep. It seemed hours passed in deep sleep when I awoke. Heavy rain poured down on the tarp. I pushed my hand up in the dark and lifted the tarp an inch just to see out the sides. The rain poured over, around, and on top of us. I watched as the water ran past me in the trench my father had dug all around us. We were dry.

I don't know if I slept again that night. The rain went on for hours. My mother, my father, my sister, the baby, and I had not moved. Wool blankets were wrapped tightly around us; my head and nose peeking out over the top of the blankets, I breathed cold air in and out.

Morning light streamed the land. I peeked through the tarp and saw the bottoms of the green-blue sage brush, the wet earth. It was damp and cold. The baby cried. I heard him nuzzle my mom and nurse.

"Well, we made it," my dad's voice streamed from behind my mom. "We made it through the first night," he repeated.

I threw back the tarp from my face and watched John, Nye, and Carey run in white underwear from the cabin door. They danced around in the mud barefoot, hooting and hollering some more, then they raced back to the door of the cabin. That was the start of a new home. It was the first place we had lived we could call ours. My father said he would get started right away on building a house.

It was the end of August, 1980. I was four years old. We spent six months living out among the trees. The small, one-room cabin became a bed for my brothers and a place for storing our things. I watched my mother standing in front of the wood-burning stove that sat out in the open, surrounded by tall, rounded piñon trees. Her auburn hair was long and silky. She stirred a pot on the stove. It was sunset. I lived and breathed the sunset since birth—it became a part of my skin seeping into me slowly. I almost didn't know it was there, except it caught the glimmering hair on the back of my mom's head. She wore a long wool dress with a blue polka dot apron wrapped around her waist. In tiny moments like these I watched my mother, not so much to learn but to feel close to her. My baby brother lay in a cardboard box beside her on the ground. I went over to peek at him. His feet were covered by little brown moccasins. He lifted his chunky legs into the air and kicked them at me. He giggled and his little round belly went up and down.

My father called it an Indian summer, which meant that winter would come late this year. Even more importantly, it meant that God was on our side in moving to this place. Because an Indian summer meant we had extra time before winter hit this year, to get ready in this strange new land. Every night I would lie down with my mother, sister, and baby brother, out under the tarp, and fall asleep.

Winter was approaching. Dad hauled loads of cedar and pine boards he had cut at a neighbor's sawmill. William and Joy Bassett were our Christian neighbors who never judged my father and would become the harbor of safety for my family over the years. They lived three miles as the crow flies, which meant off the cliff and straight through the woods. If you drove by car, it was ten miles. William was a farmer. He was a small-framed man, and always wore a black cowboy hat that looked old. He wore blue jean overalls. I don't think he ever changed them. Joy was a stocky woman with blond hair that was always pulled back in a braid. She had a garden that grew all the way around her house. William had an old sawmill that he let my Dad use.

My dad said that William Bassett was a Christian and that meant he was a good man to be around. My dad and three brothers cut down trees using a cross-cut hand held saw. The saw was six feet long and required a person to hold it on each end while they sawed back and forth, back and forth, till the tree fell. I didn't get to go on any of the trips.

I stayed with my mother every day. We made pancakes from the whole grain wheat we ground ourselves, grouty and thick. I poured goat yogurt on top of my pancakes and molasses on top of my yogurt. I ate and ate, this was my favorite food. My mom did dishes in a tin bucket on top of the stove.

"It's time to milk the goats," she said.

She handed me a pail and sent me out to the goat pen.

We had three mama goats and they each had two babies. Whitey was our best milk goat. I pulled her from the pen and led her into the stall. I had learned to milk a goat by age three; I was now five and knew well how to do it. I placed her head in the stall that had two grooved boards to hold her neck in place. I took her back leg and placed it in a sling that held the leg back from the milk sack. I put the pail down and squeezed the milk sack, then worked my hands down to the bottom of the teat. Milk shot out; it sprayed into the bucket and created a foamy layer on the top. I leaned my head into her fur and smelled the scent of the earth in her.

When the bucket was half full, I let her leg down. "Good girl," I said.

I led her back to the pen, grabbed up my bucket, and ran it back to mom. "Are we going to make cheese today?" I asked.

"Yes, we are."

Goat cheese was my favorite. It was soft and squishy on my tongue, and raw honey made it a dessert.

My sister ran around the stove. I chased her. Her legs were still a little wobbly. She had just turned two and a half. Mom got out her cloth wraps for making goat cheese, and let me pour the milk from the starter jar into the pouch. She added salt and went and hung it on the clothes line. The bag swayed there in the wind, a white, round ball.

The last days of fall were warm. Indian summer had graced us. I watched my father put up boards to hammer and nail them to build our house. He had four walls and a roof up now. My brothers hauled boards and climbed up the ladder handing him tools. John was on the roof with him, pounding a hammer. I could see the top of his baseball cap, it was on backwards and pinned tight to his forehead. Nye and Carey climbed up on the rooftop and shouted from side to side. Jacinth was crawling now. Rose and I would follow him into the empty house with dirt floors. We ran in circles kicking up the dirt and talking about where our beds would be.

On January 1, 1981, my Dad hung the large, thick cedar door to our house. We had moved inside, the floors were dirt, and there was plastic on the windows to keep out the cold. Mr. Bassett gave us an old couch and a barrel stove to fit into the living area. The cooking stove was on the floor on the other side of the room. There was a wall that separated the front and back room. The back room was split into two sides for sleeping.

Mom, Dad, Rose, and I slept on one side of the house. Rose and I shared a bed. The boys were on the other side, split by a wall, and an arched doorway with no door. My dad had built them cedar bunk beds, and one smaller bed off to the side was for Jacinth, when he was big enough.

Winter set in. Cold, hard, fast snowflakes were thick and fell softly on my forehead. When I went out to the barn to milk the goat, I would stick my tongue out and try to catch them. They were cold and then instantly warm on my tongue. By sunset we were all inside huddled by the wood-burning stove. Flames shot out the side door, the smell of pine burned into my chest.

The River of Humanity

I walked along the cliffside. The red colors of the earth meshed with the green tree branches far in the distance. This was the only river I knew, yet there was no water rushing through, the banks a steep cliff on each side. My child self climbed the cliffs just as I climbed trees, just as my father climbed in his ideals. My father lived in a river of ideals in which he wanted religion and nature to become one.

We had finally found a safe piece of land to call home. It was here that my father would work to live out his ideals; a sacred God and a sacred earth needed the tending of the heart to reap the promise of goodness. The further my father led his family into isolation, the more he felt the pressure to live up to his ideals, and the more he relied on his God to help him steer his ship. Keeping a family alive and healthy was a huge feat and the river of life that flowed through my father's veins would often burst. His temperament flowed like the ups and downs of a river, a soft rushing of water, as he erected our shelter above ground and planted our food, deep roots growing in the earth. My father's roots were deeper than the plants and he was striving to reach the sun while rising out of his past. He was letting go of an entire world he once knew, of the admiration he so wanted from a father and mother, and every idea that had been taught to him of what it meant to be successful. To be successful in the woods, one must listen to nature, hear the call of the seasons, pay close attention to the tilting sun, the moon in all her phases. One must treat work as the rhythm of life. Money is not acknowledgment for one's work. Food, shelter, and growing bodies that do not become ill are the acknowledgement. One must face fear and treat it like an old friend, turning it into song, dancing the fear right out onto dirt floors. My father was human and could not always dance it out. His flawed sense of self went straight to his religion when he could not come to terms with something, but even this he was still trying to make sense of; there was the religion that he had learned in the world, disrupted by man trying to put his own truth on it, and there was religion that came though the spirit of the woods, through the spirit of the Bible read through one's own eyes and heart.

No matter how hard he tried, my father could not completely leave the echoes of the world behind. The mounting pressures to raise a family in the woods became my father's river of life. We were on this ride with him, next to him. My mother had to be the strongest to carry all the understanding for his ebb and flow, sometimes leaning out, sometimes leaning in. When my father failed to reach his expectations, his rage would burst though, first with words, biblical passages, and then physically. The banks of the river were wide opened and overflowed. Then it was back to healing of song and dance, as my father would grab up his guitar and the softness of his truth would flow. It was in his music that my father found his anchoring truth.

Tres Palomas (The Three Doves)

The doves they mate for life
They free themselves of strife
They become one as husband and wife
The land becomes one with her children
They start out as one,
then become two
And now they are three,
a family
You and me,
you and me

We Were a Pack

We played with the sun at our backs, the tree branches reaching out to us, the golden earth spinning with shades of green. We played until dusk, where it all faded, the orange ball of fire on the horizon sunk slowly. We were a pack, my siblings and I, living on "the edge," literally on the edge of an 8,000-foot mountain range. Coyote called us into the night. We were a pack, the six of us. When the sun went down, we laid down our played out bodies, fast asleep to a world of dreams. We woke at first sunlight, the golden lines of the sun streaming through the cabin windows. Every day was new and vibrant. The same colors of the earth were spinning around us, but our hearts were a tiny bit changed by growth, by love, and by fear. Mountain lion, bobcat, deer, and coyote roamed the woods. We roamed the woods, too, looking for adventure, feeling the soul rise up to meet the mind.

The Wild West

Nighttime stories by kerosene lamp was the stage for learning to read and connecting to my mother's voice. She brought knowledge into our minds and expression into our hearts; the world was big and wide and though completely removed, we were still a part of it. During summer days, we rode bikes all up and down the road from the water well to the house, and off the property towards the mailbox, a mile away, where we got our mail. No one came to visit, except the gas man, a guy that came to check the gas meter way at the other end of our property. We didn't have gas, electricity, a phone, or a TV. But the gas company in our part of the country had a gas well at the end of the property.

At night, my mother would read to us. All six of us would line up three on each side of her in her bed. The kerosene lamp burned a dull light across the room. The cedar and pine walls glared in the light. A knitted brown and orange bedspread was flat under us, as Mom read.

Pecos Bill was the story of a cowboy, the only man crazier than my father. I think that's why she read it to us. Pecos Bill would ride out a long journey on horseback and spend his days in the wilderness, with coyotes and deer on his trail. He would then ride into town and act like he owned the place, taking up money from the bank, taking up feed from the stalls for his horse. He would ride out of town with everything, the world at his back. It was evident to me that Pecos Bill, other than the fact that he could ride a horse, was not like my father—he had no morals, and no manners either. I didn't like him much, and where was his God all this time? He didn't seem to need God, and my father had made it clear to me we all needed God.

I did like how Pecos Bill rode a horse, fast and warrior-like across vast lands, and this reminded me of my father. My father had the spirit of the horse inside of him, the wild mustang wanting to be free, and when he ran wild it was usually on a hunting trip, or a logging trip. He always carried his gun, strapped beside his saddle, and sometimes he took his guitar strapped over his back. I wondered who he would sing to, if not us?

My thoughts drifted and came back to my mother on the page, reading, reading, my brothers jumping at the next page— they loved Pecos Bill. All of them had the wild bones in their bodies, and wanted to run the mountain range and find a pot of gold, but they didn't much want to study the Bible every day as my father had taught. We were all wanting God because in the woods faith in God kept one alive, and yet not wanting God because there didn't seem to be much freedom with God, but there was freedom with the Wild West. How far was the Wild West from us? We had to be pretty close, I thought. The Jicarilla Apache Reservation was just around the corner. Wherever the Wild West is, I think we shall find it, we shall saddle it, we shall ride with it into the wind, into the blaze of sunset, and we shall do it as a family.

I looked over to see Jacinth asleep under mom's right arm. Nye, Carey, and John piled in next to each other, Rose and I spooning side by side. My father's face the only one missing. He had left to get a turkey for Thanksgiving. Said he would be back in just two days with or without a turkey. The light flickered until my mother blew it out. We slept in one big pile on mom's bed.

Two days later, I waited at the front door, then on the front porch, and then at the top of the hill. I waited for my dad. Every time my father left I felt empty inside, more scared in the woods without him. I'd wait at the top of the hill in front of our cabin and jump up and down shaking my hands with excitement when he would return. It had been two days and his time was up, he needed to show his face. I needed to see his horse, strutting down the road or coming across the field. It was Thanksgiving day. Fall was in the air, the clear crisp air of the mountain. Winter was near, but kept at bay by a bright yellow sun casting down upon us. Morning came and no papa. "Don't worry, Chlo." Carey saw my face as I looked on past the field in front of the cabin. "He's coming back."

I didn't know if he was coming back, and I needed him to return. My mother was inside baking, I smelled pumpkin pie in the air. I let my shoulders shrug and fall to a relaxed place. Pumpkin pie would make everything better. I went inside.

"Mom, you want me to kill a chicken?" Carey asked. "It's getting kinda late to wait for Dad."

"Yes, you better," she agreed.

I didn't like the killing of animals, the killing of spirit, the blood, the parts of the body dismembered. I watched John and Carey chase a chicken around the woodpile. Carey grabbed one up and flung it down on the chopping block with one hand while chopping its head right off in one smooth motion with the other hand. The head went flying in one direction and the body fumbled around on the ground a few seconds. He grabbed it up and started plucking feathers. Nye and John helped him. I ran into the back woods and climbed up to the top of a tree. Nowhere near a chicken. I didn't want to pluck its feathers. I watched the tree swaying in the wind, the needles of the pines gleaming in sunlight as a few clouds rolled in from the north.

Just as I was about to come down, I saw my father on his horse in the distance, traveling the yellow road from the east, my father straight in the saddle. I climbed down from the tree about to pee from excitement. "Dad's coming!" I yelled. "He's coming!"

I jumped up and down shaking my hands, up and down, up and down. "I told you he would come!" Carey said and looked my way with a slight grin. The boys like to poke fun at me for how much I loved Dad; they mimicked my jumping up and down and shaking my hands every time Dad was returning.

I ran out to the road to meet my father as he entered the driveway.

He and his horse looked tired. "Dad!" I yelled running out to greet him. "Did you get a turkey? Did you get one?"

My father pulled his horse up to the hitching post and sprung himself from the saddle. "I didn't get one, daughter. Didn't see a single one out there."

"That's okay, Dad," I assured him. "Carey and John already killed a chicken and Mom almost has dinner ready."

"Be good, daughter," he said his voice trailing with tiredness. "I spent last night in a rainstorm all night. It'd be good to rest, daughter." He unsaddled the white stallion and asked me to lead him to the barn. I took him by the rope and walked the yards to the horse stable in the barn. "Good boy," I said as I set him free. He stumbled into the barn, a soul weakened from a long journey. This Wild West stuff was not for babies, not for anyone but men of faith.

I ran back to the house, the smell of pumpkin pie in the air.

A Connection to Society

W e didn't have visitors often, but every now and then someone would come. We had no phone and sometimes there were no letters to let us know, just the sound of the car engine coming up the long dirt road. It was a sound you couldn't miss from a mile away. Someone was coming. My grandmother, Ogreta, my mom's mother, was the most frequent with her letters and boxes of goodies that brought more excitement than we had all year. My grandmother had visited several times when I was young and when we awaited her return it seemed like forever. My grandmother always came alone. Even before his death, my grandfather never accompanied her, and my mom's brother, Victor, had been traveling the world.

My Uncle Victor was ten years younger than my mother. He was young and wild, a worldly man of sorts who had spent much of his late twenties traveling around the globe. From China to Italy, he roamed the land with his camera by his side. He sent post cards from Guadalajara, Mexico, where he had been teaching school and developing his photography. He had long black hair and blue eyes, like my grandfather, Oscar.

My mother didn't speak of her family much, but when she did her face would light up. Now and then she would tell a story about her mother, her brother, Victor, or Blanche the maid. I'd sit in awe of this whole other life she'd had. When Victor sent a letter, it was particularly exciting, sometimes having pictures of him climbing the hillside in Rome or kicking a soccer ball with young kids in Mexico.

The day Victor arrived in his blue van with his girlfriend, Lorraine, was a big day. We didn't know he was coming and it was his first visit that I remember. He and my father didn't think too much of each other it seemed, but Victor was not a man of arguments, just a young fella looking for peace. He brought with him things of the world and was always himself, letting my father think whatever he wanted to and brushing it off. Like the time my father didn't want Victor to give John a solar-powered calculator but he gave it to him when he was leaving.

Victor always brought us more than worldy trinkets, though. He brought the promise of adventure. The six of us kids and my mother loaded into the van with Victor and Lorraine, a beautiful young woman with long, dark hair. I remember her sweetness like a touch of sugar where there was no sugar allowed. We drove from our property to a place called El Vado Lake. The northern New Mexico lake was set against a blue ridge of mountains with the Colorado Rockies to the north in the distance.

It was mid-August and the sun gleamed off the water. Victor jumped in with a head-first dive and swam till we couldn't see him. I still had not learned how to swim and the water scared me. "Don't worry, he's a good swimmer," my mother remarked. Sometime later I saw his head peeking up through lake waters. He came to shore with heaving breaths and strolled out onto the grass. John and Carey gathered around him with questions. "Wow, where'd you learn to swim like that?" John asked.

"I have been swimming in ocean waters since I was a kid in Galveston, and now I've swum in seas all over the world." We couldn't imagine there were so many places to go, so much to learn, so much to see. I wanted to swim and see the world. My body sprang with excitement, tingles moved through my fingers and out my toes in thinking about a new land, cities with tall buildings and grass growing in front of white houses. These realizations made me question my way of life and long for a bigger world that I had never seen. Victor was a walking encyclopedia.

My father had traveled much in his years before coming to live in the wilderness, but he didn't much talk about it. I secretly found bits and pieces of information about my father in private conversation with my mother. But Victor wore his travels on his shirt-sleeve. John loved this, as he had been reading the *National*

Geographic since he was ten years old. He studied late at night with a flashlight while hiding out under his bedding. My father didn't want him to get caught up in worldly things, so John found ways to learn without disrupting my father. Victor was an open book for John to source.

We gathered around a fire the boys had built in the later afternoon that day. The lake water flowed back and forth, making a shushing sound. The yellow-rabbit brush that surrounded the lake twinkled in the golden light. They boys pried Victor for more stories as we ate hot dogs for the first time.

The World is Yours

The light of gold
Comes through your voice
Your stories carry us
We have no choice
You are here to love us
To reveal the sun
To show the world
In its everything
To help us dream
We can be anything

Victor stayed for a few days, he and Lorraine camping out in the front yard in the blue van. He took some of the few photos I have from my childhood. The morning before he left, he and my father got into a yelling match. The wood-burning stove shot flames out the side of the door, and it was too late for my uncle to grab back his diary. Victor had left his diary out on the porch of the house and my father picked it up and read it. Notes on his relationship with women, his travels, his love for life, freedom, sex, all things my father saw as too worldly sent my father into a tornado of rage. There was no way for the two souls to find agreement. I thought it was rude that my father read Victor's book. I didn't know what a diary was, but learned later from my mother that it was a private book that no one else should read.

I loved my dad, despite his nonsense of a rage over things, and thought my uncle was a beacon of light. I saw clearly there was a line that divided the two men: one was of the world and one was of the woods. Victor continued to send letters, pictures and postcards from around the world. There was no keeping the outside world from us because family would always be there. I was beginning to know my father's river of life and how it flowed through his veins. Things of the world upset him; men putting knowledge and material possessions before spiritual connection triggered his rage. For he was one with Emerson on this: "Great men are they who see that spiritual is stronger than material force."

Cherry Blossoms Belong to Our Fathers

The days were short, the nights long. My father came from our neighbor Mr. Bassett's with the news one evening that my mother needed to call home. It wasn't clear why. We drove down to Mr. Bassett's to use the phone. The Bassetts lived in a typical one-level farm house, with white exterior and yellow walls on the inside. It could have been a cottage to most folks, with its one large living room, linoleum floors in a '50s style kitchen, and three small bedrooms. The small cottage was huge to me. I could not take my eyes off of everything. The front room was so much bigger than ours, with a yellow couch and chair in front of a small black and silver-screen TV, turned off. I knew what a TV was because my father had spoken about the television, "the manmade box that delivered lies and manipulation to one's mind." We were to be very cautious when it came to viewing a TV. My mother stood in the hallway and made a phone call from a green receiver that had a cord attached to the wall. I heard her voice when she spoke.

"Mama, can you hear me? It's Reva."

My mother listened for a moment, then her head fell toward her chest. I watched her face, she started to sob—the tears heavy, like I had never seen.

"Mama, I will try to make it, I will try," she said.

She hung up the phone and sat down on the floor.

I went over to her. "Mom, what happened?"

She couldn't speak. She looked down at her feet.

"Mom," I said with impatience in my voice.

"My father died," she managed to get out through her tears.

At five years old I was still trying to understand death, this being the first human death I would experience. I thought that my mother might fade away in her state of sorrow and never return. I had to get to the bottom of it. I reached out and hugged her, holding on so tight my little arms grew tired. She made loud sobbing sounds, and when I pulled away her face was all wet. What I knew of the woods was that sadness was everywhere; it was almost such a part of life, given the dying leaves in fall and the harsh wind of winter, that it *was* life and still the sun would always come and bring everything back from its sadness. This I understood, but I didn't know grief and I was quickly learning about anger.

Dad came in from outside with Mr. Bassett. He saw my mother from across the room and gave her a reassuring look.

"We better get back," he said, and tilted his head down in motion for us to follow. We loaded into the truck and drove back up the mountain. My mother wept, her tears seeming to float into the night air, the truck engine the only other sound. As we pulled over the last hill to home, she was silent. My dad leaned over and put his arm around her, holding her close with his long arms. We pulled into the front yard. I got down and went inside. I later heard them arguing from the front room. My mother wanted to go home for her father's funeral.

"We just can't do it right now," my dad said, his voice growing louder and louder. "You can't leave, Jacinth is still nursing, and we have to make it through winter."

My mother did not argue. I held onto my feelings of anger, not fully understanding them, but knowing it was wrong, just wrong that she didn't get to see her dad. I heard her leave the room. I followed her outside where she sat alone, her head in her lap while she cried and cried out with loud sobbing sounds, heavy breathing, and finally, silence. She never spoke of that day again. It was as though she had to stuff it all down to survive.

Spring could not come soon enough. The ground thawed under my feet as I ran to the goat pen. The snow was dirty from melting into the mud, the sky blue. The air was still cool, but gentle on my face as I sat and milked Whitey. She had three babies and one baby came over and started to nibble on my shoelaces. He tugged at them until they came undone.

"Hey!" I yelled at him with a smile.

He danced around me, bucking his little head that had a white diamond shape in the middle of his brow. He then ran off to his mother and nursed. The baby goats played with me every time I went to milk. It was a dance of life, young girl and baby goats twirling around the goat pen.

I loved spring, not only because it was my birthday in the middle of March, but also the warm sun started to melt the snow and the heaviness of winter was gone. Spring was full of possibilities. Hiking with the goats when they grazed all along the cliff or into the woods, riding horses, running naked up and down the road from the well after running the freezing hose of water over our heads. And the biggest necessity that came with living on the land, which was planting our food.

My dad said we would need to plant soon. My dad had a theory on the cycles of the moon and the way of the earth. He got many of his theories from studying the Bible, and from reading Emerson and Thoreau. He did not believe in going by the "bankers' calendar."

He said there are twelve moons in the same cycle for a period of two years, and every third year we get a thirteenth moon, which resets the cycle of the moon that has been behind the sun moving slowly, to moving the moon just in front of the sun, starting a new cycle over. Every thirteenth moon, spring would come later. He called it "the dance of the sun and the moon." And this determined when to plant and when to harvest the crops.

"After the last frost, we can start working the ground," he said.

My dad planted a large crop of corn in a field a few hundred feet from the house, just up a yellow dirt road and off into some trees.

I ran the yellow road from the cabin to the cornfield. The cherry tree had blossomed, white flowers were everywhere blowing softly in the spring air, bees were buzzing all around the honey box—it was a sea of white flowers and bees floating about. My dad was in the field tilling the ground around the cherry tree that stood right in the center. I raced to him.

"Dad, dad, is it time to plant the corn?" I yelled out.

"Yes'm, it is," he turned to face me, his skin turning darker from long days in the sun already, his light brown eyes glowing.

"I didn't see you last night, Dad" I said.

"Yeah, I had a late one with Carlos Werterer. We were getting some firewood on the back of the mesa."

Carlos was a friend of my dad's who showed up every so often. He was a cowboy too. He wore long-sleeved flannel shirts, boots, and jeans. He cursed—saying words like "shit"—a lot. My dad would catch him, and tell him that that wasn't God's word.

"Let's have a lesson today," Dad said.

"A lesson in what?" I looked up at him.

"In planting corn, silly," he smiled and grabbed up the bucket of seed. "Let's head out to the center of the field."

He grabbed up a shovel and a hoe. He took the hoe and dug it into the ground with the handle, making a small hole in the ground.

"About eight to twelve inches apart is what we need," he said showing me what eight inches was. "And about two inches deep," he placed a few seeds in the ground to show me.

I grabbed a few seeds of corn, poked a hole in the ground and covered them up with dirt.

"Alright," Dad said, looking me square in the eye, "now you know what two inches are—let's move on to counting. Plant them about six inches apart and see how many you can get into the ground."

I took up the hoe and made holes, dropped in a seed and began to count…one…two…three. I made it to twenty and found myself down the field a ways.

"Twenty, Dad. I made it to twenty," I yelled at him.

He came to me, and together we walked hand in hand, my small hands cupped inside his. We crossed the field to head back home as I looked toward the cherry blossoms slowly fading in the distance; they would be forever marked in my heart as the picture of spring. It wasn't often that I held my father's hand, and these moments were marked in my heart as the unbreakable bond between father and daughter. We walked the red and brown clay road to the house, where I saw my mother planting rows of cabbage in the small garden in front of the house.

My mother was in charge of planting the garden area right near our house and in front of the goat pen. It was about half the size of a football field. By May, the hollyhocks had bloomed outside the garden area where she worked all morning. The flowers were pink, white, and orange hanging off the top of the tall limbs. My mother said the flowers were her favorite, so they were my favorite too. I thought they were magical and pretended that they had special powers. I would bend the stalks over and smell the flowers, nose to petal, the scent of sweetness gathering inside me. I imagined being filled with a sap that could make me fly. I would run in and out of the garden area with Rose and Jacinth, flying my arms out like a bird. Jacinth had started to wobble on his two feet. He looked like he was going to fall, but was sturdy over every mount of dirt and rock. He had turned a year old in March.

I planted beans, peas, cabbage, carrots, and rhubarb with my mom. She held the seeds in her hand, the soft-blowing wind tossing a piece of her hair around her face. "Look," she said, this is life in our hands, Chlo."

She knelt down and put the seeds into the ground. Then she gently padded the dirt on top. My mother was softer than my father, softer in her voice, softer in her look, and softer with her words about life. I dug my fingers into the dirt two inches like mom taught me in this garden, then placed the seeds down softly and covered them up.

"How long will it take for them to grow?" I asked.

"Well, they will grow all summer from now in early May until the end of August," she said.

I helped my mom carry buckets of water to the garden and poured the water onto the planted areas.

"Now we water all summer and watch the plants grow," she said.

By summer, the plants had sprouted. Tiny, green buds popped up from the earth. Bigger and bigger they got. We hauled water from the well house that was about a hundred yards away. By August the field before the cabin was a mesh of colors—greens, purples, reds—all the plants reaching for the sky from the brown earth.

One day I was playing in the dirt next to the garden and watched a caterpillar crawl up my arm. It was the first time I'd seen one, but it didn't startle me. Everything was a part of God's land, all the animals, even bugs.

"Mom, what is this?" I yelled at her from across the garden.

My mother came to me and said, "It's a caterpillar."

"What's that?" My eyes were beaming bright.

"That's a worm-like creature that goes through a process where it splits its shell and out of it comes a butterfly."

Whoa! I had seen butterflies, they looked nothing like this, how could that be? I looked out at the tiny buds of the plants popping up. I guess it's like the garden looks like one thing and becomes something completely different. I got it in my mind, and watched the caterpillar crawl off my arm onto a flower.

When I was alone with nature, I would get a sense of life and death and all things that mattered. It was the most natural thing to me. I didn't even realize it, until I'd stop in the middle of a plant or a tree and feel my feelings. The moment with my mother and the butterfly helped me to affirm and understand that death is a part of the life cycle. I was getting these lessons every day in the woods and slowly they sunk into my body—someday I too would die. It brought up a deep sadness that I shoved into the dirt when I planted seeds with my mother.

I thought about my mother and how her father had died, which meant he had gone to be with God. I had learned this already from stories in the Bible. I remembered my mother's sad face, her broken cries, and wished in that moment that she and her father would someday meet under the cherry blossoms.

A Donkey Is a Friend

The slowest donkey in the woods was named Tawny Jack. He was a gray fur ball, large with even larger ears that stood out from his body. He was a calm donkey who let all six of us climb all on him. The six of us would get on him at once. We all lined up, Jacinth in the front with John behind him, then Carey, Nye, Rose, and me. That would only last a few seconds and he would not move. So each of us would pile off and John would load back up me, Rose, and Jacinth. Then we would nudge him in the side a few kicks one after the other, and like a slow caboose moving he would start to walk. We would ride him off into the woods. He would wander around with us on his backs. "Giddy up, donkey, giddy up, donkey," Jacinth would say to him, kicking his sides as we went. He was the most shy of all the creatures we had, the oldest, with a face of fur and sad eyes that met me right where all animals met me, right at my chest.

On Saturday afternoon, I rode Tawny Jack alone into the deep woods. We had a natural spring my father had carved out, deep into some rocks and at the edge of our forest line. I rode him there that afternoon and sat underneath the tall pine trees the wind blowing heavy. I watched as Tawny Jack's ears wriggled back and forth.

"What is it, boy?" I asked him." He was smart and could tell if a storm was coming, if the sun was going to set. If life was going to change, Tawny Jack knew it. "What is it, boy?" His ears twisted and turned, back and forth, back and forth.

Dark clouds rose overhead, and a bolt of thunder struck hard. I hopped on him, bare back—we always rode him bare back. He was a blanket of fur underneath our legs. We rode the path back to the house, half a mile before the rain started to come down hard. I leaned in around his neck and held myself tucked tight. The rain poured onto my six-year-old body, belting me hard on my legs, head, and back. We reached the house, lightning bolting from all sides of the land struck the tree branches to the sides of me, the sky now a raging sea of water pounding from the above.

I led Tawny Jack back to the barn and took cover under the rooftop. We stood side by side and watched the rain pour. "Well, boy, you tried to warn me—you did your best." I assured him. His fur now soaking wet, my hair, arms, and legs soaked. I couldn't wait to get inside the house. Summer rains were the heart of God, they brought moisture and calm to the earth, but to get caught in one made you appreciate shelter. The slowest donkey in the woods was the smartest donkey in the woods, too. Riding Tawny Jack gave me a soft and safe start to getting on the back of animal. I needed to feel safe, though I wasn't likely to admit it with three older brothers ready to ride anything. Very young I had learned how to stand in my courage, but soft fur and gentle guidance from an animal like Tawny Jack let me feel my soft side and embrace my instincts, while standing in my courage.

Pieces of the Outside World

Grandma was the book lady—with red hair and brown eyes she brought with her the world, the vision of a teacher; she was strong and capable. She came during the dry heat of summer when I was old enough to pick her some wildflowers and put them in her hand. She in return would put a book in my hand; then she would sit with me and read it aloud, her voice echoing the blue sky above. Her visits were infrequent, always a surprise, and left us in complete wonder of everything. It seemed it had been two summers since I saw her last.

It was almost August. I heard my parents arguing from outside the cabin walls while I was lying lazily on the front steps of the little cabin that was now used as a room for storage.

"It's time for a visit to my mother's," Mom said.

"We need to keep up with the garden," Dad said. "If we don't, winter will come and we will fall behind. Do you want that to happen?" he questioned her.

My mother stood her ground. "We will only go for a few weeks. The kids need to see their grandmother," she said as she walked away.

The next morning my mother told us we were going. We packed a few bags. My dad drove us to the bus station. He spoke to the bus driver, handed him some dollars, and helped us each onto the steps of the Greyhound bus. I waved to him through the window. He stood alone in the street, his cowboy hat on, his boots and jeans fitted. His face looked firm as we drove away.

"Thank you for letting us go," I whispered through the window to him.

It was a long trip to get there. My grandmother, Ogreta, lived in Houston, Texas. We lived about two hours north from the nearest town. The towns got larger and larger as we drove. We would stop in Cuba, New Mexico, to catch the first Greyhound bus into Albuquerque. There were many times in my childhood we didn't have a vehicle. This year we had my father's Chevy. We headed out past all that I knew, where the forest was thick, where the deer bounced out in the evenings, where the road was narrow and steep. It was a long journey just to get out of the property and into town. I listened to the rhythm of the truck grinding on the dirt, then on the pavement as we entered small villages and then the first town. The sound of other vehicles traveling together was a distinct noise, a grinding of many wheels packing down on the earth. I was alerted to everything. How could you hear a storm in town? I wondered. There was too much noise to hear anything but the noise.

When we got to Albuquerque, we stayed with my mom's friends Jane and Eli Rivers. Jane and Eli had lived in Albuquerque since they left the Tawapa Farm in the early '70s. Jane remained a friend to my mother and a protector of sorts, always praying for us kids. We waited at Jane's house for my grandmother to wire us money, to get plane tickets and fly to see her.

Jane had loose curls of short, dark brown hair. She was soft around the eyes and wore simple clothing. She was motherly and I felt cared for by her. My mother had kept in touch with Jane and Eli over the years by letters. Jane was one of my mom's true friends. She was from New York and, like my mom, had escaped the city to live freely among the plants and the trees. They'd wanted a new life, and they got just that. They birthed their babies by themselves without any medicine or doctors, just the men that loved them. But now Jane lived in the city.

We arrived at Jane's home at dusk on a summer's evening, a few bags in our hands and hungry.

We stormed her front door. It was teal blue, framed by a large adobe house with lots of glass windows. The trees outside her door were different than the ones at home. The leaves were softer and more delicate, dancing free in the wind. I noticed them most. The city streets were gray and hard, and my feet felt the heat rising up from them as I walked. Houses and lights everywhere, too much to look at, too much to see, my body felt overwhelmed. When we entered Jane's house, it was calm. My mother and six kids stormed into her living room.

"Hi!" is all we could say.

"You must be hungry," she said.

"Yes," John replied.

"Well, since I didn't know you were coming I don't have a dinner prepared, but we can go to McDonalds," she said.

"What's McDonalds?" I leaned into my mom's ear and whispered.

"Sheesh," she replied. "Okay, let's go."

Jane grabbed a purse and directed us toward the door.

"Will we fit in your car?" I said.

We piled into Jane's station wagon. I sat on John's lap in the back seat, with Rose in between my knees, Carey and Nye on each side of us. My mom sat in the front seat holding Jacinth in her arms.

"We only need to stay two nights," my mom said to Jane, who drove the car, not seeming to pay attention to my mother.

"My mother has wired us money and we can fly out on Thursday."

Suddenly the car turned a corner, flashing green signs lit everywhere, then a sign with a big yellow M on it appeared, and a poster in the window showed a bunch of foods I'd never seen before.

"What is this?" I asked John.

"I think it's called fast food." John was so on top of knowing things about the world.

"Is this it?" Nye shouted.

"This is it," Jane replied, "but we're only going through the drive-thru. No need to have us all get out" I was disappointed. How could we not go inside the restaurant? This was the fun part of eating somewhere.

I asked John again, "What's a drive-thru?"

He nodded his head. "This is a drive-thru."

We pulled through a tight driveway and she rolled down the window.

"Okay, what does everyone want? "

A voice came over a loud speaker from a black box. "Can I take your order, please?"

We were all startled.

"What—who was that?!?" Carey and Nye laughed out loud.

John straightened up. "It's the lady inside the McDonalds," he stated.

My mother turned around to face us. "You guys have to look at the menu on the black box and tell me what you want," she said.

I didn't know what I wanted. I looked at the pictures, a big piece of bread holding in the middle a piece of meat, stacked with a bunch of stuff but I couldn't tell what it was.

John said, "I'll have a Number One."

None of us understood the menu, so John read it out loud. John was reading at a twelfth-grade level by the time he was thirteen. He had never eaten a hamburger, but he once saw pictures of fast-food restaurants in a magazine. My mother was quiet when we went out in public and she softly let Jane know that we didn't know what McDonald's was. I heard the two of them having a side conversation from the front, while Nye and Carey were yelling out numbers for food.

"Two!" Nye yelled.

"One!" Carey yelled.

Rose didn't speak.

I looked up at John's boy face, his blue eyes smiling down at me. I pushed at his side, get me the Number One." He smiled and ordered for me.

After my mom ordered for Rose and we picked up the food, we pulled away from the strange place with an M on it. I dug into a bag stuffed with French fries.

"Mom, what are French fries?" I asked.

"They are fried potatoes."

They were warm and greasy. I dug into the bag quickly, feeling the sting of the salt around my lips when they touched. I had lots of potatoes in my life, baked, mashed, and skillet-fried in little squares, but never French fries. I did not want the red sauce called ketchup.

We drove back to Jane's in the dark. Lights—red, green, yellow, with blinking signs all over, left turns, right turns, and finally onto Jane's street. I saw the teal door of Jane's house and felt myself leaving my body with excitement. We were in the city.

There were all kinds of people—and foods—and things to do. We climbed out of the car and rushed inside. My stomach now had a knot in it. I wasn't sure if it was the food or the excitement that was making me feel sick. Jane gathered blankets and pillows.

"Boys can sleep on the couch," she said, and she pulled it out into a bed. "Follow me, girls, and I'll set you and your mom up in our spare room."

We followed her down a hallway. Pictures streamed the walls, kids smiling with Jane. It looked fun. We didn't have any pictures, or walls where you could hang stuff. I held my head down, feeling like this home was so nice compared to mine, and followed Jane into the room. It was large, a bed in the center. Jacinth was crying and mom sat on the bed to soothe him. She hummed a song out loud, and he stopped crying. Rose and I climbed into the bed.

"Girls, you can take your clothes off?" Jane stated in the form of a question.

"Uh, what? Mom?" I asked.

"Oh, it's okay, Jane," my mother replied. "They sleep in their clothes."

I climbed into the bed. It had a bedspread with blue lines and flowers knitted throughout. My jeans were snug on my body, and the sleeves of my orange sweater covered my hands. Rose and I curled up the way we always did, her in front of me, our bodies shaped together like a mama and baby lion. I lay there thinking about my grandmother and all the books she had sent us, about a city named Houston and her two-story house that sat underneath the palm trees that my mother had told me about. I'd never seen palm trees, except in the pictures she sent. I was used to the cold crisp air of the north, and those trees blew in the winds of the southern sun. It must be hot, I thought as I drifted off to sleep.

The next day, Jane drove us to the airport. It was a large

building, larger than I'd ever seen. People were everywhere. My mother carried Jacinth, who squirmed in her arms trying to make his way to the floor. John held my hand on one side and Rose's hand on the other. Nye and Carey walked side by side. We all followed my mother as she went through the gates. People stared at us as we walked.

"Mom, have I been on a plane before?" I asked.

"You have," she replied, "but you were too little to remember."

"Are we going to fly?" I looked to John for some confidence.

"Yup, we're going to fly," he said.

We moved through the inside of the plane looking for our blue seats and waiting for our fellow flyers to sit. We scuffled through the narrow lane, Jacinth now crying and Rose squeezing my hand tight. There were people on all sides of us with bags and perfumes fuming off their clothes and hair. The smell of it all was enough to make me gag. Jacinth was asleep in my mom's arms. Mom's hair was now pinned back from her face, her blue eyes looking pale and drawing the light in around the edges. She did not smile. Her dress was brown and she wore a gray wool sweater over the top. No makeup. She had gotten used to living in the woods, where there was little use for makeup or dressing for a crowd. It was enough to get somewhere with all of us tagging behind her like a row of baby ducks.

An announcement came over the airwaves through the room, and my mother said it was time to take off. The lady on the plane, who my mother said was a stewardess, would help us to feel safe on the flight. The lady came by and requested that we put on our seatbelts.

"What's a seatbelt, Mom?" I asked.

John pulled the strap over me and connected it around my waist.

"That's a seatbelt," he said.

The plane took off. I felt funny in my stomach and hoped I wouldn't throw up. My mom sat across the aisle from me, nursing Jacinth. He was falling asleep on her nipple. Her shirt covered over most of her skin. His green-steel blue eyes softly lulled opened and closed, until lashes were all I saw.

"Don't throw up!" I told myself.

I sat near the window, and did not look out. John held Rose's hand as the plane leveled out in the sky.

"It's a short flight," Mom said low in her voice.

Nye and Carey were in the seats behind us. I heard Carey laugh, and Nye tell him to shut up. I laid my head back and fell asleep. I awoke to the plane landing, wheels scraping down, a huge push, the seatbelt pressing against my belly, and a jolt as we slowed down.

"Are we there?" I mumbled from my seat, my hair tousled around my face.

"We are here," Mom said.

Grandma's...
A Whole Other World

We made our way through the crowd of people till I caught a glimpse of Grandma's red hair. She was waving from outside the gate. She was taller than my mother by a few inches, with a tight, athletic frame and the most impeccable posture. We ambushed her with hugs. She stood strong, like a force—determined, ready to go.

"Let's get you to the car," she said.

We followed her toe-in-toe, but with her fast pace I could not keep up. We piled into the car, like we had in Jane's. Cars and buildings zoomed past us, and we zoomed past them. Signs, letters, words written on buildings, I could not make it all out.

"My friend Ruth is making lunch for us," she said. "Do you remember Ruth?"

"I do," Carey said.

"Me too," John followed.

"Tomorrow we can go to the zoo," she added.

"The zoo? What's that?" I asked John.

"It's a place for animals." He explained.

"What kinds of animals? Horses, goats, like we have?" I said.

"No, not those kinds of animals—the kind of animals that live in Africa and other countries," he said.

Other countries...I didn't exactly know where he was talking about. John had been reading books for a long time and he knew things from all those books. This made me want to read.

"When will I know how to read?" I asked him.

"Hmm, well, Mom is teaching you now. You'll learn," he said.

I felt comforted by his affirmation that I would read someday, even if I didn't go to school. He didn't go to school and he learned to read, so I guessed it would be okay.

When we pulled into the drive, two palm trees greeted us like giants, standing free, their long leaves blowing in the wind. I remembered them from the pictures and felt at ease.

Grandma's house looked bigger than I had remembered. It was white, with the green trim around the windows. It had two stories, a large living room, a dining room, a kitchen, and two bedrooms downstairs and two upstairs.

So much room, I thought. Why would my mom want to leave this place?

We entered the house through the garage. The sticky humidity seeped into my skin, my face melted, my arms fell to my sides. It was hot. The door to the house opened and a whoosh of cold air brushed past me. We went inside. The living room was a huge square, with large windows at the back of the room, and a door leading to the outside yard full with green hedge grass. It was late afternoon. The light was different. I saw bushes along the fence, but no trees. A TV sat in front of a couch that faced the back door. Carey and Nye ran to sit on the couch and plopped down.

"Can we watch something, Grandma?" Carey asked.

"Give me a minute," she called out as she carried our bags into the room next to the dining area where a large table took up space with green chairs all around it.

I was excited about the food and wondered what we would be eating. Grandma helped my mother put her things away while we all sat on the couch. I was exhausted, but excitement pumped adrenalin through my body like the electricity brought light through the plug on the wall. I couldn't sit still. *Inspector Gadget* played on the TV set. He was funny, this Inspector Gadget guy, in his long overcoat and funny looking hat, not a cowboy hat, one to keep off the rain I supposed. He went up high into the sky with an umbrella that lifted him magically. I didn't understand how that was possible.

Sometime during the show, the outside lights came on, and I noticed the sun was gone, but there had been no sunset. Grass glistened in the nightlights that filtered across the lawn. We were in another country, I thought.

Grandma knew we loved macaroni and cheese and she made it for dinner, along with a salad she said we needed to eat. We cleaned our plates.

"Now up to bed, wash up and get into some pajamas," she said.

"Pajamas? What's that?" I asked.

She gave my mother a look, took my hand, and walked me up the wide stairway that was carpeted.

"Most people," she said, "when they go to bed, they change out of their clothes they have worn all day into what we call pajamas."

"Hmm…but, why?" I asked.

"Because it's not good to go to bed in dirty clothes," she said.

I realized my grandmother had a lot of different ideas about how life should be. But I liked her so I listened to her. She put me to bed in my underwear. "Tomorrow we will buy you some pajamas." She looked at me, her brown eyes were deep and round, and they sparkled.

"Night, Grandma."

The soft bed was piled with a thin, white quilt that had gold trim all around the edges. I laid my head back, picturing Rose asleep with my mom in another bed. This was the first time I had slept by myself. I liked it, and started to dream about how someday I might get my own room. I didn't know how that would happen, but I thought somehow it could happen. I closed my eyes and drifted away. The next morning Rose and Jacinth charged through the door, piling on top of me.

"Let's go, let's go!" Rose shouted.

Jacinth did his bow-legged baby walk around the room and looked into every drawer he could reach. He dug his fingers into the drawers and pulled himself up, and then fell back on his butt. I pulled on my pants and helped Jacinth down the stairs.

Pancakes for breakfast, but they were the fake ones. The flour was mushy and soft, and syrup ran out the sides of the plate. My brothers scarfed down their food like wild wolves that had mistakenly entered into a civilized place, and then asked to go out and play with the neighbor kids. Grandma tried to wipe their hands before they headed out the door, but they dodged her and ran. I sat and ate my pancakes, slowly, bite by bite. I never knew when I would get to eat them again.

My mom sat in the living room while Grandma cleaned up the kitchen. *Deserving,* I thought—my mother was always doing dishes at home, cooking, cleaning, and never sitting. I didn't know how she could like that.

I helped my grandma carry some plates into the kitchen, and propped myself up on a red stool she had near the kitchen window. Perched there, I could see my brothers running across the street with two boys. The boys' skin was black.

"Why are those kids black?" I asked.

Grandma stopped for a minute. Then she paused and said, "Well, those are black kids, and there are a lot of blacks in my neighborhood."

"Oh," I said.

I didn't press her but that didn't answer my question. The only kids I had seen of another skin color were Indian kids, and they didn't seem that different. I had never seen black skin. It was neither good nor bad, just different.

When the dishes were done, Grandma and I headed back to the living room; Jacinth and Rose were running circles around the round glass coffee table that sat in front of a long oval-shaped green couch. It was fancy.

"Watch them with that glass," Grandma noted, to my mother.

"Hmm…huh," my mom responded.

"I will pack some lunches for the zoo," she said as she exited the room.

Grandma called out for the boys to come inside. They rushed in through the front door, gleaming sweat dripping from their faces and arms.

"Alright! The zoo!" Carey said. "Bet I can tell you the names of all the animals."

"Bet you can," Grandma said and she squeezed his hand. "You are one smart boy."

We loaded back into the car. The heat melted us together against the seats. The air came on quickly and saved us. We drove and then parked at a place that looked like a huge park filled with grass and hills and some type of dome.

"What's that for, Grandma?" I asked.

"They sometimes have music here at the zoo," she said. "It's called the Miller Outdoor Theatre. All the musicians get up on that stage and perform for all the people sitting on the grass."

"Can we go?" I shouted.

"Sometime," my mom responded.

I thought about my dad for the first time since we had left him. I wondered if he played his guitar when we were gone. I didn't know why he never came with us to Grandma's. I guess he was too different himself. Grandma never said anything bad about him, but then again she didn't say much of anything about him. *Someone had to take care of the animals,* I thought, and was glad my Dad was loyal and stayed behind with them.

We ran into the zoo, Grandma yelling at us to slow down.

First I saw a giraffe, with its long neck hovering over a huge rock wall, then a lion in the distance, behind a wire fence, with a bushy, yellow mane. Its eyes were sad and drifted off, not looking at us. I also saw kangaroos with a belly pouch.

"What's the pouch for?" I asked John.

"It's to carry their babies in," he replied.

Next I saw a polar bear. That was my favorite. John pointed out the animals to Rose and me, telling us each of them by name.

"But we can't touch them…why can't we touch them?" I said.

"Yeah, why can't we?" Rose asked.

"Well, because they live in their cages. They have a different life than the animals we are used to seeing," John said.

I believed him. They just had a different life. My heart was sad for them. I wanted them to be free from their different life.

We ate lunch on the green lawn in front of the outdoor dome. There was no music, but it was pretty. Grandma knew how to keep us happy with our favorite foods, peanut butter and jelly sandwiches. She handed them out one by one, wrapped in little bags. Grandma knew how to wrap things well. She was well wrapped herself. Her clothes were clean and she wore a green, relaxed pant suit that looked vibrant against her red hair. She had red lipstick. I wondered if my mom ever wore red lipstick or if I would ever wear it myself.

By late afternoon, the humidity was stuck to my skin like my own freckles on my arm, and we said goodbye to the zoo. I ran to the top of the grassy hill and watched the sun fade behind tall buildings to the west. Tall buildings got in the way of everything important—the sun, the trees, the land. I felt closed in by the city and longed for a moment to stand in the woods with the doves. At home on the mountain, the evening was marked by the sound of cooing doves. I wasn't sure I liked the zoo. I didn't care whether we went back.

The Ocean Is Full of Love

"We can plan a trip to Galveston this week," Grandma said to my mother in the front seat.

My brothers shouted out, "Galveston! Have I been there?"

"Mom, have I been there?"

"You have been there," Grandma said. "The beach, remember?"

I was seven now and vaguely remembered the gray sand and the seagulls flying overhead. Now they seemed happy, those seagulls.

The week went quickly and we headed for the beach. We drove and drove. Long hills, lots of buildings, towers so high I wouldn't want to climb, and so many cars. I noticed all the many colors of the cars as we neared the ocean.

Roaring water and loud crashing waves came rolling toward a cement wall we sped past. We drove down into a sandy area and parked. The boys rushed from the car, screaming. I stepped out into the sand, warm, smooth and slippery under my feet. It sparkled almost like the snow at my house in winter. We walked toward the water, my mom in a breezy, white dress. For once I could see the skin on her arms, as she was always covered up; she was pale white with a few freckles. Her hair was bright and flowing in the air, the sun bathing it. I watched her walk and thought she looked pretty. The water kept on roaring as the boys ran in screaming, splashing, and tumbling over and under the waves.

"Let's go in," I told Rose.

We squeamishly made our way toward the water, first touching our toes in and then running out. My mother and grandmother sat on the sand, looking out at us. Jacinth played in the sand next to my mom. His hair was blond, and cut just above his eyes. He sported a cloth diaper that made his butt look bigger than it was. His legs were chunky and sturdy as he marched through the sand. He bent over and dug his hands into the wet sand, picking up gobs of it and throwing it back down.

Rose and I ran for it, dipping in and out of the water. The salt burned my lips when the water rose too high around me. It was deep and we didn't know how to swim, so I only went as far as my feet could touch. I could see my mom watching from the sand, a blue beach umbrella now over her head. Rose stayed near the edge and I went back towards her.

"Let's go lie down," I said.

My skin was turning pink. We made our way to the big umbrella.

"You need more sunblock," Grandma motioned for us to come to her.

She applied globs of white goo onto my skin. It was cooling. The heat felt like it was vibrating from my body. I lay down on a green towel under the umbrella, listened to the waves, and watched the seagulls swoop overhead. The sand was still stuck to my feet, and I brushed them back and forth to get the sand off, off, off. The boys ran in from the water and their flailing bodies soaked me while plopping down on the towels.

"Time for lunch," Grandma said and pulled out some bologna sandwiches stuffed with lettuce, tomato and mustard all in between two slices of bread.

It tasted weird at first, but then I liked it. The afternoon sun was plain hot. I rested on my towel and drifted off to sleep. When I woke, Grandma was packing the bags.

"Aw, we have to go?" I lifted my head in sadness.

The waves rushed ashore, my mind was still. It felt similar to when I fell asleep in the woods far from our cabin. But there was no water, no water like this. And there was no Grandma, no peanut butter and jelly, and no grassy hills, and no palm trees. I sat still for a few more minutes. The sun was fading in the sky, the light grew dim, and my eyes became dull with the changing light. I wanted to rest there forever.

Then we drove. Night came, the city lights popping on all around us. The car moved fast. I fell asleep leaning against John's shoulder. The whole car was asleep, our pack piled together in the backseat, leaning on one another.

We had stayed three weeks at my grandmothers when my mother said, "We have to leave in two days." From my child's point of view, time was an elusive thing; there was rhythm in the woods that was not in the world when it came to time.

The last night there, I sat on the long, oval-shaped couch in front of the glass coffee table. I noticed the picture of a woman that hung above the fireplace. A painting that looked formal, with gold trim around its frame. The young woman had no lines in her face, soft skin, red pouty lips. She wore a black blouse, loose and flowing with a deep neckline, and a red skirt that was above her waist with the blouse tucked in tight. Her auburn hair was thick, and piled high upon her head. Her eyes were blue. Her lips were pressed softly together with no hint of a smile. She looked sophisticated, elegant, educated.

My grandmother sat next to me on the couch. She had been teaching me some numbers and letters. I stopped counting and looked up at the woman in the picture.

"Grandma, who is that?" I pried for a response.

"That's your mother," she replied, proud.

I stared at the picture. My mother had never worn a fancy dress, at least not the mom I knew. Her hair was pulled back in a bun most of the time, and mostly she looked older and sadder than the woman in the picture. I couldn't believe it was her in the picture. My mother was upstairs reading and my grandmother took the liberty to keep going with her show and tell.

"You want to see some other pictures?" Grandma asked.

"Sure I do."

She brought out a bunch of photos. They were all in black and white.

"Did you know your mother was a ballet dancer?"

"No," I said with a question. "How do ballet dancers dance?"

"Look at the pictures. You see how your mother has on tights and a little dress, and those pink slipper-type shoes? That's what ballet dancers wear, and they move light on their toes like birds floating in the air across the stage."

"Really, Grandma? Mom was like a bird floating across the stage?"

I imagined her floating and happy. In the picture, her hair was neatly combed around her ears—she had lots of hair—and a bow wrapped around the middle of her head was tucked behind her ears. She was bent forward, holding her dress out slightly with one hand, taking a bow.

That was my mother, and I wanted her to still be that girl, but she was someone else now. I had never seen her dance. I moved my eyes away from the ballet pictures, pushing them aside.

"Thanks, Grandma. I am going to go lie down now."

I climbed the stairs to my room, lay down in my underwear, closed my eyes, and listened to the fan blowing loudly on the floor near my feet.

The next morning, my grandma made us our last pancakes. We ate them and then ran around the living room while Mom and Grandma gathered our bags.

"You know, you don't have to go back," I heard her saying to my mom.

"Oh, Mom, we've had this conversation before." My mother shrugged her shoulders and walked away from my grandma.

We piled into the car one last time, the heat of Houston pinning us to our seats and to each other.

The center of the city had taller buildings than I had ever seen. The airport was waiting for us. People hurried with bags over their shoulders, suitcases on the floor beneath their feet. People sat in chairs, thumbing through books, and many staring off into the distance.

I didn't want to get on the airplane. My insides tugged at me. Grandma held my hand tight, she squeezed and squeezed it, she held Rose with the other hand, and guided us to a seat near the gate.

"Girls, I want you to practice your letters every day, you hear me?" She looked me in the eyes, expecting me to do it.

I wanted to read. I wouldn't let her down. She hugged John, Nye, and Carey tight in a group.

"You keep reading," she said to John, "and you boys keep learning all you can," she said, cupping each of their faces in her hands.

I watched her walk through a crowd of people, her red hair going, going…gone. We boarded the plane.

We flew. I didn't throw up. We landed, and Jane picked us up.

We were tired, worn out, and no one spoke.

Normal as We Knew It

My mother had already spoken to my father, and he wanted to meet us right away at the bus station in Cuba. There would be no overnight at Jane's.

"I can give you a ride to the bus station, if you guys want," Jane said.

"That will be fine," Mom replied.

We stopped at a pay phone that stood outside the bus stop in Albuquerque. My mother made a call to Todd's to try to reach my father; they spoke briefly and he would meet us in Cuba, New Mexico, by sunset. We rode the bus to Cuba. My dad was there when we got off the bus at the bus stop. He was happy, and talking a lot to my mom. They embraced each other, both smiling. My dad knelt down, his frame towering over me. He hugged Rose and grabbed us up with both arms.

"Okay, Dad," I hugged him and insisted he put me down.

"So, we have a ride home?" Carey asked.

My dad was on foot.

"Truck broke down right after ya'll left, and I haven't been able to get it running," he said.

"I am trying to get a hold of Mr. Bassett for a ride," he said.

"Let's move from the bus station," John said as he lifted Rose onto his shoulders.

We moved from the bus station across the street to a Circle K gas station. We had a round, tin washing tub holding all our clothes and bags. We sat in front of the Circle K, the red lights blinking from inside.

"Let's go in and get a hot chocolate," my dad motioned for us to follow.

"Yay!" Rose and I pushed behind the boys through the door to get hot chocolate.

My dad used the last of his change to buy the drinks. We sat in front of the Circle K, the red lights flashing. A sign on the front door said "Open 24 hours."

Night was all around us. Sounds of car engines came and went, and slowly settled into the darkness. Jacinth lay asleep in the bath pan on top of the clothes. Rose and I leaned in over the bags. It grew later and later. A few people stopped and went, looking strangely at the family of eight sitting on the front steps.

A tan car pulled up, and two women got out. One had neatly combed brown hair, and wore green earrings, and a black pant suit with a red undershirt tucked inside her pants. She was the driver. The other wore a pair of jeans with a white blouse and a tan jacket over the blouse. She had blond hair, cut short. Her face was round, and her skin delicate. They went inside chatting it up. When they came out, they approached my dad.

"Sir, might we help?" the driver of the car offered.

"Well, that's mighty kind of you." Dad replied, "But I think we are doing just fine."

The other lady spoke up. "Let us get you a hotel room for the night, let your children sleep," she requested with pleading eyes.

"No Ma'am, I can't let you do that. We have a ride coming in a few hours," Dad put his hand out to thank the women and move them on their way.

I lay against the clothes, so tired, and a bit cold. I had never been in a hotel room, and it was a dream that wasn't going to happen. The two women got in their car. I watched them back up slowly, their eyes looking at me, Rose, and Jacinth laying on the steps. Dad went to make another phone call. He came back in a few minutes, the night lights the same, blinking off and on, off and on. Darkness was beyond the edge of town.

"Okay, Mr. Bassett is on his way," Dad said. "He'll be here in less than an hour."

I had drifted off to sleep when I heard Mr. Bassett's voice trailing under my father's. I pulled myself up from the clothes. My dad loaded the bags. My parents and Jacinth got into the yellow truck with Mr. Bassett. The rest of us climbed into the back of the pickup, the bags of clothes packed around us. We all laid back, the wind blowing overhead, the twinkling lights of the city disappearing behind us.

All Our Friends Have to Leave

Summer was nearly gone when we got back to the mountain. I slept till the sun was brightly streaming through the windows in the backroom. I woke excited to see the animals. I ate my cereal quickly and ran out to the barn. The goats were already gone for their morning grazing, the dogs gone with them. I looked everywhere for Tawny Jack.

I ran back to the house, "Mom, where is Tawny Jack?"

"Ask your dad," she said.

I found my dad and John out near the barn, lifting bales of hay.

"Dad, where is Tawny Jack?" I yelled up at him to the rooftop.

"Don't know where he is. I haven't seen him for about a week."

"A week! He never leaves for that long…Dad, Dad are you listening?"

"Yes. I don't know, something might have happened to him. You're going to have to check the woods."

I ran back to the house to tell my mom that Tawny Jack was missing.

"I am going to look for him, Mom. Be back soon."

I let the door shut before my words could get out.

I took off though the woods, calling out his name, "Tawny Jack, Tawny Jack!"

Nothing. I went all the way past the well house, and then cut back through the woods to the edge of our property. Back by where my dad had dug out a natural spring, where we carried buckets of cold water for a half a mile before the well was dug for us. I wandered through the woods, my gut telling me he was there. I sat down on a fallen tree now rotting at the roots, the forest alive around me, green branches reaching out, the soil soft under me. I hung my head down.

"Tawny Jack," I said in a low voice.

I gazed out across the forest and saw something. I jumped to my feet and raced over.

"Oh no."

His body was mostly decomposed, his rib cage sticking out, his head already gone, his hooves black and intact. I stood over him and cried.

"Tawny Jack, what happened?"

I sat on the tree log a while until my tears ran out. He was gone. I got up and walked the half mile back to the house. My father saw me coming through the woods with my head hung low.

"What happened, you find him?"

"Dad," I said, my tears returning. "I found his body."

My tears burst from my eyes; I could hardly speak. My dad hugged me.

"Well, he was old, that's all. Nothing bad happened to him, he went out there to die in his favorite place."

"Okay," I said.

But I wasn't consoled. Nothing could console me.

Things die, even if they are really important to us, they still die, I thought. I made my way toward the house. I couldn't tell Rose about Tawny Jack. I went and lay down in the back room.

Apples Are the Soul of Life

Fall was around the corner. I buried my grief in all the other animals, holding the baby goats and playing with the dogs. My dad had learned that dogs became good herd dogs if you had them nurse on the mama goats from a very young age. We had just had a new litter of pups. They were an Australian-mix breed with brown and white patches of thick fur. I would hold up a round, fat-bellied puppy to the mama goat, and squeeze the goat's milk into his mouth. The puppy would start to nurse just like a little goat. This bond was then unbreakable and the dogs naturally became goat herders. This new form of life healed me, and I moved on from Tawny Jack's death. The puppies started to grow and they followed the goats right out the goat pen, and on to their hikes for grazing.

"Keeps the mountain lions and bobcats from attacking," my dad said.

The air grew colder and Dad said it was time for a trip to pick apples. Old man Gildo lived about twenty miles away; he had an orchard with fifty apple trees. He offered for us to come and pick whatever we could and take them home. We piled into the back of my Dad's Chevy truck, running again now. My mom came with us, holding Jacinth in the front with her. The air flew past us, and we pulled into the apple orchard. Green leaves and red apples hung low, the branches heavy with life.

"I can't believe it," I yelled. "Look at all those apples!"

We all jumped down. Rose and Jacinth ran free through the trees, their little blond heads dipping in and out of the brown tree bark.

"Get any good ones you see from the ground first," my dad said, "Then we can get up in the trees."

John ran alongside me as I raced past three trees, bright red apples overhead and on the ground. We raced and he let me win. Carey and Nye caught up to us.

"Let's race to the end of the orchard," Carey told John.

"Okay!" John was already running.

Nye ran after. My feet froze, I couldn't move. *I am too slow,* I thought, *I'll let them race.* I wandered off through some trees. I didn't mind being alone; it was my sacred time in which all of the earth messaged me through her sounds of life. The sky was a dim gray that day, making the apples look even more dark red. I wanted to eat them, but thought Dad would get upset if he saw me, but he was at the end of the orchard. I didn't really know if he would get upset, but I had been taught so well to conserve, to moderate my desire, as winter was no fool when it came to her harshness, and food was sacred. I felt this inside and then let my child wisdom rise to the surface; I was no fool and there were tons of apples all around me.

I sat down, picked one from beside me, perfect, ripe red, delicious. I ate, and in seconds I looked down; it was all gone. I threw the core as far as I could to get rid of the evidence. I ran back toward the end of the orchard where Mom and Dad were picking apples together. They looked happy working side by side, my father's strong arms lifting buckets while my mother's soft hands laid apples gently in the buckets. I helped them fill up buckets.

"Fill 'em to the top," Dad shouted from a tree up above.

Rose and Jacinth gathered some from the ground and proudly put them in the bucket.

"Look, Mom! One, two, three…"

Rose counted to twenty. She had gotten big—I didn't know she could count. My mother was randomly giving us school lessons, mostly reading, writing letters to my grandma, with some mathematics, but Rose wasn't consistent with her lessons yet, so I had not heard her count. Our schooling happened when my mother could fit it in between chores, and in the rare moments she could keep us all calm sitting at the table.

It got cold, and my hands were numb as I put the last few apples into the bucket.

"Let's load the truck!" Dad called out to the boys, who came from the other side of the orchard carrying buckets full of apples.

Wow, how would we ever eat this many apples? I didn't know.

It was the one snack we were allowed to have, no candy or sugar of any kind, so apples were the real deal. We loaded the truck. Gildo showed up as we were headed out the gate. He was a Hispanic fella that talked fast. My dad greeted him.

"Hola, amigo."

They spoke a few minutes, my father thanked him, and we drove away.

Buckets of apples surrounded us in the back of the truck. I felt rich, rich with apples we were. The next morning we helped my dad unload the apples into the bins in the root cellar. I never wanted to go into the root cellar by myself. The door was opened, the steps laid out before me, pitch black twenty feet below. I climbed down, down, down…and then decided that I couldn't do it and ran back up as fast as I could. Carey and John came running.

"Let's get them apples in the cellar," Carey said.

Good. I pushed my way out the door and let them go down before me. My dad then carried a lantern down into the cellar. It was solid earth all around us. A large dugout house in the dirt, cold and damp, bins lining the back wall of the cellar. I went in and looked at all the red apples beaming with the light of the lantern. Fall was here, and the bins were full. I felt relief, now having survived so many winters, and knowing how important the food stock was. I looked up to the shelves along the walls, full with canned jars of apricots, beans, peas, and carrots. We were set for winter.

Winter hit fast and hard; the snow blew in by late October. The plastic on the windows held tight with the wind pressing the plastic in and out; it made a popping sound every time. We couldn't go outside, it seemed, for days. My dad and brothers went to gather wood, kept the fire going, and fed the animals. I worried about the animals during the storm. They had half of the barn covered with a roof, but snow could still come in through the open front porch. They would pile together against the back wall of the barn; the hay bales were piled on top of the barn covered in blue, tied-down tarps. Everyone was hunkered down for a blizzard.

Wild Horses

My father began his love of horses young. He had been going to visit his grandmother and grandfather, Jewel and Lonnie Baxter, on their ranch in Clovis, New Mexico, since he was a kid. Outside of my father's summers, he spent most of his time in a suburb of Dallas, Texas, where his father had gone from being a judge to becoming a Christian minister. Ira still wore the cloak of the law, but now he wore it with the larger purpose of a Christian movement. My father felt called to the land at a young age and spent his summers helping his grandfather herd hundreds of cattle by horseback across dry desert lands. He loved the vastness of the land and his grandfather was a gentle leader.

When my father left the world, he left all that was offered to him in the world, but he had taken with him his ability to connect with the wild bronco of the west. Living in northern New Mexico gave lots of opportunity to train and ride wild horses. He rode on horseback all over the Sangre de Cristo Mountains for hundreds of miles into hundreds of sunsets and sunrises. Some of the years were before my birth, but I didn't miss anything because he told me the stories of being in the wild, with little food, few supplies.

Some of these trips, John and Carey were with him and my mother. The ballet dancer was now a horsewoman. I'm not sure my mother loved the stories as much, for she seemed to fade away in the kitchen whenever he talked about them. The true cowboy in the room was my father, wild like the horse, sincere in his best moments, strong in will and fiery in his conviction. I think my mother wanted a soft place to lay her head and her heart. Cowboys can sleep on rocks on the ground and get up to keep riding. I admired my dad and thought I might be so tough as to sleep on rocks too.

My brothers sure were and they proved it every day by being as dangerous as they could. They ran the cliffside that outlined the acres of wilderness. They rolled huge boulders off the cliff and followed the trails off thousand-foot drops. They were like mountain goats with sure footing and big grins on their faces while they ran. They helped my dad train horses by throwing on motorcycle helmets and hopping on wild horses, only to be tossed into midair, sometimes landing on their butts and sometimes on their feet. Nye was much shyer than both John and Carey, but he learned to be strong inside his smaller body and rode with them, did everything they did and more. He was like David in the story of David and Goliath. Nye was kind and sensitive, but when it came time to cowboy up, he was the first one to get on the horse. It was a boy's world. I spent a lot of my time watching and building strength, in my mind, on how I would be a champion in a boy's world.

The Horse Whisperer's Hands

The middle of winter was quiet. A blanket of snow cupped our house like the hands of God, holding us up under the weighted white of winter. The kerosene lamp flickered, casting shadows that danced against the back wall. The large cast-iron wood-burning stove shot flames out the side of the door.

My father, Nye, Carey, John and I sat around our little wooden kitchen table. I listened, my eyes big, my heart opened wide. My father talked about a horse he had seen earlier that week.

"He is straight off the Apache reservation," my father said.

He had been left on old man RC's property. RC was an old-time farmer who owned hundreds of acres, and didn't have the patience for training wild horses.

The thin boards of pine and cedar could not protect us from the outside world. There was two feet of snow outside our doorstep; I understood well the plight of a horse trying to survive the winter without assistance or its herd.

"I am going down to RC's tomorrow and see if he will give me that horse," my father said.

My father stepped away from the table to stoke the fire, his long arms and broad shoulders blocking the light from around the room.

"He's not much of a horse from what I saw, looks to be half starved to death."

"Can I go with you tomorrow, Dad?" I asked.

"Better stay here and help your mom," he answered, a sternness in his voice.

I felt broken and went to the back room to lie down next to Rose. I thought about the horse running wild and free through a green meadow. But I knew that was unlikely. RC traded for wild horses and then didn't have the patience to train them if they became difficult. At the end of winter's harsh underbelly you could drive by his property and see the remains of a horse or two left behind to starve to death, and fade away under the snowdrifts. *Maybe Dad can save him,* I thought, and I came back to good thoughts about my dad and fell fast asleep.

The next morning, I made my way to the goat pen, trudging through snow up to my knees. I sat down and milked one of the goats, keeping my hands warm with the kneading of the goat teat. My father and brothers had already left.

By afternoon when the sun finally burst through the clouds, the snow looking like a thousand tiny diamonds, my father returned, leading a white horse.

"His name is Juniper," my father said.

Juniper was thin and frail looking, with his ribs poking out the sides. His eyes were sad, and his mane tangled.

"Is he going to die?" I studied my father's face closely.

"I think he will make it," my father tugged at Juniper's rope and walked toward the barn.

Night fell and Juniper stayed tucked away in the barn. He had eaten some hay, at least. The next day I came from the barn where I had been closely watching him in silence.

During this time, I was beginning to see more and more of my father's river of emotions, not always knowing what triggered his anger; it was a flood coming out of nowhere. I heard yelling from the cabin, and made my way to the window. My father was raging about our living room, his arms flying up and down like a Roman soldier high atop his chariot with his left hand held in a fist, and his right hand clasped on the Bible. He erratically made his way around the small living room.

My mother sat in the corner, her auburn hair falling slightly around her neck, her head tilted down in submission. Her youthful face gave way to lines of sorrow. It was as though she had checked herself out, and I worried she would check herself out one too many times, and never return.

This burned a hole in my heart, my stomach was tight with knots. I wanted to throw up my fist and hit him, but in moments like these I feared my father too much to confront him. I made a fist with my hand and voiced to myself that I hated the way he acted, then I stormed to the barn with tears streaming down my face. I found Whitey and one of the baby goats in the corner near some hay bales and curled up next to them, wrapping my arms around them; I breathed in the smell of baby goat fur, and tried to quiet out the yelling from my mind. I couldn't wrap my head around the two men my father was—the wise shepherd of the land and the broken soul of the seeker were both inside of him. He seemed to be riding an emotional wave and didn't have control of the reins, which made no sense because my father always had control of the reins.

Hours passed. It was dusk when I got up and walked back to the house. It was silent. Carey and John were sitting at the table. I sat with them, and ate some fried cabbage and potatoes.

For the next few months, I heard very little yelling and my father worked with Juniper every day. Bringing food and water, he would then retreat to the opposite side of the pen, and wait for Juniper to eat and drink.

"The best gift you can give a horse—especially a wild horse—is the gift of your time," he explained.

He said that Juniper would need time to heal, and the first part of his healing would be learning to trust. Horses are emotional creatures; they feel all emotions that we feel: pain, anxiety, hope, fear, and joy.

I often watched my father while he was training Juniper, my face pushed up against the fence as close as I could get. At first Juniper would run and buck when my father tried to bridle him. His eyes were dark and his vision fueled by fear. I was astounded by my father's voice. Always strong and compassionate, his voice never altered as the hours of sunlight faded into the darkness of night.

By late April, the oppression of winter was lifting. I took off my snow boots, slipped on my tennis shoes, and ran out to the barn. It was late afternoon. The descending sun cast a golden glow that lit the branches of the piñon trees.

My father sat at one end of the barn. Kneeling down on his left knee, he placed his black cowboy hat on his right knee, and his working hands fell humbly to his sides. Juniper approached slowly, and placed his forehead against my father's forehead.

I held on tight to the wire, my eight-year-old child hands freezing from the sweat seeping through my body. I didn't know what to make of my father. So opposite was this man before me from the man who raged about our living room.

It was becoming clearer that my father had two sides, two men in him. One life that was bound in nature and love, and another life that was bound in fear and anger. I wasn't sure how he became two men, but I needed him to be healed. My admiration of him hung on one half of my heart while the other half of my heart lived in defiance of his ways.

Friends Are the Way Out

Sage was two years older than me. She was smart, smarter than me, taller than me, more worldly than me, and she wore it all in style with the rustic look of a boy, but the charm of a girl. I had met her when I was only four years old, but not being able to visit her much left years of unearthed friendship. She lived just down the mountain with her dad, Todd Colombo, and her mother Becky. She was an only child, making her lucky or unlucky, I could not decide.

My first visits that I remember well were when I was about six years old. I would ride horseback down off the mountain with my father, and through the open fields of wheat and grass, till we arrived at Sage's house. The valley down below the mountain was serene, calm feeling, far less lonely than the mountain. Their house was nothing like ours. Her dad was a real carpenter, and lived all his ego and pride of being a man in everything he built. His sword was the hammer and nail, and my father's sword was the word of God; the two men, not seeing eye to eye on much of life, could agree on a piece of wood and how to put it together to build a solid structure. Todd had helped my dad on many occasions in his life with a job here and there, or lumber for building. They needed each other as there were so few of us in that area, and it worked for me because I needed Sage. I needed a friend who could understand how crazy my dad was, and how outrageous our lives were. Sage had a crazy dad too, one that she also loved, but needed to get away from as much as I needed to get away from mine. There was much unspoken dialogue about our fathers, a knowing between two friends that floated around in the air like oxygen. You could say Sage and I needed each other to breathe.

She would meet us at the door of the cabin upon our arrival from the hour's trek on horseback. She usually was wearing something cool like a cotton dress with some jeans underneath, or a pretty blouse, and her hair was always combed. My hair was a mess flying around my face. To my mother's credit she did at times try to comb it, but I'd go roll in the dirt and make it feel natural again. Upon our arrival, Sage would barely greet my father and drag me straight to her room, where she would talk at a fast, pace and move around me like a dancing cowgirl assured of her steps.

"We are going to do a play today. I will be the lead actress," she would say and throw back a fluffy feather boa around her neck. She sat me down on a stool that faced a mirror. I could see myself for a rare few moments, with all my long, loose, brownish-red locks, untamed.

"Let's comb your hair first," she said, no judgment in her comment, just matter-of-fact, let's get down to business and make you fancy. Ten minutes later I was fancy, with my hair all dolled up with curls, and a new dress covering over my jeans, leaving my cowboy boots on to give me a little height.

Sage knew all about movies, actors, and Hollywood. Her father proudly displayed black and white photos of Marilyn Monroe and James Dean on the walls, plus lots of Hollywood décor, and fancy lit signs from the '60s straight out of somewhere I had never been. She knew how to act, and would stand me up from the seat when my hair was done. She moved her arms back and forth, dancing across the room like a butterfly; she flittered and mouthed out the words of some famous actress. I followed along, my body holding me up for balance and fighting back my insecurities of knowing nothing she talked about but enjoying the ride.

I knew not to talk with my dad about anything we did, as we played late into the afternoon hours. Somewhere in full steam of our acting routines, she would break and say, "Let's go outside." Lighthearted, I would respond quickly. Outside was something I knew how to do well. We would gather up walking sticks and head into the woods behind the house. She had an old donkey named Sugar who would follow us into the woods. We would roam around the pine and piñon trees looking for keepsakes, old Indian pottery, arrowheads, and bones.

Sage's father had been in the film business. He was a film editor who had worked on the film *Easy Rider,* co-written and directed by Dennis Hopper in 1969. Sage told me stories about how after the release and fame of the film, nearly the whole cast and crew was wild with ambition, fame, and reckless daredevil schemes, each of them trying to one up the other with who could push the limits, who could come close to death and still return. My dad later explained to me that Todd had wanted out, so he'd up and moved to the sleepy town of Lindrith, where he could use his hands and quiet his mind. Their house was a large cabin with a living room and two large rooms in the back. It was a real-looking cabin with round logs to support the outside structure, and smooth edges put perfectly together inside, the floor a nice, polished wood. Sage showed me a secret trap door to a basement, where she said the ghosts of the past lived. I immediately felt fear in this and did not want to go into the basement.

But I never gave way to my fear and followed Sage down the stairs, my tiny fingers running along the cold damp wall as we went deeper down, till we hit pitch black. Sage grabbed up a lantern and lit a match to flame the lantern. We stood in the dark basement.

"Where are the ghosts?"

"They usually come out at night, never during the day."

The story goes that this was an Indian burial ground and all the dead of all the families in the village are buried right here under her house. She said it like it was cool thing.

"Hmm," I said, not sure I believed her. My father had taught me not to mess with those of the past, not to pay heed to ghosts, if there were such a thing as spirits lingering on earth. My insides started to boil up and fire grew along my arms. "You better get out of here!" a voice yelled inside my head. I turned and ran back up the stairs.

Sage followed me up, blowing out the lantern. "You don't have to get so freaked out, they won't hurt you, ya know." She put the lantern down on the counter and motioned for me to follow her outside. We ran back around the house and up through some rocks. We watched the sunset standing on a large boulder, golden lines of light cascading through the forest. This made me feel so much better about the dark basement. *If there were ghosts, I'm sure God knew about them and had a plan for them,* I thought. I heard my father yelling for me and we raced down the hill to the house. I climbed on my horse and we rode toward the mountain.

Books Are Knowledge

I only saw Sage every few months, usually on a trip with my father. On rare occasions my father would be gone for a day hunting or logging and I'd sneak off to Sage's by horseback. I was now eight years old and had been riding a horse named Dallas all summer. Dallas was given to us by a neighbor who felt he was too rough and wound up for his young girls to ride. I was one with Dallas like I had been one with nature since my first years of playing in the dirt. I arrived at Sage's house on a fall afternoon. She was home from school and had been scheming in her head since our last visit.

"Hey, I have been saving some books out here," she said. "I know your dad doesn't let you read science books, but I took them from the library at the school, and you can keep them." I was blown away by her boldness to take something. "Holy man, Sage," I said. "If my dad finds me reading this, he will spank me."

I thought about it long and hard as we sat together in the dirt, our jeans worn and tattered. "Hmm, I really want to teach Rose to read," I said. "I really would like to use these to teach Rose."

"Ok, I'll do it," I said and grabbed them up. "I'll take them back on my horse tonight and hide them out by my hideout in the woods. My dad will never find them there."

"Awesome," Sage said. She lifted three books from the dirt and we rushed back to the house.

"I'd better go."

She gave me a little white cotton cloth bag and I shoved the books inside. I climbed on Dallas and rode toward the woods. I looked back to her standing in the dirt, the evening sunlight aglow around her freckled face, her blue eyes dancing.

"Thank you," I whispered back to her.

I rode home nervous. Climbing the high mountain range always put things in perspective, the hundred feet below, the pull of the saddle under the horse's back, the heavy breathing to make it to the top, held me in quiet space the whole time, and only by the time we reached the top had I gained full courage. Rose was two and half years younger than me, making her six now. I would teach my sister to read, I would bury those books near my hideout and we would both read till we knew what was in those books cover to cover. I rode past the well house and down through the woods to my hideout. I hopped off Dallas and grabbed up the books from the saddle. I took a stick and started to dig into the ground. The dirt was soft and came right up. I had a large hole within minutes and laid the books inside the hole. The last one with a green cover had a picture of frogs on the front of it.

I rode back to the house. It was a new day filled with new possibilities, and tomorrow I would take Rose to the woods and show her the books.

My father read from the Bible that night, a passage of warning that was brought to the people of Abraham. Lot was warned by God that he was to leave the towns of Sodom and Gomorrah or he would be killed. The world at that time had gone mad with evil, and corruption was upon the heart of man, the sins of the heart, sexual promiscuity, and the like. I lay there thinking about Abraham and how God had warned him. God had warned me to get out of Sage's basement, but why hadn't He warned me about the books? I wasn't supposed to lie to my father, and for that I felt guilt, but the books, they didn't make me feel guilt. I went to sleep next to Rose in the back room.

"I have a secret," I whispered to her.

"What," she responded in the dark of the bed.

"I will show you tomorrow."

"Okay," she said with a sleepy voice. I slept solid, no guilt could keep me awake.

Morning sun filtered the room, it must have been 7 a.m., the light already awake in the house. I rushed out to eat. Rose and Jacinth were up and at the table.

"I slept in, Mom, why didn't you wake me?"

"Your trip to Sage's must have made you tired, I figured you needed the rest." I never slept in, what was my deal, I thought.

Is it possible guilt makes you tired? I shrugged it off and ate my ground wheat cereal, yogurt piled on top with deep, thick black molasses over it all. My belly was full and I ran outside with Rose and Jacinth. We ran to the goat pen and pulled the baby goats up to our chests, holding them close until they squirmed their way out of our arms. Jacinth ran up and down the fence. "You can't catch me, little goat!" he sang, "You can't catch me, little goat!" He pressed and pressed his way till he was out of breath.

"Let's go out to my hideout," I told Rose. "Jacinth, you gotta stay here with Mom," I told him. "No," he cried. Rose and I ran, leaving him crying in the goat pen, sitting in the middle of the goats.

We scraped our arms against tree branches and dove head first through the forest. Finally there, I knelt down to the ground. "Look." I dug in the dirt and pulled the books out.

"Where'd you get them?" Rose asked in surprise. "Why did you bury them out here?" She seemed puzzled.

"Because they are science books. Sage got them from the library at school." My father had made it clear that he didn't' agree with the teachings of science. He went on and on about how Darwin's theories of evolution were not true, making a mockery of man's identity and his connection to God. I knew the Big Bang Theory and the story of how man had come from apes. Whenever my father would get upset, I'd listen closely for his words, then I'd go to my mother in private and ask for clarification on what he was talking about. She would explain the different points of view.

"You know Dad only likes for us to read the Bible, and some of those *Little House on the Prairie* books," I said, kneeling down to pick up the book with the green cover. "Why does Dad just want us to read the Bible?" she asked.

"Because these books don't talk about God, they talk about man-made things. Dad doesn't like man-made things," I explained.

We sat down in the dirt, our legs crossed. Rose lifted the book with the frogs on the front. She opened it to see more pictures of animals, and descriptions of the animals.

"Here, let me see it," I said, and grabbed it up. "This one is talking about elephants and how they roam the grasslands in Africa."

"Where's Africa?" she asked.

"I'm not sure," I said, "but really far away." I knew that much. In our studies with Mom, we wrote letters to our grandmother, read select books, and read the Bible. We didn't study geography much, so I didn't know locations of the rest of the world, but I did know that we lived far away and in a much different way than most of the world lived. I knew this from John and my mother, who had a great deal of knowledge about the world. John had been sneaking books for many years, but I didn't know it. We all had our little secrets, the boys kept theirs hidden and now Rose and I kept ours hidden. The only one with no secrets was little Jacinth, Dad's strong horse, who seemed to be his favorite. I wasn't jealous of this and knew it was because Jacinth was the baby.

We sat in the dirt looking at the books and reading what we could. I showed Rose the polar bears and read about their natural habitat in the ice. I loved those polar bears and how free they seemed in ice water. I didn't like the cold. Summer was my favorite—no cold buckets of snow to melt on the stove for a bath, we could go up to the well house and take the water from the hose, spraying ourselves silly.

"Let's put these back," I said. We buried the books back in the dirt, our lifeline to the rest of the world. All the other kids were reading those books and now we could too. The books got boring fast and I told Rose we should run up to the well and spray ourselves with cold water.

We ran to the road and there we saw Jacinth, muddling along by himself. He ran to us and we grabbed him up. "Let's go to the well house and spray ourselves with water," I said. "Let's go," he repeated, and together we ran the stretch of yellow road to the well house. We stripped down to our underwear as we always did, and the freezing cold water rushed my body from the hose pumping water from three-hundred feet below. It was June, hot summer heat poured onto our skin, pink color tones gathered around our shoulders. We would strip down and pour water from head to toe, then run to the top of the hill up past the well and back down feeling the cold sting of the body rushed by the warm sun overhead. I had forgotten about the books, as we played in water all afternoon.

We made it back to the house by early evening; my mom was cooking dinner on the wood stove. "What's for dinner, Mom?" I looked into the black skillet and saw fresh squash from the garden with orange carrots and potatoes mixed together, frying in vegetable oil, and herbs all over the top. "Yum, I'm starving," I said.

The boys arrived home from a trip into town. I didn't care about going this time because I had wanted to show Rose the books. There was no better day than a day my dad was gone the whole time. I was leaving behind that little girl who stood at the top of the hill jumping up and down for her father. Part of it was my age and part of it was my defiance of his river of emotions.

The eight of us gathered around the wooden table, the kerosene lamp burning bright. The boys talked about their day helping Michael Gold work on a geodesic dome. It was some kind of structure they had been putting together for our neighbors, Michael and Patty, to help out with the camp kids. I wished I had seen the dome. Why didn't I get to see these things? How did my father want me to learn without seeing things? The Bible is not the only place you can see things.

My insides started to swell with anger at the thought of not seeing more things of the world. I left the table and went to lay in the back room. The dark vigas overhead gave me comfort as I pushed back my feelings about not seeing the world.

I didn't want to read the Bible anymore. I wanted to see the world we lived in now. The Bible was old, and its people were old; what did it have to do with the world now? I shut my eyes to cry. God came to me through a deep knowing, a sense of peace that came like a soft wind. I wasn't sure what it was, but it was also more real than anything around me. This thing called God, Jesus, light, was still my guide even when I didn't want to believe. I felt the presence of soft hands on my forehead, I was a child lost in the woods, a child screaming for grace.

I woke the next morning. It was Saturday and Sage would be home from school. "Dad," I caught him as he was going out the door.

"Dad, can I go down to see Sage today?" I asked with a pleading heart.

"Help your mom with all our chores, and you may go," he responded.

I rushed through the morning milking the goats and feeding them, piling hay into the horse stalls, and back to the house to help Mom clean up the kitchen. Dishwater ran through my hands, warm water covering over my sorrow, a wilted flower needing water, needing space, needing to be free.

"Mom, I'm done!" I yelled, finishing the last dish, and ran toward the barn to saddle Dallas.

I looked back at Rose sitting on the front porch, and my heart ached that she had to stay. That's how it was—the oldest got to do the most, and the boys got to do more than the girls. We would always try to follow the boys and they would yell at us to stay back. "Go back with Mom," they would yell. "You can't come on this trip, it's not for little kids!" Carey would shout at us to stay behind. Rose and I would grab hands and walk back to the house, letting the boys go on yet another trip without us.

I would never yell, and Rose, I just couldn't take her with me, but I would bring as much of the world to her as I could. I rode off. The cliff was there, as always, steady and ready to calm my emotions as I came to the edge—time to focus my mindset in deep, as Dallas made his way down the steep trail. Once at the bottom, we would gather up a gallop and run toward the woods. Freedom was just the other side of everything.

I got to Sage's to find her out by the barn. She was crying.

"Sage, what is it?" I lifted myself from the saddle.

"My parents are getting divorced. My dad is such a jerk." She kicked the dirt. "I can't stand him," she mumbled. I walked up close to her.

"I hate our dads, both of them." I said. "They are so mean."

She looked at me. "Listen," she said. "I'm gonna have to move with my mom."

I broke down. "You mean I won't see you anymore?"

"I'm sorry, Chlo," she said. "I have to move to Albuquerque with my mom."

That was so far away I would never see her, never.

I slumped my shoulders. "Man, I can't believe this."

"Listen, I have a plan. I think you should go to school."

"Well, nice idea, but I can't go to school. My dad won't let me."

"I know, but that doesn't matter. Look, I have a plan. My mom has that cabin back in the woods that's near your Dad's and no one lives there. My mom and I are leaving next week to Albuquerque. I know I can catch a bus ride to Cuba with my bike on the front, and then ride my bike all the way to the cabin. I can meet you there next Monday. Gather up as much food as you can this week. Hide it in the woods, and meet me there by late afternoon on Monday."

My insides were terrified. *How would I gather up stuff?* My dad was going to notice if it was gone. How was Sage going to make it all fifty miles from Cuba on her bike? How was I going to go school?

"We will dye your hair red, cut it short, and you can catch the bus straight from my cabin. No one will know it's you."

I didn't even know you could dye hair. It sounded like a pretty good plan actually, and I had no choice but to believe it. My only friend was leaving and this was my chance to get out.

"Okay." I said grabbing her on the shoulders and giving her a shake. "Okay, we can do this."

She told me to go home now, as her parents would not let me stay around today. She hugged me tight, pulled back from my face and said, "Monday, I will see you next Monday."

I mounted Dallas, bewildered by what had just happened. We rode the long trail home that seemed even longer today.

My life was a gripping force unrecognizable to me. My face, my insides were changing, the time was coming, it was coming hard, though I didn't completely understand it.

Dallas hit the trail front at the bottom of the cliff and I didn't want to focus. I didn't want to let go of my sorrow to climb up that cliff. I just wanted to sink back into the saddle and wake up from that dream.

I rode the yellow road to the house. My somber mood was noticed by no one. Mom was cooking. Her life was not changing, I thought, and Rose and Jacinth sat on the floor looking at picture books.

"How was Sage today?" my mom asked.

"Fine," I replied. My mother couldn't get close enough to me to know my insides. I always knew her insides, but she was too busy, too worked, too heavy with her burden to know mine, and this time it was to my advantage.

I couldn't tell anyone my plan. I barely even let myself feel my own plan. I had to leave Rose, and I knew that wasn't fair to her.

That week I took apples from the root cellar, oil and flour from the cabin. I slowly took small bags of things out to my hideout. I put them inside the hideout. My dad never went inside the hideout, things would be safe in there. I didn't mention a thing to Rose and made my trips to and from the hideout when she was playing, or when she was with Mom. She would grow bigger and read the books on her own, I thought. She would make it. I would to go school and at some point I would come back for her.

Monday morning came like a black storm, I was to leave my family and make my own life. I was to stay it through with my friend and go to school with other kids, and finally be part of the world. I went through my daily routine, milking the goats, one drop of milk at a time in the bucket, the white suds bubbling as I worked.

I leaned my head in against the goat and felt the warmth of her belly on my forehead. My mom would have the goats, I thought; she would be okay. Jacinth would have the forest, Nye would have his bike to ride off anywhere, and Rose would have my hideout in the woods. My hideout had saved me on many a day. I would go and lie there in the late afternoon with the sun streaming through the cracks of my makeshift ceiling. Rose would have her books, and I would leave her some apples to snack on.

I finished all my chores.

My mom was sitting in the afternoon sun, in her knitting chair in the corner of the house. Her auburn hair glistened, her hands moved quickly with her needles. Dad was gone with Nye, and wouldn't be back till after dark. Rose and Jacinth were looking at books spread out on the floor. Jacinth was learning to say words from books. "Ball." His tiny voice brought to life inside the cabin walls.

"Ball." He liked saying it out loud.

"That's right," Rose said, and patted him on the back. "You can read."

"Mom, I'm going to my hideout and be back." My mother never lifted her head, she kept her eyes on the knitting needles. I watched the three of them there, the sunlight shining upon their heads as I exited the cabin. I ran through the woods, focused and at full speed to my hideout. I grabbed up the white bag Sage had given me earlier and loaded it full. I grabbed up another bag, and pulled both of them out from the hideout. Ugh, heavy, I sighed, and lifted the bags onto my shoulders. I would make it one step at a time all the way to Sage's cabin. It was two miles. I didn't know that then; I only knew distance by how it felt on foot or horseback. I started out through the back woods. No one would see me go.

I hauled the bags about two-hundred yards at a time, then dropped to the ground for rest. I made it by late afternoon. My shoulders searing with pain, my small body ready to collapse, but I made it. I sat outside the door of the cabin with the bags beside me. It was late in the afternoon, the sun moving toward the west already. I wondered when she would get there. I didn't want to go inside for fear of mice or other animals that may be inside, since no one had ever lived there. From the porch, I looked through the cabin windows. Empty walls on a solid earth, empty walls with the birth of my past running through me, a message swooped down into my lungs, this was not my path to take. I stopped peeking through the windowpane and lay there on the porch in the sun with my head against the bag of flour.

I had fallen asleep without awareness and startled myself to wake. Geez, what time is it? I looked up at the sun now on the horizon. Oh man, it's late, where is she? I thought. I waited and waited as the sun went below the tree line and the silhouette of tree branches bundled in close to me. There is no way she is coming this late, I thought, there is no way. I stood up from the steps and sighed. Something happened, something had to have happened. I wasn't staying there alone, and hated that I had to walk back in the dusk of evening, but took my feet off the steps of the porch, leaving behind all the bags. I marched forward across the forest line and up the hills in the dark, until I could see the kerosene lamp burning in the window of my house. I didn't have to leave my family after all, and that was such relief that my sadness over not going to school had washed away. I ran toward the house.

Rose and Jacinth came running to me in the front yard. "Chloe, where did you go?" They yelled at me from across the yard. I didn't respond with words. I ran to them and embraced them both at the same time.

A full month passed, and my dad said Sage was coming up from Albuquerque for the weekend. "Do you want to go down and visit her?"

Do I want to visit her? What kind of question was that? Early Saturday morning I saddled Dallas and rode the same trail to her house. She met me outside the house.

"What happened?" I jumped down from Dallas.

"I'm so sorry. My mom caught me, she totally busted me the day before I was trying to leave. I was grounded, and in so much trouble. I haven't even been able to visit my dad this whole time.

"I had no way to call you or get you a message. What a bummer," she exhaled.

"Man, I waited for you all day. With all the bags."

"I know, I'm so sorry. I got in so much trouble."

"Well, I'm just glad my dad never found out."

We walked over to the barn where her donkey, Sugar, was lying in the sun.

"How do you like it?" I asked

"I hate it. School sucks, and my mom got this new boyfriend, he can bite me."

"I will find a way out, and you will find a way out too," I said. We both crouched down inside the barn, rubbing Sugar's belly. Soft donkey fur in the summer air, the sky will hold you, the sky will hold you, until you are safe. I never spoke about God with Sage. She wasn't a Christian, but she knew God in the earth, in the trees, and in all the plants. She knew it like the back of her hand, and together we let our beliefs live side by side. I didn't see her much after that visit. Life took her away.

Medicine Is in the Mind

My father attracted old vehicles like he attracted wild horses—they came to him by trade or by serendipity. Carlos was my father's friend from years past. The two of them were on the front lines of living in the West, befriending the wild horse and conquering the woods every day. Carlos had given my father an old, two-ton logging truck to use over the winter. The truck was a character in itself, with dual wheels and a winch attached to the back of the bed for pulling logs up; it was dark green with one large cab for sitting and the cab had no doors on it.

My father often took Nye with him on trips to get firewood. The river of humanity was catching up to my father and he often got into it with Carey and John. John was an old soul with much wisdom inside his fifteen-year-old body, and he had taken it upon himself to work for a neighbor who lived fifteen miles away. Carey, a year younger than John, too was venturing off the property, making friends with country boys who lived miles and miles from us. Nye was still young, ten going on eleven, and wanted to be a companion to my father. Father and son left the house with rifles, saws and axes for cutting wood one August afternoon. I watched them drive away, standing on top of the hill, a light rain drizzling on me.

I heard the engine of the two-ton winch truck thunder up the long drive over the last hill into the property. Nye and Dad had left just one hour earlier to make a logging trip to the far East; they were supposed to be back two days later. The truck etched its way into the driveway, stopping right beside the house. The engine cut. Dad climbed down from the driver's side, and made his way to the passenger side of the truck. There were no doors on the logging truck, just a step to put your foot on and pull yourself up to the seat.

Dad's face was solemn, his head was down, and he did not flinch in my direction. I watched him closely while making my way toward the truck. There was no Nye and then he pulled Nye from the seat of the truck! Nye was passed out, his body was limp, and my father hoisted him over his shoulder. Nye's head dangled over the back of my father's shoulders.

"Dad, what happened? What's wrong with Nye?" My voice cracked. "Dad!"

My father did not respond, he carried Nye inside the house, his face serious. He bent down so he could get him inside the front door without hitting his head. Nye was not responding with any movement. Mom rushed to the front door as they entered.

"Oh, dear God," she gasped.

My father's voice quivered, a rare thing that I'd never borne witness to. "He's gonna make it, Lord have mercy he's gonna make it," he mumbled under his heavy breath. He knelt to one knee and slowly let Nye's body down to the floor, holding him tucked like an infant in his large arms. I ran over to my mom's side and watched. My mother brought blankets and pillows from the back room. Nye's face was pale.

"What happened, what happened?" my mother pried for attention from my father who was in a trance now leaning in over Nye's body.

"I had to run over him, I had to run over," he repeated, the sound of defeat in his voice.

My mother clung to Nye, wrapping her arms around him where he lay flat on the floor, a wool blanket propped underneath his head. "Nye, Nye," her voice called out to him. He was unconscious and did not respond. I stood back from them and watched. Rose and Jacinth rushed through the door and over to me. "What happened, Chlo?" Rose's voice whispered in awe. "What's Nye doing on the floor?"

"He got hurt," I responded.

"Hurt," Jacinth chimed in a tiny voice from beyond.

"Yes, hurt, but he will be okay." I motioned for them both to move back to the other side of the kitchen. "Let's let Mom and Dad take care of him."

"Papa, take care of him." Jacinth spoke in tiny voice again. "Papa take care of him."

I had seen my parents battle many a time with our wounded souls, high fevers, earaches—and Nye had them the worst, but now he wasn't waking up. My father knelt down beside him on the floor and undressed him, pulling his blue jeans down to his ankles. He felt his way down his legs. "Not broken, not broken," he said, as my mother sat back trying to pull herself together.

"He's not broken, God have mercy, in Jesus's name, Father, Your glory is upon us, he is not broken." My father pulled another knit blanket from the couch and laid it across Nye's body. "Get me the olive oil from the kitchen," he directed my mother. She came quickly with a bottle of oil, and I watched as my father pulled back the blanket from Nye's limp frame, his white underwear cupping over his waist and tucked in tight at his upper thigh. A purple tint started to form around this waist and hips.

"He is swollen," my father said. He grabbed up the oil and anointed him while praying. The words of Christ spilling from his heart, spilling so soft and low, I couldn't make them out, but the room spun in rhythm to his words, his strong hands touching oil on Nye's body. He repeated the motions over and over, bent down on his knees on the floor, hovering over Nye. My father seemed more broken than Nye, who lay there in stillness. I was aware that Nye's body shouldn't look like that; his eyes should be opened, he should be talking.

It seemed he was there for thirty minutes or more. I took Rose and Jacinth outside. We ran out back to the woods and darted in and out of the trees. The whole while my mind on Nye's unconscious face, his lips pursed together, his brown hair falling toward his eyelids. *When was he going to wake up,* I thought, *when?* It was taking too long for him to come to and I needed him to wake up.

I left Rose and Jacinth playing hide and seek behind the large juniper tree with all the berries dangling. I ran back to the house and rushed inside. My father was still leaning over Nye, my mother beside him. I approached, Nye was speaking, he was speaking. "Dad, I need water," he said.

"Water," he motioned to my mother, and she quickly brought a glass. My father put his hands around Nye's neck, cupping his head and lifting him. Nye's face looked with extreme pain, but he made no sound. My father held him with his whole arm and brought the water to his lips. "Here, son, drink." He pushed the glass up against Nye's lips. Nye drank small sips, then lay back into my father's arms. No more words. My father rested him back onto the floor and pulled the wool blanket over him. He rubbed his forehead, with smooth motions, rubbing, rubbing, until Nye closed his eyes and off he went into silence again.

"Dad, why didn't you keep him awake?" I asked.

"Dad, should he be going back to sleep like that?" I pried further, my insides telling me my brother's body may not be broken on the outside, but maybe it was broken on the inside.

My mother asked me to go get Rose and Jacinth. She saw my face and gave a reassuring look, but I didn't trust her. I knew her fear like I knew my own, bottled up inside my chest, inside her chest, it came spilling out through the eyes.

"Okay, Mom," I replied and left to get Rose and Jacinth.

I ran behind the woods of the house, the juniper trees were of blue and green shades in the evening air, the piñon a brilliant green. Surely all of life is alive, God is alive, and my brother will continue to be alive, I thought as I planted my feet into the dirt, hoping for God to speak some kind of affirmation to me.

I could hear tiny, tin-sounding voices counting out loud in the woods. "Two, three, four, five…here I come!" Rose and Jacinth were playing hide and seek. Rose yelled out, "Here I come!" and ran out from behind a large piñon tree. "Rose, where is he?"

"I don't know, he's hiding," she said.

Rose and I marched around from tree to tree looking for our little brother. "Jacinth!" I called out, "Jacinth, come back in." Jacinth was like this. He would disappear into the thick woods, no mind of anyone else, or bears, or lions, or bobcats, just a little guy running wild. I guessed it had been twenty minutes at least and he wasn't anywhere to be seen.

"Oh geez," I said to Rose, "we gotta go tell Dad we can't find him."

"No," Rose said, "let's just keep looking." She didn't like asking my dad for help. She would rather be alone at sunset into the dark looking for him than ask my dad for help. But I knew better.

"We better tell them, he has been gone too long."

My father came through the woods to find us. "Let's eat," he said.

"Dad, Jacinth was playing hide in seek with Rose and we can't find him. We have been calling to him, and he's not coming back." I looked for the sun setting low in the sky, the tree branches were preparing for evening's call.

"Jacinth," my father called out in his loud voice. "Jacinth, get back here now." He walked off a ways in the back woods, and called out to him. *My little brother,* I thought, *he is going to get a spanking.* He was the baby of the family but now and then I did see him get a spanking. I heard my father one last time. "Jacinth, get back here, son! It's time to eat, the game is over."

Jacinth came running from the back woods with a big grin on his face. He had duped us all. He ran straight to my father and rushed up to his arms. "Strong boy," my father said and lifted him into the air.

That little rascal, I thought, *he never gets in trouble the way the rest of us do.* The sun set as we rushed into the house. Nye lay on the floor. We ate beans and rice at the kitchen table. Jacinth stuffed his mouth with bread that he broke off from a whole loaf. No one spoke a word. Our hearts were in prayer, tiny fingers digging at food, grown spirits lifted to the heavens for guidance. God, come into our house now.

I walked past Nye where he was still lying on the floor.

"Will he talk tomorrow," I asked Dad. "Will he walk tomorrow?"

"Not sure if he will be walking that soon," my father said. "It might take him some time, and the swelling around his hips needs to go down."

"Help me move him to the couch," he requested of my mother.

She came from the kitchen, and stood at Nye's feet. He

looked dead, silently breathing; I could see his belly moving ever so slowly, in and out. I knew he wasn't dead. The breath is the one true sign of life.

My father stabilized himself around Nye's upper body and laid him on the couch. Nye lifted his eyes for a moment, looking at the both of them. He was a lost soldier in the woods asking, *where have I been, where am I going,* but had no voice to ask.

My father put his hands again upon his forehead and prayed.

"God, almighty Father, there is no rock unturned by you. No life can be saved but through you. I commit to you now the life of my son, Father, take him and make him whole again."

I left my father leaning in over Nye and made my way to lie in the back room next to Rose, who was already asleep. I got in under the heavy blankets and tucked my body in next to hers, spooning her with my side against her back. I wrapped my arms around her, feeling her belly breathe in and out.

I awoke at the crack of dawn; the light was gray and revealed its beacon through the plastic cover over the window near the bed. My arms were still wrapped around Rose. I pulled my arms back, keeping my whole body under the covers, and stretched out my toes. I could hear my mother in the kitchen and crawled out of bed to go help her.

Nye was laying on the couch, in the same position, his head propped up and his legs stretched out before him and his eyes wide open. He was looking up at the ceiling.

I approached. "Nye, are you better?" I knelt down next to him. He turned his head over to me, no smile, lips still pursed together, no words.

"It's okay, you don't have to tell me how it feels," I said. I put my hand on his arms and squeezed down hard. His eyes lit up, but still no words.

I ran over to the kitchen to help my mom cook eggs in the black skillet. She and I stood side by side, and again I could feel the fear in her chest, pounding, beating hearts waiting for relief to come.

Rose and Jacinth ran past me in the kitchen. "Eggs, eggs, eggs!" they shouted.

We sat at the table. Dad came in from outside, his cowboy hat tucked down on his forehead a man on a mission. "Today God heals," he said, "today, Nye, you will be better."

I took eggs over to Nye on the couch and my Dad lifted him up again, propping a pillow behind his back.

"Do you want to eat?" I asked. Nye dug his fork into the eggs and pulled a bite to his mouth. He couldn't take the whole bite in, and put it back on the plate. "Water," he said to my Dad. I got him water and watched my Dad hold it to his lips again. This time he drank the whole glass, gulp after gulp. No other words. He lay back down.

I walked backed to the kitchen where my mom was cleaning up. "Mom, why can't he talk?"

"The accident shocked him," she said. He will talk again. "He is probably still in shock and his body is trying to come back to itself."

Come back to itself. Hmm, what did that mean?

The day was otherwise normal. I milked goats and ran alongside them out by the cliff, and for a few hours I forgot about Nye. The sky was with me, the sky was around me, the sky grounded me, heaven and earth becoming one. I felt my footsteps on the dirt pressing on with the herd as they grazed along Dennis's hill, the red and brown clay glazing in the sunlight. It seemed it was late afternoon, and I left the goats in a patch of green grass and sagebrush down below Dennis's hill. There was a large hill that peaked the top of the mountain above the cabin that Dennis Hopper had. The original cabin that my father had played music in when he negotiated to live on the property. We kids called the steep mountain of a hill "Dennis's hill." I walked the mile toward the house on the yellow road. Maybe Nye would be talking again when I got back.

I got to the house and saw Nye asleep on the couch. I wondered how he went to the bathroom, or had he not gone to the bathroom in two days? My father came in from outside and my mom left her knitting chair from the back room. They gathered around him.

"Let's check his body again," my father said and knelt down next to him on the couch. Nye did not stir. My father lifted the blankets from his body, still in his shirt and his underwear. His legs and waist were completely purple. I stood behind Mom and Dad as they leaned in over him. Nye woke up and watched them steadily as my father ran his hands over Nye's body again with the oil. My mother heated some hot water on the wood stove and brought it over to my dad. He dipped a white cloth in the water and slowly washed Nye's body, from the feet up to his hips, in soft slow motions. When he got to the waist, Nye cried out, "Ow, Dad, ow! That hurts. Don't touch me," he said pulling his head away.

Nye put his hands on his waist. "No more, Dad, no more," he said.

My father knelt beside him and prayed silently. He was crouched down with one hand over his heart and his cowboy hat hanging over his bent knee.

While my father was in silent prayer, I too silently prayed. *God, when will you come to us, God, when will you come to us?*

When will my brother be healed? I asked.

I felt guilty about my prayer because I knew we were not supposed to doubt God. Sometimes I did doubt God. It just didn't make sense. If he *could* heal my brother right away, like Jesus did the man with leprosy, why wouldn't he heal my brother right away? The stories of the Bible didn't make sense. Was it just a matter of believing? And could I believe for Nye or did he have to believe on his own?

I went outside with my questions. This is where I always went with questions, to the woods, to the sky, to the land. The land made more sense to me than anything else. The sun always rose, the moon was always there, whether in a sliver or a bright round ball; they were consistent. I believed the earth to be a place of magic and if it could run so perfectly then God must be able to help humans run more perfectly, if he was in charge of all this, as I had been told. Why all the flaws all the broken pieces? The trees knew how to grow, and how to beat the harsh winter. Then I recalled a tree that had been struck by lightning right before my very eyes. Its branches fell to the ground. That tree never healed, it died. I had seen animals die, my grandfather died. I couldn't attach any of these lessons to my broken brother; he was not any of those things. *There must be a reason for it all,* I thought, and ran back inside to sit next to Nye on the floor.

I took out *White Bird,* my favorite book, one that my father let us read. I had mostly memorized the book with my mother reading it to me, as many of the words I couldn't yet pronounce. By memory I read the story to Nye.

> *A man was traveling west by wagon. The wheels of the wagon turned and turned, until they came to stop. The man got down from the carriage, and saw a white bird injured and lying on the ground in front of the carriage. He went to the bird, picked him up, and put him inside the carriage. "You will live," the man said. He gave the bird water for thirty days and thirty nights, and on the last night the bird woke and spread it wings. The man took him from the carriage and held him out on his hand to fly. "Go," he said. "You are free."*
>
> *The bird flew in a big circle up above the man and then came right back to land on the man's shoulder. "I told you that you are free to go," the man said.*
>
> *But the bird had found his place and from that day forward he would watch over the man, guide the man, and warn him of all evils and all good that was to come his way.*

I looked up at Nye's face. With the story vibrating in our tiny beating hearts, we both knew that within thirty days, with bread and water, he would walk and talk again. I smiled at Nye, set the book in his lap, and ran outside.

For two weeks, I helped Nye onto his bike. Helping him up from the couch, and letting him steady his body on me to throw one leg over the bicycle. He would hoist himself onto the seat, and hold onto the handlebars. I would hold him and the bike up and push him a hundred yards to the outhouse. Then I would help him down off the bike, and into the outhouse. Every day we did this in the morning and in the afternoon. Two weeks passed.

Nye still did not talk, so we did the journey in silence. His body was still in shock, I somehow understood, he needed the silence to come out of it, so quietly we walked. Until one day I went to get him on the bike and he stood up from the couch, took three steps forward and he was walking. I ran outside and yelled for my mom. "Mom, he is walking! Mom, Nye is walking!" I yelled at her into the front yard.

My mother came running inside. Nye passed her going out the front door. "I'm walking, Mom. I'm walking!" he said and kept going. I watched him go out to the front yard, past the goat pen, out past the root cellar and he just kept walking. A few hours later he came back.

My dad had been out gathering wood, and returned by evening to a walking son. Nye lifted his shirt and showed us all that the purple was gone.

The purple never came back, and Nye was stronger than he had ever been. One evening I was sitting alone with my father before the sun was to set. It was Sunday and he didn't work on Sunday; it was the day of rest. I asked him what had happened that day he was with Nye. "How did you run over him, Dad?" I asked.

We were headed up Pine Grove Hill, he explained, and Nye reached down to grab the lunch box, next thing I knew he was out. He flew out the side of the truck. I started to put my foot on the brake, and God spoke, *'Take your foot off the brake, Jerry.'* I pulled back my foot and just then I rolled over him. Lump, lump, the wheels rolled right over his body. I rushed out to find him smashed into the dirt that had been softened from new rainfall. I ran right over his whole waistline. God saved me from braking on him, daughter. I would have killed him."

My mouth hung open, tears swelled in my eyes and in my father's. "Bless Jesus, bless you, Father, bless you, Father," he said, bowing his head.

My parents had taken a leap of faith to raise us by the rules of nature, to bring all healing to us through nature and the power of prayer. Until this point we had only suffered from ear infections, winter colds, and sore throats. We used plants and herbs for treating illness and preventing further sickness. The wild oregano plants with the purple stems were not just for show; oregano is an antioxidant, antifungal, antibacterial and supports the immune system. We drank sagebrush tea to support any stomach, throat, or eye issues. The taste was a bitter astringent that coated my throat with years of wisdom pouring into me. The smell of osha root was in the air of our cabin during spring and fall, used to support respiratory and digestion function. I felt the colors of the earth spinning inside of me when taking herbs, a connection to everything. Raw honey was a staple of healing on our kitchen table and spreading mud onto wounds was the healing salve of the earth. I knew this connection to earth and spirit had saved Nye from dying. I would never forget his purple skin all bruised from being run over, but he was walking and talking like nothing had ever happened to him.

That summer the purple clovers were all I wanted to see if anything was going to be purple. I ran out past the root cellar to see Juniper in the field. I crossed the field and looked down at all the purple clovers beneath my feet. *Purple is good,* I thought, *but only if it's a flower.*

The Heart of God

Wolf Draw was the place of magic where I saw my first bear when I was six years old. It was the forest of aspen trees towering over the purple fields of oregano, the forest that held for me all the secret messages. I had first encountered the bear and the heart of God in these woods.

Wolf Draw had become a yearly event for picking raspberries and gathering wild oregano. My father wanted to go an extra time this year. We had already been once, but he needed more wood, and decided to only take John, Nye, and Carey. I felt it unfair and stamped my feet into the ground making off around the back of the house.

I was upset until I found a blue jay sitting perched on his branch, his feathers gleaming in the sunlight. It was late August of 1983. I roamed the woods that day looking for my own adventure. I took with me a sheet from my bed and went out to my hideout to make a tent. The tent was better than the hideout, because I could lie under it and feel the warmth of the sun on my body. I could see the shadows of tree branches and birds perched upon them from my inside my shell of warmth. I tied a string from one tree to another making a tight line. After draping a sheet over the line, I nailed it down on each side, creating a tent that had two sides and flaps on the ends for doors. It was my own glowing room filled with warmth and light. I lay for hours gazing at the shadows of the trees, listening to the wind blowing through them. The blowing wind almost sounded like the ocean at my grandma's and for a moment I was transported there. I fell asleep and when I woke it was almost evening, I went back to the cabin as the sun was going down.

I helped my mom cook deer meat and mashed potatoes. The boys had just gotten home and were hungry—no one spoke at the dinner table. Silence streamed through the room as everyone took long bites of food. Dad's face looked stern, not a hint of joy was evident to him, and the boys wouldn't make eye contact with him.

Something had happened.

I lay down on the couch, darkness all around, the last breeze of summer seeping through the cracks, cool air coming through the walls. I fell asleep and awoke to my Dad's voice, loud and piercing tones echoing within the room. He was yelling something at John. I saw from the front room they were in a wrestling match, my father trying to pin him down. No more sounds of voices, only heavy breathing. John swirled out from under Dad's arms, and when he popped up I saw his face streamed with blood. With startled eyes and heavy breath, John ran toward me and out the front door. My dad gathered himself and went after him. My mom was awake in the back room.

"Mom, what happened?" I sat down on her lap, holding back my tears. Rose and Jacinth climbed on top of both mom and me.

"Your father was upset with John for carving his name in an aspen tree up at Wolf Draw.

"Why? Why would he get mad about that?"

"Because he thinks the trees are sacred and he doesn't want your brothers carving their names in something sacred."

"That's stupid," I said, annoyed at my father and remembering John's face.

Now I understood what was going on when they returned home that day. My father was upset that John had carved his name in the aspen tree. He didn't like for us to mess with the trees, unless that messing had a purpose.

Not only had John carved his name in the tree, he'd carved a date and year that were both incorrect. It was August 1983, and using his pocket knife John etched into the aspen tree, October 1984. *Why would he write a different month and year?* It made no sense to any of us.

"Where will John go?" I asked Mom.

"He will come back. Don't worry—they will work it out," my Mom said.

I fell asleep there with her in the bed. In the dark, my dad returned and moved me over from his bed to my own bed. He climbed in with my mom. There were no words spoken.

The next morning, I woke to look for John, but I didn't see him. Nye and Carey were at the table eating. Silence again.

"Where is John?" I asked.

No one spoke. Carey's face was red. He got up and left the table, and Nye followed after him.

"Mom, John didn't come back?"

"No, but he will," Mom said.

Rose and Jacinth ran around the kitchen stove, with pancake in their mouths, laughing out loud. I thought about how they didn't understand what was going on. Days went by, no John. Now it was late September, and he had left in August. A few days later John returned. He had worked for the past two weeks on a neighbor's farm that was fifteen miles away. John was so tall I thought of him as grown up. He was taller than Carey, almost reaching my dad's eye level. He continued to read his books by flashlight under his covers at night and was looking for more connection to the world. He and my father were splitting apart on their ideas of life. John wanted more independence; he wanted to work and my father wanted him to stay at home. They danced around each other for an entire year, trying to find a place to land as father and son, but the gap between them was too wide and another argument came in the fall of 1984.

It was September again, the same time of year as the last argument in which John had left for weeks. I awoke one morning and John was gone; the settling of loud voices from the night before still carried in the air that morning. *How many times would John leave and would he come back?* I felt the question on everyone's hearts. John had come into his own manhood that summer when he turned fifteen on June 21st. He was training a wild paint mustang for Jack Bechdol, the rancher he had worked for previously. My brother's heart and the heart of that wild paint were one and the same. No one could break that paint; he bucked like no other mustang my dad had trained. Carey and Nye both got bucked off him like two sheep flying into the night. But John stayed at him, on him, next to him, the two became a pair by the end of summer. Now John was gone and the horse, Painted Brush was his name, waited for him at the fence. His brownish-red coat with white patches spread throughout glistened in the light. He was young with a white diamond on his forehead; his mane was blowing in the wind and his eyes captured the earth and sky in their reflection. Animals expressed sadness through their eyes in such a way that it penetrated my heart and rang right out my feet. I wanted to hug Painted Brush. My father decided to take Painted Brush back to Jack Bechdol. Jack owned pigs, cattle and many horses, he was a likeable fella who wore overalls and a straw cowboy hat. He had a wife and three daughters who all rode horses and were as "country" as you could get. We all went for the long ride and while we were there Jack offered up full bounty of the apricots that were on his tree. We loaded bags of apricots and drove home. Jack came to our place the next day, picked up Painted Brush in his horse trailer, and drove away, leaving the sadness of the earth and sky with us.

I was standing in the kitchen next to my mom. The pressure cooker was on the stove cooking apricots for canning. All the jars lined out on the counters, the lids off to the side. It was afternoon, and the sunshine was streaming the house, light all around. I felt the warmth of the sun penetrating the back of my neck, the steam from the pressure cooker rose in the air in front of me, the sound of steam coming from the spout loudly pulsated the room.

I turned around and John was standing there. He was wearing jeans and a white T-shirt with brown trim on the arms, and his brown baseball cap was on backwards.

"John!" I screamed.

Mom and I turned to greet him. He hugged us both, a big smile, blue eyes glistening. Mom was so happy.

"Where have you been?" she asked.

"Well, all over," he said, "I tried to write you. You get my letter?"

"I did, I did," she said. "The letter said you wrecked on a motorcycle. I was worried."

"I'm fine, Mom. I didn't get hurt bad," he said.

"Have you seen your father yet?" Mom asked, hoping for some resolution.

"Not yet." John was there most of the afternoon. He hung out with Nye and Carey, chatting it up in front room of the cabin. By sunset he was gone. I had been out in the back of the house helping my mom with the goat cheese and when we came inside, Carey said John had left. He didn't say where he was going.

"Will he be back?" I asked Mom.

"He will, he is probably going to find some work or something, then come back."

"Okay."

I put my head down and walked away. I didn't believe her.

Dad came back from hauling water, and Mom told him that John had been there.

"Well, where did he go?" Dad asked.

"I don't know. He looked good, though."

My father left the room.

A few days passed, no John.

October had come quickly. The leaves fell from the oak trees, leaving the ground yellow amidst the green piñon. The sky was still blue during the day, but the nights were freezing. Winter was upon us. We gathered around the wood-burning stove that evening as the wind howled outside. John had still not returned. He was at Carlos and Jill Werterer's house earlier that week and had called our neighbor, Todd Colombo, to ask if my dad could come for him. My father went the next day and he was gone. We hadn't heard anything since. It was like chasing a ghost. John was there and then he was gone; traveling boots and a traveling heart were his ways.

"It's going to be a rough one," my dad said as he walked out the door to gather more wood.

The cold air sucked through the door and wisped over my face. I stuck my face against the window and could see the snowflakes blowing wildly outside. It was a blizzard.

My dad came in with wood, stoked the fire, and then sat down to play his flute. The flute sounded the room, echoing the flames from the stove. I dozed off to the music floating around the room. Dad woke me and told me to go to bed. I climbed into bed; the covers were cold in the back room. I could hear the storm raging outside the house and finally fell asleep. I woke startled, to the muffled sound of a vehicle driving up the side of the mountain.

"Dad, Dad! You hear that?" I sat up in bed calling out to my dad, who was in the same room.

"What? Hear what?"

"I hear someone coming," I said.

"Yup, now I hear it," he said.

He climbed out of the bed. Nye and Carey came from the other room. My dad stopped at the door and slid on his boots. Very few people came to visit in waking hours and no one ever came at night.

"Be right back. Let me see who it is," he said.

He stepped out the front door. We waited. My mom came into the front room. We waited. Dad came back.

"Who is it?" Carey questioned him.

"It's Doyle, the postman."

"Why, what's going on?" Mom spoke up.

"The police called Todd. They couldn't make it in to tell us, so they sent Doyle. John is in the hospital," Dad said.

"What! What?!?" Carey questioned him.

My father sat calmly on the couch, lacing his knee-high leather boots, crossing the brown laces one by one over to each side. I watched his face to see how upset he was.

He was solemn, determined.

We all stood there frozen, Mom had no words.

Carey spoke up, "Well, what happened?" What happened?"

"I don't know, son," Dad replied. "I have to go with them now. I will find out."

He grabbed his heavy jacket from the wall, and shut the door behind him. Carey started a fire that lit slowly; the cold air of late night seeped through the walls, as we all huddled together.

"I bet he broke his leg working on some oil well," Carey hypothesized. "He told me he was going to get a job doing that stuff." Carey stoked the fire with confidence.

We waited around the fire, silence among us. I don't remember anything else from that night.

The next day the storm had come in so heavy the roads were blown over with snowdrifts. I made my way to the goat pen. The blizzard was coming right into my face; I could barely make out my path as the snow swirled around my body. I thought about how none of us had ever been in a hospital. John was there. How long would we wait until we knew of something? The heavy snow packed down on the earth like the weight of not knowing packed down on my small body. I was eight and a half years old now. I had come a long way since being five and learning about the passing of my grandfather. I had learned to be calm in the midst of a storm. I sat down in the goat pen and watched the baby goats gather around me, I was zoned out with my heart beating slow and deep, the blizzard forming around me. Our neighbor, Todd, made his way into the property the next day. He had gotten the call the night before that John was at UNMH, University of New Mexico Hospital. All he knew was that John was injured badly. He had broken legs and a broken shoulder—we needed to go, we needed to get out of the blizzard, we needed to see him. He was hours away, lying in a hospital bed. Todd couldn't confirm what happened to him as the police were short with their responses when they spoke to him. There were no answers. The snowflakes fell, Mother Earth was consistent in her form, the storm would rage on. It was October 1984, the date John had carved his name in the aspen tree a year earlier, when he and Dad went to Wolf Draw.

By that afternoon, the blizzard was still going when Carlos Werterer, my father's friend, drove into the property in his big logging truck. He wore working gloves, and a cowboy hat, with heavy winter boots strapped high up to his knees. Carlos was rough around the edges but always told it straight. He stepped down from the truck. He was an old cowboy true to form, had manners when it mattered most.

"Well, seems you got a rough one on your hands," he said in his kindest tone, looking at my mother.

My mother did not speak. I could hear her silent voice underneath, cracking in two.

"I am here to give y'all a ride into town. Take you straight to the hospital, if you need."

We loaded into the truck—no bags packed. Just climbed in and off we went. The snowdrifts were piled up around the house. The goats were huddled together in the goat pen under the sheltered roof. I could see their faces in the distance as we drove away. Snow blew heavy, thick flakes dancing through the windshield wipers of the old logging truck. The engine huffed as we turned the hills out of our property.

There was no sun in the sky. I don't remember the rest of the drive. Carlos took Rose, Jacinth, Nye, and me to his house in Cuba, New Mexico, and dropped us at the front door with his wife, Jill. Carey and my mother stayed in the truck.

"Carey and I will go to the hospital," Mom said as she waved us toward the front door. I wanted to go, I wanted to see John, but I was frozen inside. I couldn't respond to my mother. *There must be a reason she doesn't want us to go,* I thought.

Jill stood in the doorway. She had a long, blond braid that was twisted around to the side of her neck, and her skin was pure white. We stood at the doorway, not one of us making a sound.

She shuffled us inside and took off our jackets.

"It's better if she and Carey go. A hospital is no place for you guys to be," she said matter-of-factly, and walked toward the kitchen to get us food.

"You guys must be hungry."

"Starved," Nye and I replied.

We had not eaten since the night before.

Carlos and Jill had two children, Carmen and Lon, who were older than us, about John's age. They knew John, but when they saw us they didn't mention a thing, just came to us with smiles. I didn't quite get it, *why was no one talking about my brother who had broken his legs?*

Carmen and Lon played card games with us. I didn't understand the games. My face would go red with embarrassment, when it was my turn to "Go fish." Night fell, we slept somewhere. It had been two days since getting the news that John was in an accident. No one called. We didn't know anything else.

A Birthday to Remember

It was October 21st, which meant Rose's birthday was coming the following week on October 27th, so Jill decided to make her a cake.

We waited around the kitchen stove, the smell of vanilla throughout the room. Jill told us not to jump up and down on the hardwood floors because the cake might collapse. We immediately started to jump up and down, our little heads bobbing up and down in front of the stove. The kitchen window was large and showed a gray sky outside. Rose was excited—it was going to be her birthday.

Jill finally checked the cake, poked it with a toothpick, and said, "Cake is ready."

"Yay!"

Rose ran around the kitchen with her hands held high in the air. Then we all sat at the table. Jill smothered the cake with white frosting. She put six candles onto the cake. We sang "Happy Birthday" to Rose. The candles flickered in the afternoon light, there was a quiet stillness in the air. Rose made a wish and blew hard. Jacinth was now four. He stuffed his mouth full with cake, the white icing sticking to the side of his face and his blush-red cheeks. Rose ate slowly. She licked the frosting and took small bites of the cake. Nye and I sat still at the table. We dug in our forks to eat. He sat across from me. His face was sad, his eyes were sad, his body motionless, there were no words to be spoken. Cake wouldn't fix anything; Nye's face showed me and I followed his emotions down to the bottom of my own heart.

We drank cow's milk with the cake. When we finished the cake, Jill suggested we play outside. Outside was the one place that the heart had to keep pumping blood—there was no sitting around in a puddle of worry; nature forced one to be alive in the hardest of times. The ground was frozen but the snow had stopped falling, the air was thick and damp. We had knitted gloves Mom had made us, and hand-me-down jackets from years back that barely fit. Rose and Jacinth ran circles around me.

"Let's play hide-and-seek," Jacinth said.

Carmen came out the front door and offered to play with us.

"Can you count, Carmen?" I asked.

"One, two, three," she started off, her eyes closed.

We ran together and hid behind a large maple tree. The leaves had fallen, the tree was huge, with a light-gray trunk. We tried not to giggle as she stomped her feet around the yard pretending she didn't know where we were hiding.

Then she bounced upon us like a lion and roared, "Rawrh!"

We threw ourselves at her and ran. Jacinth was still bow-legged, and his little belly gone, but he was strong and fierce, and tried to climb on anything he could. He pulled himself up on the wood porch in front of Carlos and Jill's house. He held on with two hands and hung there, waiting for us to see him. Carmen came over and insisted that he get down before he got hurt. He held on a bit longer, then dropped to the ground, and looked at her with a smirk on his face. It grew colder, and dark within minutes.

"Let's go inside," Carmen said.

My fingers were growing numb inside my wool gloves. I wished my mom were back; I wished they came for us and had John with them. We went inside. The fire was warm. A pot belly stove sat in the corner. Wood floors ached with noise as we walked across them in our socks. Night fell. No news from Mom, Dad, or Carey.

The Sun Rises Even
When We Cannot

It was day three. I stirred from the blankets, my feet warm. I listened with one ear outside the blanket, and heard my father's voice carrying across the living room next to where I slept. I jumped from the bed and ran out. He caught me in the doorway.

"Dad," I exclaimed, "you're here."

He knelt down next to me, and sat me on his knee. His black cowboy hat was placed on the floor next to him. Anytime my father took off his hat, it meant that life had brought him to his knees. I looked at his face. His eyes were dim, tired, holding back a thousand emotions.

"Where is John?" I asked.

He put his hand on my back, and held it firm.

"God took him."

I looked around the room and saw Nye lying against the wall on the floor, curled up in a ball, like a baby, his sobbing started to echo the room. I didn't need to ask my Dad what it meant to die. I knew when I saw Nye. I looked for Carey and saw him standing in the kitchen, the morning light cast across his face. His jaw was tight, and his arms were crossed. He did not make a sound, did not move. He had his hiking boots on, and looked like a soldier returning from war.

I looked for my mom and didn't see her. My dad held me on his knee. I looked at Nye once more, his little blue jacket raised above his back, his skin showing a little. He faced the wall, his body still in a ball, his knees tucked tight to his chest, his arms tucked in close and his hands over his face. This was the meaning of death. Nothing could prepare me, not Tawny Jack, not the loss of my grandpa, not the killing of animals for food; there were some losses you could not prepare for. Heaving sadness came up through my body and out of my chest; tears swarmed my eyes like the snowstorm that had swirled around me earlier that day.

My dad started to pray. "God in heaven please receive us now, Grace of God be upon us. Your salvation, Father, is our only light, our only way."

I let my head fall, my chin drop to my chest. My memory fails me following the next few hours, I don't recall seeing my mother at all.

The Sparrow Knows No Such Sorrow

You were bold, strong, with a young man's body but an old soul. We watched you walk away. I had seen your tear-stained face, blood running from your nose, as you crawled out from under Dad's fatherly arms. The rage was in you both. You couldn't take anymore, better to be gone.

You ran, you kept running, till God called your name.

It was raining. You were hungry, and in the city. Late-night lights streamed the wet pavement. You wanted to cross the street to get food at a 7-Eleven. Red and green neon lights lit up your fifteen-year-old face. Handsome, blue eyes, tall, strong—you thought you were invincible. You were born in the woods, on a dirt floor inside a tepee. You thought you were an Indian when you were little, but you were a white boy born in the woods. A boy who loved the earth. You were connected to every plant, to every tree, to every bird. That night you stood in the paved street, your feet planted firmly on each side of your bicycle, and you waited, cars passed, you lifted yourself onto the seat of your bike, tucked your head down, and pedaled hard.

The green and red neon lights of the 7-Eleven flickered across the street. Rain poured onto your green army boots.

You saw the headlights coming at you and you jerked the bike hard to miss them. You didn't see her, the woman driving the car. No time left. Bam! She hit you straight on. Your legs hit the front bumper and broke right above the quads. Your body catapulted forward, no helmet, head to windshield.

God called your name. John.

You flew over the car, landed onto the wet pavement. Your bicycle tires still spinning, the pedals stopped. The bike lay twenty feet down the street from your body. Headlights of the car streamed across the scene, your body on the ground. The lights from the ambulance lit up the night air moving toward you.

No father knows how to say goodbye to his son. I wanted John to know how much Dad loved him. I still want this.

That first night he drove to the hospital and asked for God's guidance.

God spoke to him and said, "Do not weep for the one who is dying, weep for the one who is running away."

He arrived at the hospital, rushed through the emergency room, passing beneath all the fluorescent lighting, holding his Bible in his right hand. The doctors and nurses swarmed John's body. White overcoats and stethoscopes moving back and forth. Dad saw his body, strong muscles protruding, a naked boy on the bed. He had tubes attached to him, coming in and out of his mouth and from his chest. They had strapped him down on the bed, and he was convulsing and fighting to get the tubes off. Like Samson from the Bible, ready to pull down stone pillars holding up an empire. His head was swollen like a basketball. Dad walked slowly, feeling God's hand on his back, and approached the bedside. Thoughts swirled around in his head.

"This is not my son, I don't recognize him."

God spoke, "Whose son do you want it to be, Jerry?"

He knelt down next to John, and reached for his hand. John's hands were large and strong, that of a working boy. My father conceded, it was him. He held his hand and leaned in close to his ear.

"Your mother loves you, your father loves you, and your Creator has got nothing against you," he whispered with devout faith.

John's body fell to the bed, he stopped fighting, and let go. The moment his head had hit the windshield, God had called his name, but the moment that Dad whispered the truth in his heart was the moment he heard God calling him.

Dad was asked to leave the room; tension was growing heavy as he proceeded to preach his faith out loud. My father knew inside that John wasn't going to make it, but no one was ready to let him go. That's how we are in this world, we can't let go, we don't know how, we don't know when, we keep holding on till it's definite, till the soul has left the body. My father wanted to believe in these men and women trying to save his son. He let go of his ideals and surrendered to his son being in a hospital. Maybe with the help of God, they could save him. They told my father John had lost a lot of blood, that he needed a transfusion or he wouldn't make it. My father argued with them, "My son's blood is pure, he's never had a pill inside his body, he can't have someone's blood inside of him." The lead doctor spoke calmly to my father, "Sir, you must calm down and let us do our job, you must let us give him the blood. We are trying to save him." My father conceded again, and gave his permission for the blood transfusion.

They cut open John's head, to relieve the swelling, to help prevent brain damage, and finally gave him a blood transfusion. He was gone, but his body held on a little longer, until finally, it flat-lined. The nurses' faces were white; the doctors squirmed in their overcoats. They waited a few minutes before they had the courage to tell Dad. The attending doctor was a young Lebanese man. He met Dad in the hallway. Dad was still holding onto his Bible.

"Is that your medical book, Mr. Gallaway?" the doctor asked.

Dad nodded his head to confirm.

"The best one you can find," the doctor said.

"We did all we could for your son." The doctor gave his truth and looked my father in the eyes. "We couldn't save him."

My father knew it was coming, this knowing had been there since he left the house three nights earlier, when God spoke to him on the drive to the hospital. In the middle of the trauma, he did not want to hear his internal voice. My brother had been hit by a car straight on, his legs were broken above the knees; his head had hit the windshield before he flew over the car and landed on the pavement. There was no fight left in him.

My father walked the hallway of the cold corridor until he found a pay phone, put two quarters into the phone, and called his dad, Ira. I believe my father's heart was much like mine, in that on one side of his heart he was full with admiration for his father, and on the other side he was in complete defiance. The years of disagreement and struggle between the two men came to a halt.

Dad summoned his words to come up through his strained voice. "Dad."

Grandpa answered the phone. He knew his son's voice.

"Jerry, what is it, son?"

Dad's voice shook. This was the first call he made to anyone.

"John was in an accident."

"Oh, son," Ira's voice fell on the line.

"He didn't make it, Dad, he didn't make it. Dad, I need you to come and get him, I need you to come and help me with his body, I can't handle it." My father had made his request. At the time, my grandfather was leading a congregation of over a thousand people at a church in Peoria, Illinois. He had been traveling the world, leading religious tours and writing books. His love for my father was defining and clear in that moment.

"It's okay, son, it's okay, son, it's in God's hands now." Ira spoke the words strong. "I will be there in the morning."

My father hung up the phone.

My grandfather flew in the next morning, and went down to the morgue where John's body was kept. My father had requested that John have a natural burial, that he not be taken to a funeral home and be processed with any chemicals. Grandpa did exactly as his son had asked him to do. He anointed John's body with oil, and wrapped him in white linen as they did Christ. He had a plain pine coffin crafted in one day by an old Spanish fella who lived in the South Valley of Albuquerque. He laid John's body in the long, rectangular-shaped box. He rented a van to carry the box and we met him on the road going to our cabin.

A rally of people gathered around us, all at once everyone knew. My mother's friend Jane picked us up from Jill's house and drove us out to the property.

I sat in the car next to Jane, my mother's friend who had helped us to get to my grandmother's. Jane was sweet toward me, and leaned in to give me a kiss. I wiped it off my cheek. I couldn't receive this kind of affection; the heart must be tough to keep beating. We drove the long two hours out of town. Grandpa had rented a white van to carry John's body. We followed in Jane's blue station wagon, the white van in front of us. We climbed the dirt roads headed toward our cabin in the woods. The roads were muddy. Heavy snowdrifts from the sides of the road melted into the road, leaving piles of white on the sides and all brown mud to swerve around on. The van swerved back and forth as it climbed the steep hills onto our property. The back doors to the van flew open. There inside the doors sat Dad on one side, and Nye and Carey on the other, holding down the coffin.

The van got stuck in the mud halfway up the hill. The few cars behind us came to a stop. I watched as Dad and the boys pulled the coffin from the back of the van and lifted it onto the back of a pickup truck. They got in the back with it and continued up the hill. We drove into our property. The cabin stood beneath the trees, surrounded by white snow and patches of mud throughout. People were arriving by horseback, on foot, and by vehicle. Neighbors had heard of John's death, and found a way into our property to say goodbye. I don't remember all of their faces, except for that of Mady, who brought with her a cherry pie. I saw it sitting on the kitchen table. It was wrapped with clear, film-like paper; the cherries where bright red and held together with some kind of clear-like sticky glue. I wanted to eat it right away. I hadn't seen Mady in a few years, since the Mesa when we played with Micah and Medea. She was another one like Jane, who brought me love through her eyes, through her touch, and through her baking.

People moved from inside the cabin to outside. I looked for Mom, and did not see her. I had not seen her face since finding out John died. Twenty feet behind the cabin, back past the tallest piñon tree, I had my platform tree house built at the top of the tree. There I could see the mailbox a mile away. Back past that tree, the coffin sat on the ground. I walked over to the spot where Dad and Carey dug at the cold solid earth with shovels. I watched pieces of the damp dirt flying slowly into the air. The tree branches were frozen stiff, there was no wind, but winter was piercing our backs. The sky was gray, a dull vastness above.

I got down and walked closer. I stood a few feet back from the box that I later learned was called a coffin. The pinewood looked new and the smell of fresh pine was in the air. There were no nails to hold the lid shut. The lid was smooth and creased shut, making the box look like it had no lid. My grandfather walked over to the other end of the box, and lifted the lid.

"His head is on this side," he announced. "He should be buried with his head facing west to meet the rising sun from the east."

He shut the lid and walked away.

I made my way closer to the box. The adults clambered around me. Voices rose and fell in the air. I could see people's shoes as they walked past me, their coat hems at the sides of their hips. No one noticed me, no one spoke to me, no one offered to hold me. My heart grew thicker inside like that of an old tree growing strong branches with every storm.

I had learned to count four summers ago in the cornfield, and I knew well what a foot was. I stood at one end of the box and set one foot in front of the other, and counted, one, two, three, four…when I got to twelve my voice trailed off to a whisper.

I bent down to the box, tucked my fingers inside the lip, and lifted as hard as I could. Someone grabbed me up around my waist from behind, and the lid fell shut before I could see anything.

"I want to see my brother."

"Let me see him!" I screamed kicking my whole body.

Grandpa held me tight around my belly till I stopped squirming.

"Grandpa, put me down," I demanded and pried his fingers from my body.

"You don't need to see him, honey. His body is not the same." He put his hands on my shoulders, and looked me straight in the eyes. "John has gone to be with God, dear."

Someone called out that the neighbor was bringing his backhoe to help dig the grave. I heard the engine blowing its way up the hillside. Everyone stood back. The hole was small and my father and brothers put their shovels down and let the neighbor dig. The backhoe backed away from what was a very deep hole. The driver cut the engine. People gathered around the space. John was beside us inside his box.

Dad stood beside the coffin, holding his cowboy hat to his chest, his face white and his head shaking. Carey and Nye stood next to him. I stood in between my Grandmother Sally and Grandfather Ira. Rose and Jacinth must have been with my mother, but I have no memory of them. Silence grew around us. Grandpa read from the Bible. I don't remember the words. I only saw my brothers' faces, their heads bent down in submission to the earth, tears running down the sides of frozen cheeks. We lowered John's coffin into the ground. Men grabbed up shovels and started to throw dirt over the top. I hadn't forgotten about the cherry pie. I watched the dirt cover over the box, snowflakes landed on the dirt, white on top of brown. Drifting snowflakes fell softly till someone ushered me away from the site. I can't remember seeing Mom the whole time. I don't remember her face at all. It's as though she was gone too.

Everyone gathered inside the cabin, except for Carey. He stayed outside sitting on the frozen ground next to John's grave. Dad went out to get him, then Mom, but no one could get him to come inside and eat. The walls felt thin and the air came through, a brisk chill at my back. There was food, lots of food. I ate and ate, and still had not forgotten about that cherry pie, until finally, Jane asked me if I wanted a piece. I sat on the floor and dug my fork into the cherry filling. It was sticky and full of sugar. I licked my fork and my plate till there was none left.

It was getting dark. Finally in the last hours before he could have gotten frostbite, Carey stumbled inside the house and went to lie in the back room in his bunk. People started to say their goodbyes. One by one, they left on foot, in trucks or on horseback. The last car to leave was Grandma and Grandpa's. I had seen my Grandmother Sally only a few times in my life. She had silver hair and clear blue eyes. Her lips were pink and soft, and her skin even softer. She spoke sweetly, was gentle, and moved gracefully.

She stood at the door of the car in a long, black overcoat. She had already hugged me goodbye. I watched her hand as it came up for one last wave. She was a pillar of grace, my grandmother.

As I stood in front of the cabin to watch her go, my heart cried out to her, *Don't leave me, Grandma. Don't leave me. Please don't leave me.*

The car drove away, the taillights a fading red in the foggy gray air until they were gone.

A Mother's Love Lost

Winter was a blanket that covered over the land. It seemed to cover Mom, too. There was an invisible veil of sadness that covered my mother that even the sun could not penetrate. She was physically there, but I had no memory of seeing her. I don't know how we made it through that first winter after John died. We just did—fire by fire, bite-by-bite. By spring, I saw Mom's face again. I saw her standing at the clothesline hanging white cheesecloths. The cloths were blowing in the wind and she was graceful in her movements. I saw her from the back of her head, her auburn hair blowing in the afternoon sun. I strolled around to the front of the clothesline to see her face. Her cheeks had color, but her eyes had lost a part of their light. In my young body, I didn't know exactly what it meant, but it struck me right in the heart, making my knees weak. Somewhere inside of me I knew that my mother would never be the same again.

We existed now in a river of loss, the flowing grief pumping through the blood. Nature was the one healer that could break through the walls of grief. I watched the sunset through the trees, the last bits of golden light dropped from the earth. The pack was now broken, but nature's love was full in her presence. The sound of the wind cut sharply through the walls where we slept. The sun rose and fell, the sky opened her arms wide with twinkling stars, and a moon smiled down on us. John was still alive somewhere but it would take some time for me to feel him.

A Brother's Bond

John had been born on June 21, 1969. Carey was born the following year on September 23rd, 1970. They were almost like twins, both nursing at the same time, as my mother held two stout, chubby-legged little babies in each arm. They would be suckling and get into a hand-shoving match, both pushing the other's hands across my mother's chest. Their playful battles and self-discoveries continued for the years to come. John walked and Carey had to transform his little body to follow. Follow the leader was the game and out the door they went one day. My parents were living at the Mesa at this time. They lived in a two-room adobe house that had been gifted to them by Jane and Eli Rivers.

The adobe sat high on a hilltop with acres of green hillside spread out to meet a thick forest line. The two boys with golden hair played from sunup till sundown. They watched the land change underneath their feet, until one day they were running, fast and furious, out the door and toward the woods. My father did a lot of hunting and logging in those days, and was usually gone for hours. My mother knitted in her kitchen chair facing a south window with bright beams of sunlight pouring in, a red geranium plant hanging in the window.

One afternoon, out of nowhere, heavy clouds gathered and quickly a massive storm ensued. Rain poured down on the high Mesa. They stayed inside and waited for my father to return. He made it by evening and together they ate dinner under the kerosene lamp. The storm brought a strange quietness across the land. The next morning John and Carey rushed the open fields of wet, soggy earth and bounced around splashing in puddles. Later that afternoon while my mother made goat cheese, the two boys disappeared. My mother took no notice as they were always wandering off. A few hours later they returned soaking wet from head to toe.

They stumbled in the door. "Mom! John almost drowned in the pond," Carey announced. It was rare that the ponds in that area would fill up. My brothers had never experienced this heavy of a rain and when they went to play in the shallow pond, the waters had engulfed them. Neither of them had learned how to swim yet. Carey walked on foot with his head far underwater till he made it to the other side of the pond and climbed out onto the bank. He rolled onto the bank and didn't see John. John was nowhere. Carey went after him and dragged him out of the water. He patted John on the back, helping him to gag up the water and stabilize his breathing. They both lay on their backs in the sun. They had defeated death.

> Little boys like warrior men
> Now you come to defend
> To make real your strength known
> To bring the brightness of the sun
> To hold the snowflake in your hand
> To know one day you will be a man
> You will have made
> All this way
> We bid you farewell
> The boy inside
> The light that shines
> Now has died

Boys Become Men

Carey could not save John this time and his world would never be the same again. He told Dad that he was going to school. He had made a decision and was resolute, despite my father's wishes. He told a neighbor, after sitting in their living room trying to read a third-grade book and unable to do so, that he would go to school. Some things he voiced and others he kept inside. When we were grown, Carey would explain to me his thoughts at that time. He felt John had died because he went into the world without an education. He would not suffer the same fate as his brother; this idea became the foundation for his strength in starting school. Carey and Dad danced around each other like Dad and John had, but now my father knew how harsh the results of loss could be, in that he tried for weeks not to go into battle with Carey. Carey alike tried not to upset my father, staying calm and steady in his words, never disrespecting my father, but toeing the line to complete his mission to get an education.

The school bus driver would pick him up en route through the back canyon to get the few kids who lived miles apart from each other. It was a damp spring morning when the bus driver bellowed up the driveway and pulled into the yard. It was the first time I had seen a school bus up close. I watched through the window. After a few weeks of this routine, my father's river of emotions broke through a dam and he marched out into the driveway and spoke loudly to the bus driver. "I'm not giving you permission to take my son with you." My father was on fire, his arms flying about, his words piercing the air. "Do I tell you how to raise your children?" he questioned the bus driver. "No I don't! And to be a neighbor is to respect a man in all his ways. I'm not coming onto your property telling you how things should be done." My father couldn't stop himself.

Carey marched right through my father's fire and climbed on the bus, he never spoke a word. The bus drove away. That evening Carey returned on foot where he had hiked the mile from the mailbox to get home. The bus driver, too afraid of my father, would no longer pick him up or drop him off. Carey sank more into his resoluteness.

When my father sang there was an outpouring of love, and when he raged there was an outpouring of fear. This was his river of humanity, the ebb and flow of my father's life that we couldn't understand, that we couldn't fix, and we couldn't' hide from.

Early one morning, I heard loud voices from the front room while lying under my quilt in the back room. I jumped out of bed and stood in the open doorway between the back and front room of the cabin. Dad and Carey had gone from shouting to a silent struggle, a fourteen-year old boy and a man under the arms of war. I watched as Dad pinned Carey up against the front door. Carey broke loose of him, never raising a fist to my Dad. My dad swirled around and threw a right punch straight at Carey. Carey weaved down like a pro and my dad's fist struck flat on the heavy cedar door. My father's heavy breaths turned to a bear-like growl when his fist hit the door. Carey, in one full motion, swerved out from under him. My mother stood silently in the kitchen. Carey ran past me in the doorway and out the back door of the cabin. I watched as he ran through the woods behind the house, his body moving at high speed, past John's grave, and onward until his head disappeared beneath the piñon trees.

That evening, he did return. We were all aware of Dad's short fuse and broken state that could erupt at any time. There was little speaking of any kind and this pattern seemed to go on for days. I found my solace, as I always had, by lying in the bales of hay holding onto a baby goat, the warm blood of the animal keeping me alive, keeping me hopeful, allowing me to feel something.

Weeks later, Carey walked up the front drive one afternoon. He looked like a man, walked like a man, but still sounded like himself. He brought with him a hacky sack from school. We clamored around him in the front yard.

He tossed the hacky sack to Nye. "Hey, bro, wanna play?" There was no one more relieved to see Carey than Nye. They played with that hacky sack for hours until the sun fell. Carey stayed the night. At dinner, he spoke in a calm tone his truth to my father and told him that he would be living with a teacher from now on, as he would be going to school and it just seemed like the better thing for everyone. My father did not argue. His resistance showed through his eyes, but he did not speak. His stout body seemed to be weakened. His silence said it all. He could not win this battle, he couldn't seem to win any of his battles, or to even remember why he was fighting them in the first place.

On March 11th Nye turned eleven and on March 12th I turned nine. Mom made our favorite carrot cake. The days were getting longer with the sun keeping the evening warm. We gathered outside on the front porch to sing "Happy Birthday." Nye and I stood side by side, with our hands folded at our waists. We had learned to let happiness in when it came. It came with the spring air, with the smell of horses, with the sound of my mother's voice singing, "happy birthday to you." Rose and Jacinth were gleeful, jumping in circles around the cake. Carey was not there, but I got the sense that he was more than safe and that he may be having more and more happy moments. I was split in two with wanting Carey to return and my own ideas about someday being free, going to school, and having friends. The ice cold of life was always there, peeking through my child eyes. Somehow the sun would melt the ice and my heart would thaw in the chirping of a bird, in the neigh of Juniper, in the ba ba ba of a baby goat. I don't remember my father being there for that birthday. He normally played the guitar for us, but that evening he was not present.

The less my mother was present, the more I needed to feel safe and to process all the loss that had taken place. My mother was drowning in her own grief. I could see it, but didn't know how to help her. Rose was seven, and I mostly felt protective of her, but secretly without my knowing she had become a lifeline to me. Inside a masculine world we were two brave little girls that could feel and touch the sadness and joy of life like no one else.

My sister was always quiet, a radiant beauty shining through her blue eyes. She seemed to find a way to just be amid the chaos, the loud voices, the sounds of life that she had grown accustomed to. We had both grown accustomed to this life, and at the same time we knew there was something different, something more. At night we lay together in one bed, whispering to each other about the day or making up stories.

One of our favorite stories to read was called *Flicka, Ricka, Dicka and the Strawberries,* a story about three little Swedish girls who lived with their mother in the deep woods in Sweden. The three girls go out on their own one day to pick wild strawberries. They end up getting lost and crying alone in the woods. When the sun is about to set and they could be overcome by the darkness, this is when they rise up in courage and decide that they must find their way home. Which is when their real adventure begins and they make it home to give their mother full baskets of strawberries. The mother makes jam from the berries, and they all sit down to eat. In the story there are no males, and yet the women are strong and capable and completely safe. My sister was my strong, capable, and completely safe place to go. We lay there into evening drawing circles on each other's bare backs.

"Guess what it is," Rose would say after drawing a few lines up and out.

"A tree!" I would respond. "Now, it's my turn."

I would draw circles, squares, and sometimes attempt a goat or a horse.

We did this until we fell asleep.

Sisters and Cupcakes

Most of the neighbors were about a ten-mile drive from us, and few of them ever visited. Joy and William Bassett had become a rock, a place to go for refuge for all of us at different times. They were walking in faith as soldiers of Christ, and I was learning by their every act of kindness. They were the neighbors we visited most frequently, and they also seemed most aligned to my father's religious ideas. Well, I'm not sure they were aligned but they didn't seem to argue much with my father, and as I had learned in my time many could argue with my father on his beliefs, but most did not want to go there.

Mr. Bassett looked like a farmer, if I'd had officially known what a farmer looked like. He wore the same blue-jean overalls, with a white, long-john undershirt, and a black cowboy hat that was curved in the front. He was slender and shorter than my Dad. He had a soft voice, and did not speak much. Mrs. Bassett was a stalky woman, taller than my mother, reminding me of a Russian woman who picked potatoes. That's what I always thought when I saw her, *hmm,* I would say to myself, *she must be from Russia and know how to pick potatoes.* I had no idea where Russia was on the map, but I knew that my grandfather, my mom's dad, had emigrated from there when he was four years old, and I knew that it was cold, very cold.

Joy had the bluest eyes, even bluer than my mom's, and she told me she had thirteen kids. That seemed like more than a herd of goats, I couldn't imagine. Their house was three miles from our house, off the front of the cliff and through the woods. I had walked the trail with my dad and brothers many times, but now and then my sister and I would sneak off and make our way to their house. They always had some kind of treat waiting for us. Macaroni and cheese from a box, cheese that tasted salty and different than any I'd ever tasted. All I had eaten was goat cheese, so I didn't have much to compare it to. The mac 'n' cheese was worth the three miles down the mountain and the three-mile hike back up the mountain.

It was the end of summer and the root cellar was full of harvested vegetables. Yellow and orange pumpkins peeked through the bins at the back wall of the cellar; bushels of apples lined the side walls; green beans, carrots, peas, corn, all took up rows of wooden boxes my dad put together to hold the food. Nye and Jacinth had made a trip down to Mr. Bassett the day before. They had been gone all day and my Dad was slightly upset upon their return.

"Where have you boys been?"

I could hear his voice with the stern pitch coming from the front room. "Uh, just down helping Mr. Bassett," Nye said.

"Well, I could use some help here today," my father's voice receded.

"Sorry, Dad. We helped Mr. Bassett load hay all day," Jacinth chimed in.

How could my father refute helping out a neighbor? After all, Mr. Bassett had helped us twenty times over. My father often caught himself in these moments of contradiction, telling us children one thing that went against something else he had preached from the Word of God earlier. He would sometimes catch himself after a few upset breaths and let it go. Occasionally he would admit that he was wrong. Nye and Jacinth sat down for dinner and ate their food like starved orphans gobbling up beans, mashed potatoes, and pan-fried squash strips, with homemade bread still warm from the oven, a round loaf that smelled of yeast and oil, the brown crust shining in the evening lantern light. After dinner Nye sat next to me on the couch in front of the tin-barrel stove, the flames burning hot. Summer was just leaving us.

"Hey, go down to the cellar tomorrow and check out the black bag in the back," he whispered to me.

"What is it?" I probed.

"Goodies from Mr. Bassett," he smiled, keeping his attention away from Dad standing in the kitchen.

I immediately ran to the back room to tell Rose. She was lying on our bed. "Nye got us goodies from Mr. Bassett."

We both knew what that meant. Every now and then, once a year or even a longer stretch, Mr. Bassett would make a trip to Farmington, New Mexico, where he would buy a lot of things from the store. We were never allowed to have these things, and had never even set eyes on them until the first time we got them from Mr. Bassett. We were not allowed to have candy or sugar of any kind, only desserts that my mother made for us, usually with molasses or honey. I liked the desserts from my mom, but could not resist something different from the outside world. Rose and I went to bed with wired minds thinking of what waited for us in the cellar. We woke before sunup, helped Mom make breakfast—eggs and potatoes fried in the black skillet. The boys always ate with Dad before us, and then left to get wood around the back of the mountain.

Rose and I glanced at each other with a mischievous grin. We couldn't go down to the cellar yet; we had to help Mom milk the goats. I rushed toward the goat pen, my feet fumbling after me, the milk pail spinning in my hand. I rushed to the goat-milking stall, shoved her head into the clamp of the headrest, and lifted her leg into the holding hoop. I pulled the wooden sitting stool under me and milked her. Milk shot out through my hands, onto the floor and missing the bucket. Mom entered the goat pen, annoyed at the milk pouring onto the floor. "Chloe, watch what you're doing."

"Okay, Mom," I said with a hint of sarcasm, and focused my hands back on the goat teat to finish up the job. My insides were screaming to get out of there. I had half a bucket of milk and hauled it to the house, and poured it into the white container where Mom would use it to make goat cheese later.

Rose waited for my cue and we rushed out, letting the heavy cedar door slam behind us. Mom passed us on her way inside. "Where are you girls going?" She caught my eye.

"Nowhere, Mom, just gonna go down to the field and check on Mule." Mule was my father's horse in training. We both ran before Mom could get another word out. We flew like birds in the open air, landing on the doorstep of the root cellar. I opened the door and started down the wood steps dug into the dirt, the dirt walls growing deeper as I descended. The outside light gave me just enough light to see the bins in the back and make my way to the left-hand corner where Nye said the bag would be. I felt my way in the dark at the back wall and got a grasp of bag in my hands. I pulled at it, the heaviness tugging me down. *Geez, what's he got in there,* I thought. I dragged the bag into the light. A black plastic bag with a white string tied it together. I pulled it further out into the sunlight that lit the path straight down the steps into the center of the underground dwelling.

"Open it, let's see what it has." Rose said. I untied the string and reached my hand inside, pulling out a box of Twinkies, eight Twinkies in a box. Rose's eyes grew big. "What are those?" I set them on the floor and pulled out another box. A smaller package of cupcakes, two in a set, wrapped tight inside a plastic casing. "Cupcakes!" we both exclaimed. We pulled the bag back to the corner and tucked it away in a sure spot where Dad would not see it if he came into the cellar. We grabbed the Twinkies and cupcakes and climbed the stairs out of the cellar. We sat in the sun on at the front of the cellar, the heat beating down on us.

"Let's eat them," Rose said and opened up the box of cupcakes, her tiny fingers tearing at the wrapping. She handed me one large, round chocolate cupcake with a white frosting laced across the top center. We lifted them to our mouths and ate from the edge, large bites till we made it to the center of the cupcake—a white, soft, all-sugar frosting. I had only had Hershey's cocoa that my mom used to make a cake for Carey's birthday one year. It was bitter, even after we added honey. This chocolate was pure, sweet, deep, rich, moist cake that stuck to my tongue and got all over my lips, the white frosting gooey, soft, and pure sweetness, too. We ate it all and looked at each other.

"Wow," our eyes exclaimed.

We waited a few minutes and dug into the box of Twinkies, tearing at the plastic wrapping paper. We each got a whole one and bit off a huge bite. It had soft, fluffy, yellow cake mix, with white, creamy filling; it was even sweeter than the cupcake. By then we were melting in the hot sun, our backs leaning against the closed root cellar door. We each ate one more Twinkie, pushing it slowly into our mouths and swallowing with will.

"No more."

We lay in the sun sick with sweetness. It took thirty minutes for me to move. Rose was almost passed out next to me. I shook her after what seemed a long while. "We gotta get back, or Mom's going to start looking for us."

"Okay." Rose rolled over to her side, looking pale and sick in the eyes and face. I grabbed the box of Twinkies, wobbled down the cellar steps, and stuffed the box in the corner next to the bag. We walked the fifty yards toward the house with slow dragging limbs and our bellies full with sugar. Once inside the house, Rose and I each grabbed up a large glass of goat milk and drank it all down with five big gulps. We would never speak of our gluttonous act to anyone, not even the boys.

At lunchtime, it felt good to eat Mom's left-over squash with beans and potatoes. The real food went down slowly but welcomed itself kindly in my belly that had ached and twisted for the past two hours. I felt more tired than usual and went to lie on the front porch in the afternoon sun. I laid my achy body down on a quilt from the bed in the back room onto the wood panel flooring that faced south. The sun was tilting toward the west, and a few clouds rolled in creating a shade spot that hovered over me on the porch. I lay there letting my eyes drift open and closed; the stillness wrapped around me, the clouds taking me with them as they moved across the sky. I thought of my dad and how he didn't want us to eat the cupcakes. I wondered if he had eaten them when he was little, and maybe he knew they would make us sick. Maybe he wasn't such a mean guy after all.

Girls Can Be Cowboys Too

Dallas was the only horse I could call mine. I was now ten years old and after watching John and Carey rebel against my father, I was finding the courage to take my own steps into the world, no matter how small those steps were. Dallas had been a rebel of a horse, according to the neighbor, and I was right there with him finding my courage.

From Dallas, I had learned that you needed to meet the spirit of the horse right where he was. I never wanted to be a mustang runner. My father taught me it was about connecting to the energy of the horse—honoring his stride, his breath—and moving with him. I didn't so much think it as I knew it when I climbed up on Dallas's back. A horse needs you to lead and if you don't feel strong enough to lead, he will doubt you for certain, and this will show up in all sorts of ways, from moving a few feet when you attempt to climb in the saddle, to bucking, stalling, or sharp movements.

What started out as a normal ride brought me quickly to my senses. Dallas spooked, and was suddenly in a full-speed run through the woods. I dug my cowboy boots into the stirrups, and pressed my thighs hard into the saddle. Holding the reins in a tight grip, I tried to pull back. I lifted my head slightly, and... SMACK!...a piñon branch whisked across my face. I tucked my body tight against the saddle, feeling heat rising up through him. As the last tree branch disappeared behind me, I sat up, pushing my weight down into my boots. I pulled back on the reins. "Whoa, whoa," I yelled out.

I felt his body shift under me as we came to a sudden stop. I leaned forward into the saddle horn, and doubled over.

"What was that, buddy?" I said, short of breath.

Dallas walked slowly, his heart pounding. I had gotten Dallas a few months back for my tenth birthday. He was a bit ornery, but I trusted him and felt confidence in his response to my voice and grip on the reigns.

"What happened, buddy, did something spook you?" I patted him firmly on the neck, my hand sticking to his gray, sweaty coat.

It was one of the last days of spring, just before the sun melts into summer. The fresh air gathered around me. It was half a mile more to the end of our property, brown and red hills stretching out to meet the yellow road. There was no fence to mark our property line. A dirt trail continued off through the woods and past a small pond with tall green grass. We stood at the edge of the pond for a few minutes; Dallas's neck drooped while lapping up water. It was a risk to leave our property without permission. Adrenaline pumped through my veins. The ride on Dallas had sparked gumption in me, and anger at my father brewed deep, like that of an old underground well. We headed east down a narrow dirt trail weaving along a cliffside, making our way toward Rainbow Mountain. Rainbow Mountain got its name from its brilliant majestic colors that caked the eight-thousand-foot cliff with purple, pink, white, and red earth tones.

Just off Rainbow Mountain and half a mile through a thick forest was Michael and Patty Gold's summer camp. Cedar Mountain Camp was founded years back after Michael had made millions designing his own clothing line. The family came out every summer from Studio City, California, to vacation and run the camp for kids living in the city. Michael was a short, muscular, confident fella. He was a businessman of sorts, sharp and witty, with worldly ideals; he seemed so opposite to my father, I didn't know how to approach him. I had been around him many times, as my father worked with him from time to time on building the camp. Patty, with her long, wild hair and strong body, seemed more of the wilderness type. She was a hands-on, get-down-in-the-dirt kind of woman, with a soft smile if you caught her at the right moment. I felt a kindred spirit in her. Michael and Patty had three children, Daniel, Damon, and Kamala. Daniel was the oldest, close in age with John, Damon close in age with Carey, and Kamala, the youngest, just older than me. The boys were a bit wild and playful in manner, while Kamala seemed softer and country-like. I wanted to be friends with them, but had only seen them a few times in my life. My life that seemed completely different in every way possible. I knew they went to school, lived in the city, ate normal food, and had lots of friends and money. My father had set out to have as little money as possible, which I couldn't fully understand. But I was learning that living in the world was a battle and this battle had a lot to do with how one used money—that money brought greed and despair in the form of lying governments, and a society unaware of their need for Mother Earth and God.

California kids were different. One visited our house once. He took one bite of goat yogurt and spit it out. I knew I'd be seen as an outsider at the camp, but figured I could fake my way around any conversation and just maybe I'd make a friend.

The moon was a half sliver in the sky. My heart raced as we approached the trailhead. I had been down the trail but once on foot. Dallas and I stopped at the top of the trail. The smell of freshly uncovered dirt, sage, and piñon rose up to meet me. The trailhead started at the far west side of the mountain, with hundreds of feet to descend. Expansive views went on for miles, blue mountain ridges far in the distance narrowing across patches of light, dark, and muted greens, forest-deep, thickly meshed together like one large family. Dallas's breathing was calm and mine began to pick up.

"Let's go," I said, and nudged Dallas with my boots.

He took his first steps onto the trailhead, my body pushing forward in the saddle. The trail was narrow, slipping its way through small crevices, with brown and yellow clay underfoot and small red pebbles dotting the path. To my left was a fifty-foot drop, to my right a brown and purple clay wall. I breathed in and out to the rhythm of Dallas's footsteps. At first my mind raced, but as the trail grew narrower my adrenaline kept my thoughts at bay as we pressed through two large boulders. Small rocks shifted underneath and rolled off the side; silence gathered in the air as they landed below. We etched our way smooth and slow like molasses, until reaching our final descent. Once the trail grew wider, my shoulders dropped with relief.

Blue-green sage dotted the outline of the path. Indian paintbrush, with tiny spear-like orange blossoms pointed to the sky. There were a few overhanging clouds that cast a shadow across the earth. We stopped behind a boulder. I took my canteen of water, and guzzled it down. I didn't think once about having to climb back up the cliff. I strapped my canteen to the saddle horn.

"Let's go, buddy." I shook the reins and we were off.

We rode into camp, my body calm from the journey that was more than an hour's time. We traveled down the long stretch of red dirt road toward the first compound, a brown adobe house with a red tin roof. Patio chairs outlined the front porch built of dark wood. The windows reflected the outside light, and I could not see in. There were no children in sight. We took a left and passed a large pine tree that stood in the front yard; a tire swing hung from the tree. I thought I heard voices of children echoing through the soft wind, but it was only in my mind. Excitement rose in me from my boots and up through my body. And then, panic—it seeped into my head with questions. Who would be there? What will the kids be like? I wasn't usually too concerned about my looks. At my house there were no mirrors for the daily routines of getting ready and viewing oneself. My hair was either a tangled mess flying around my face, or pulled back in a ponytail. I now wondered what I looked like.

I sat tall and proud on Dallas as we rode toward Michael and Patty's large, three-story, cedarwood-paneled home. To the left was the property caretaker's residence, a two-story adobe with blue shutters, a screened doorway, and a red tin roof overhanging the front porch. I passed the chicken coop and the garden area, glancing at tiny green vegetable tops sprouting from the ground. Past Michael's house, the road continued into the thick woods where four pine cabins retained the surrounding beauty of Rainbow Mountain.

Dallas walked with a lazy step as we neared the chicken coop.

I heard someone call out, "Hello there."

Cornplanter, who was the gardener and caretaker of the property, stepped out from the gate to the garden. He approached, his straw cowboy hat making him look taller for what was a thin, blue-eyed, pale-skinned New Englander. He was awkward like my father, a man seeming to be from a different planet in the way he spoke, soft and low, and how his legs bent slightly at the knee. His boots rugged and dirty, he loved the earth. But he was not religious like my father and that set them apart greatly. I didn't feel judged when I saw him. When he looked at me, I sank into my jeans and knew they fit just right.

"Ms. Chloe, what brings you out this way?" he asked as he approached Dallas.

"Just thought I would come by today," I responded.

He led Dallas by the bridle and tethered him to a post in front of the chicken coop.

"It's good to see you. How's your father doing?" he inquired.

"Oh, Dad's just fine, I guess."

I was waiting for him to question whether or not my father knew I was there. He smiled the best smile he could. It was not infectious. His lips were thin and he showed no teeth.

"The kids are all out on a hike. I assuming you'd like to hang out with them this afternoon?" he asked.

"Yeah, if that's okay."

"Fine by me. Michael and Patty went into town, won't be back till later this evening. Camp staff will be back with the kids for afternoon snack. Why don't you come in for a bit," he asked as he walked toward the adobe house.

I followed, my feet moving slowly. We entered the house. Light streamed through the windows from all angles. I glared at the clean white walls, the high ceilings, and bright décor; a yellow tablecloth that overhung the sides of a smooth wooden table shone brightly against the blue kitchen sink.

"You want something to drink?"

Cornplanter reached for a glass from the cupboard.

"How about some grape juice?"

He poured a glass of purple juice and set it in front of me. I moved my hand cautiously to grab it, this being my first time trying grape juice. I hadn't finished the glass when I heard a rustling of voices and footsteps traveling loudly outside the adobe windows.

"And there they are," he stated, as he started toward the front door and motioned for me to follow.

A stream of kids—boys and girls, light, dark, and blond hair all neatly groomed with fresh clothes and new shoes marched down the road, clumped together like foreigners to this land. I followed Cornplanter steadily. We met the kids on the road. The adult woman traveling with them greeted us.

"I am taking the kids up for snacks." She stopped and looked at the both of us.

"Great," Cornplanter said, and pulled me to the front of him.

I was startled and quickly gathered myself to stand upright.

"This is Chloe, she lives up above Rainbow Mountain."

The kids all stared. I kept my eyes focused on the adult woman. She wasn't tall, and had brown hair that wasn't fancy. She wore jean shorts with a white T-shirt and hiking boots with red shoe laces.

"This is Mary Ann," Cornplanter stated.

"Hi, Chloe, would you like to come up and eat with us?" she asked.

"Uh…sure." I moved a few steps forward, aligning myself next to her.

Cornplanter waved us off and we walked the dirt road to the adobe house I passed on the way in. I stayed next to Mary Ann. The boys giggled in the far back, as the girls chattered about things I couldn't make out. We arrived at the front steps of the house, where Mary Ann directed us to sit. I stepped onto the front porch; the dark wood creaked underneath my feet. The kids gathered quickly, clambering for a chair. Two girls sat next to me. One blonde, with neatly combed hair clipped up with two purple barrettes. The other a brunette with her hair pulled back from her face. They were clean, neat; I couldn't smell anything but knew they smelled good. It had been weeks since I'd had a bath, and as the realization set in I pushed back in my chair, hoping no one would notice.

"Hi, Chloe, I'm Emma," the blonde said.

Emma looked a little older than me. Her voice broke a silence inside.

"Hi," I replied with a half-smile.

The noise of the other children was drowned out by this grand gesture of friendship.

"So you live here?" Emma asked. "I think that's great. I love coming here—it's my favorite thing for the whole year."

I listened as Emma spoke rapidly.

"You live in California?" I managed to get into the conversation.

"Yes, right near the ocean," she gleamed. "My Daddy's a lawyer. What does your dad do?"

My mind froze, my eyebrows twitched. *What does my Dad do?*

Mary Ann approached carrying a tray of peanut butter and jelly sandwiches. Everyone scrambled to their feet and grabbed a sandwich. I timidly reached for one. I'd had it twice in my life, at my grandmother's in Houston. I held the soft bread between my fingers and ate slowly, the strawberry jelly gushing out the sides of the bread, the salty peanut butter sticking to the roof of my mouth. Emma had stopped talking while she ate her sandwich. Blackish purple clouds gathered in the sky above the porch.

"Looks like it might rain," Mary Ann said. "I'm going to take a group of students with me now back to the cabins."

Mary Ann looked around and then made eye contact with Damon, who was Michael and Patty's son. "Can you bring the others when you guys are ready?"

Mary Ann left. As soon as she was out of sight, Damon started up. He was charming, clowning around, making jokes. The group seemed to like him a lot, but I was suspicious of his cantering around like a clown.

"I have an idea," Damon blurted out. "Let's sneak up to my parent's house and watch a movie!"

My mind began to swirl with thoughts. My father's presence loomed over me, the lines in his face serious, his thick beard partially covering his facial expression. He had always said television was bad for your mind, even worse for your heart. I wasn't sure if this was true. I had only seen *Inspector Gadget,* the cartoon about a private investigator, while sitting on my grandmother's couch after the sun when down in Houston. I had never seen a movie. I didn't know the difference between a movie and a TV show. The kids all gathered around, hushing their excitement of disobeying the rules. I followed the group reluctantly toward Michael and Patty's home. My feet grew heavy, my shoulders tight; my desire to fit in was stronger than my intuition. I picked up my feet and walked faster. I was going to watch my first movie.

I was last in the group to enter the house, letting the screen door slam behind me with a clang. Damon led the group toward the living room, a wide-open space with wood floors covered by fancy rugs. The rugs meshed softly under my feet, the afternoon light shone dimly through the windows that spread across the southern portion of the house. A dark, leather, L-shaped couch sat at the center of the room. The kids pushed and shoved one another all the way to the couch until they plopped down. I wanted to sit next to Emma, but it was so crowded, I couldn't fit. I sat down on the floor beside the couch and pulled my knees in close to my chest, wrapping my arms around them.

"What are we watching?" someone yelled out.

"You'll see," Damon replied, as he slipped the video into a small box underneath the TV.

The TV screen reflected sunlight; small dust particles floated in the air. The movie began to play. The scene was a campsite on a lake, similar to the camp where I was, except with thicker woods and a lake with dark blue water. Teenage boys and girls gathered in a small cabin set in the deep woods. The girls were in a living area combing their hair and talking about which boy they liked. The boys were in the kitchen, one of them hunched over the stove.

A girl with dark brown hair and blue eyes approached the boy near the stove.

"Hey, Steve, I am going out for a walk," she said.

My heart pounded. I wasn't supposed to be watching this.

The movie continued. "You want me to come?" the boy asked.

"No," the girl smiled and made her exit from the cabin entrance.

She walked slowly toward the woods, the light around her grew dim, and a heavy sound of music started playing.

I felt my body shift under me. *It's time to go,* my intuition pressed against my insides.

The girl walked, making her way through a clearing of trees, and out jumped a man wearing a white facemask, carrying a chainsaw.

I pushed back on the floor and covered my hands over my face. Sweat melted against my cheeks as I peeked through my fingers. The man in the movie raised his chainsaw toward the girl, and she started running, her screams loud and echoing through the room. The kids broke out in laughter, the sound of laughter drowning in with the sounds of screaming on television. The room started to spin. I kept my hands over my face, my stomach sick, my mind in a panic. I jumped to my feet and ran for the front door, threw open the screen and ran as fast as I could toward the chicken coop.

Dallas stood tethered to the post. My hands fumbled for the reins and untied them. I threw myself on and kicked him hard to start down the road. I didn't look back. Dallas broke into a fast trot as we made our way off the property. My hands shook, still sweating, my heart rate elevated. I tried to calm my breathing, and then came the tears. *I knew I shouldn't have been watching that,* my mind went 'round and 'round. We rode through the wheat field, the sun sunk low in the sky, golden streams of yellow cascading across the land. Tears rolled down the sides of my cheeks, my chest pushing in and out.

The sun moved quickly toward the horizon as we pressed on towards the woods ahead. We entered the trail to the woods. Shadows of light disappeared, drawing darkness around the trees.

My imagination ran wild. Did men like the one in the movie really exist?

The forest felt thick, heavy, and deep in the midst of darkness. I wiped away my tears and gathered my body in close; my instincts to lead my horse lay dormant in me. I held tight to Dallas, wrapped my arms around him as far as I could reach, his heartbeat pounding through the saddle.

I leaned in and whispered to him, "Please take me home, boy."

Dallas moved quickly, his footsteps trotting against the soil. Noises rose and fell throughout the landscape, the crackling of tree branches and animals bustling through the night. My insides injured as though a parasite ate at me. Every time I heard a noise, all I could see was the man in the white mask. Holes poked out for the face and eyes, behind the mask a man with no soul. I lifted my head to make out the clearing as we rode out of the woods and toward the cliffside.

The trail was a thin, ghost-like vision ahead of us, boulders shadowing the sides. Dallas did not slow down. I felt the saddle sway backwards underneath me; sweat creased his neckline. The air was cool and damp as we approached the high point of the trail. I couldn't make out the clay wall but could see pure darkness where the trail dropped off the side. I could hear Dallas's heartbeat, his footsteps, and the weight of his body shifting. I didn't know what would be harder: facing my father, or getting up that cliff. As the trail leveled out, I patted Dallas firmly.

"You did it boy, you did it."

We rested for a moment and then rode. My body settled into the night air. The yellow road was visibly different from the rest of the earth as we approached the cabin. There was no place to go but home. I could see the kerosene lamp burning in the window, my father's shadow lit against the back wall of the kitchen. I was exhausted. I would never sleep again if the man in the movie never left my mind. I wanted to tell my father about the movie. I wanted him to tell me these things were not true about the world. I choked back my thoughts of telling the truth. I was already in so much trouble.

We rode into the front yard. I tethered Dallas to the hitching post, removed the saddle, and began to groom him. As I ran smooth motions with the brush across his fur, a million stars gathered in the sky.

"What a good boy," I spoke, my mouth close to his ear.

I leaned in and hugged him tight. I took my time, until my stomach growled from hunger, and I had to go inside. I walked Dallas to the barn and set him free, watching his gray coat shimmer in the night air as he trotted to the feeding stall. I turned and walked toward the cabin. It wasn't cold, but my hands were frozen, my face was changed, my eyes twitching. I pushed with all my strength to open the front door, the thick cedar door feeling so much heavier than it ever had.

I entered the house. Dad sat at the kitchen table reading the Bible. He maintained his composure and did not look at me.

"Where have you been?" His voice was low.

I held my hands in my lap, my head down. I was ready for my punishment.

"I rode Dallas to Michael and Patty's house," I said.

"You must be hungry." He sat a plate of pan-fried vegetables in front of me.

We ate in silence.

"Go to bed. We will talk about this tomorrow," he said as he looked up from the Good Book.

I went to lie down. Rose was awake in the bed. She looked at me, her green eyes gentle.

"Chloe, where were you? Dad has been upset all day."

I lay next to her in the dark, the lamp giving a tiny hint of light from the other room.

"Want me to draw on your back?" she said.

I turned over and pulled up my shirt. She went round and round in circles.

"Okay, my turn," I said.

She rolled over and pulled up her shirt. I wrote out letters as best I knew.

"What did it say?" I asked her.

"I don't know," she said, "something with 'a' in it... apples?"

"Apples."

Whenever we were sad, Rose and I drew on each other's backs. It was a game we played for years.

The next morning I sat at the table eating my ground cereal. My father came in from outside.

"Why don't you help me out with the horses today?" he said.

His anger was gone. I didn't know what happened. Maybe he knew I had been punished enough somehow. I would never tell him about the movie—it was my cross to bear.

The Spirit Calls Out to Us

It was August of 1986. I had made it to age eleven; it had been two years since John died. I felt like a grownup, ready to make decisions for myself. Life in the woods is all about being grown up in so many ways; the spirit of the child is alive but the harshness of reality requires one to grow up quickly.

I came in from the goat pen. It was late evening and the sun was going down. I heard my father yelling. His voice grew louder and louder. He talked so fast, his words were fumbling out of his mouth. I would later learn that my father was being triggered by many things: the school board was sending him letters about putting us in school, the State of New Mexico was inquiring about our immunizations, the walls of society were closing in on him, and my mother was the only person he could tell.

Not again, I thought.

I peeked in the window. My mother sat in the corner, this time her knitting needles in her hand, her head down, her fingers moving fast with the purple yarn weaving through her hands. The faster he talked, the faster she knitted. It was as though they were in some kind of rhythm together. He was preaching out lines from the Bible, and she was taking them onto the edge of her needle and shoving them together piece by piece. She ignored him and continued to knit until he settled himself down. I walked around the back of the house, where Nye was sitting out near John's grave. I watched him sit there, my heart splintering into tiny pieces.

"It's gonna be okay," I whispered to Nye.

I sat down in the dirt with the noise of the argument swirling around me. My father always talked about when he was young and how he hated being popular. He had told me a story about when he played football for the University of Texas. He was the quarterback of the team, and he had led the team to victory many times. And after the victories they would shove him into the cheerleaders' dressing room. Girls loved him and swarmed around him for attention. He said he hated this whole game of win and lose, and the way people admired you for something that was not really you. Even though he had always been mostly on the winning side, he hated the notion of competition, this idea of pitting people against each other for one person to win and another to lose. How could anyone really win? It was a contradiction of sorts, flames coming from my father's mouth, all around the desire for a calm and peaceful people. *If he wanted calm and peaceful, why couldn't he communicate that in a peaceful way?* As a child on the verge of womanhood, it was utter confusion to me. I looked for truth in my father's behavior with animals and nature, with neighbors and the natives; there he was in his truest form, bringing love into action. The world was a scary place, a place where men were rampant with greed, women were confused with morals, and children were defenseless against an indoctrinated society. All of this mattered to me, but my own desire to be in the world would not stop prying at my insides, until I got there and found out for myself the truth of it all.

I got up from the dirt and dusted off my pant legs. The trees were blowing softly in the wind, as the night doves cooed from tree branches in the distance. I felt God reach down to me and put his hand on my back. I tried to breathe. I didn't believe my father about the world. I needed to find out for myself if it was a good place to be. I didn't believe that he hated being popular or smart.

I walked around to the front of the house. The sun had set. I waited till everyone fell asleep. Quietly, I tiptoed past my mother and father's bed. I grabbed my tennis shoes and a bag with a pair of jeans and a white shirt that had red hearts scattered all over it. I put the shoes outside the door next to the bag. I snuck back into bed. Before dawn I woke. I could hear my father snoring a few feet away. I tiptoed past him once more. Quietly, I opened and shut the front door, and put on my shoes, pants and shirt.

I ran as fast as I could, trying to beat the sun before it came over the horizon. My dad would be awake by then, so I had to make it off the property before he could get to me. I ran past the root cellar and into the open field of green grass and sage. The path was a straight line to the cliff, and I didn't slow down till I reached it. Bent down onto my knees, my breath heavy, I looked out over the cliffside. Brown and red clays rolled for half a mile to the east, hill over hill of jumbled, jagged rocks. To the south, gullies and arroyos dim in the early morning light. A barely seen path curved up and down until it reached the forest.

Just follow the path, my head said.

I would be at the Bassetts' in one hour or less if I ran the whole way. I could catch a ride with them to the Baptist church twenty miles into town. There I knew I would meet people and somehow my life would be changed. I stood up and started down the cliff. My feet flew under me; I slid down the hundred feet of red clay and brown dirt. If you move quickly enough you won't fall because your feet will never catch. I made it to some rocky points, and climbed foot to foot, hand to hand, and then the trail opened up with those tiny red pebbles dotting the path. I started to run, and my foot slipped on a pebble. I flew in the air—my body flipped completely over. I went over the side of a drop and landed ten feet below.

"Ow, ow, ow!"

I came up head first, holding onto my leg. I couldn't move it, it was heavy and felt like it was going to fall off. I pulled my right leg to my chest.

"Oh, God! Oh, God!" I cried out and then real tears came, fast and hard.

My leg was broken. I moaned, cried, and held my leg tight for a few minutes, my sounds echoing to the canyon walls far to the east.

The sun was up. It glared into my face, my eyes and my skin. I stopped crying, no one could hear me—what was the point? I needed to make a plan. I sat in the sun for what seemed a few hours, lying back on the dirt under me. I was dehydrated. My mind drifted to a tall glass of water, then a pitcher of lemonade with bright yellow lemons floating on top. My options were try to climb back up the eight-hundred feet of cliffside or go three miles on one foot to Mr. Bassett's. If I made it to Mr. Bassett's, he and Joy would take me to the hospital.

This was best, I thought, as I had never been to the hospital.

I imagined the hospital room with white sheets, white clean walls, and a pitcher of lemonade sitting beside the bed. I wanted to go there. I pulled myself up and scooted on my bottom all the way to a large rock. I pushed myself on my butt, holding up my leg with one arm and moving my body with the other arm and hand. I lay behind the rock in the shade.

Tired and hungry, for hours I couldn't move. The sun moved toward the west; it was getting late. I could not make it three miles to Mr. Bassett's, but I could not risk waiting for anyone to find me. At dark the mountain lions and bobcats would be prowling. I knew they could smell the injured, so I had to move. My fear gave me energy and clarity. My dad would be the best one to help me. He had helped Nye when he was run over; he had helped all of us heal from many wounds and infections. *The world was not good at taking care of broken people, maybe they wouldn't be good at taking care of a broken leg.* The moment it popped into my head, like the burning sun above, that John had died in a hospital, my dream of clean sheets and white walls was stopped right there, hitting a blank space of fear. I worked backwards, making it to the trailhead. I pushed my body on my butt all the way up the trail till I hit the rock formations. Now I had to climb. I turned my body over and lay on my belly, on my left side, dragging my right leg that was broken. I pulled myself a few inches a time, then pulled my leg up with my hands. I dragged myself, pulled, and turned my body every way possible to get over the rocks. I made it to the steep clay. Two-hundred feet left. I broke down and cried.

I wanted to leave my father so badly. I wanted to be with the rest of the world. There were people in the world and I wanted to be with them. I knew there were good people!

I put my hands over my face and cried out to my dad. "Daddy!" Daddy!"

I sat on my butt again. My leg ached and splintered with pain, but it was growing numb. I pushed my body backwards up the hill one inch at a time. I pushed, and pulled my leg, pushed and pulled. The hill got steeper and I had to reach out to small, brush-like plants to hold myself in position so I would not slide back down. I gripped the earth with my good foot and dug in with my palms, fingers into the dirt. I needed to pee. When the sun fell to the horizon, I made my last and final push over the cliffside.

I heard voices.

They were looking for me and yelling out, "Chlo, Chlo, where are you?"

I pulled myself over to a log, leaned my back against it, and pulled down my pants to pee. I struggled to get my pants back up and hoisted my body onto the log.

I yelled out as loud as I could for my Dad and Nye, who were calling out to me. I sat and waited as they came running. I saw my father nearing the cliff, his beard twitching, his eyes filled with worry. I was scared, but he approached and lifted me into his arms.

"Wrap your arms around me," he said.

"I broke my leg, Dad, it's broken," I cried. I could smell his skin near my face tucked into his white, long-sleeved cowboy shirt, his red bandana slipped around his neck like a necklace.

"I'm sorry, Dad, I'm sorry."

"What happened," Nye walked beside us.

"I was running and I fell," I said. "I don't know how, I just fell."

Dad carried me to the house, where I was swarmed by Mom, Rose, and Jacinth.

"She will be okay," my Dad spoke clearly.

He lifted me onto the bed, both my knees bent up to my chest.

"It hurts, it hurts," I cried out. He put his hands on my shoulders.

"Listen," he looked at me and his light brown eyes showed strength. "I have to set your leg," he said.

He worked his hands down my leg and felt around the bones.

"No, no, I don't want you to touch it," I demanded.

My arms and hands wrapped around him tightly.

"Don't move, just take a deep breath," he said.

"No, no!"

I took a breath. He placed one hand below and one above my broken leg and with one smooth motion he shifted the bones into place.

I held onto him, no words, but loud sobs. He held me there for a few minutes, and then laid me back onto the bed. He pulled my leg down to the bed.

"I am going to make it stay with a splint," he said.

I put my whole arm over my face. He braced it by wrapping two boards on each side. I felt the pressure of the boards and the tape cradling my leg, it gave some comfort, and I lied back and passed out.

"God heals all wounds." I heard my father say this as he left the room. I crawled on my hands and knees for weeks on end. Nye would put me on the bike and push me to the outhouse. It was his turn now; we knew well this walk of silence together. He would lift me off the bike and set me on the potty, wait outside, and then help me back onto the bike. The woods were calling out to me; it was fall and the leaves on the oak trees were turning yellow. I wanted to play and thought it would be genius if I got onto my bike. My plan involved leaning toward the left side of my body, away from the right foot, and pedaling with the left.

I stabilized myself onto the bike from the front porch. I pushed off the porch, immediately the bike tilted to the right. I instinctively put my foot down, and tumbled over.

"Ow, ow, ow!"

My foot hurt like hell. I came to sitting, and promised I would heal before trying anything again. It took about two and half months before I was walking.

Life was a gift, and the injury had given me new strength for my life. I could run, play with the baby goats, and ride my horse again. Carey came a few weekends to visit us, and talked about his adventures at school. He liked living with the Shear family; they had a son named Sky, whom Carey had become close with. He talked about all the friends he had made, how he played basketball, and shot three jump shots in row. He didn't have a girlfriend, but there were some pretty girls at the school. I still longed for the outside world. Carey made the world appear safe.

Though he was far behind in his reading, he was way ahead in his math. Everyone is born different; Carey was good with numbers, whereas John was good with words. Naturally John had picked up reading and was way ahead of his grade level, according to my mother. Carey found math to be easy. I wondered about the rest of us. I had never taken a test, so it wasn't clear what I was good at. I guessed reading, because I was reading a lot of books on my own: books on nature that my father allowed, the stories from *Little House on the Prairie,* and science books that I kept in my hideout. I didn't read the Bible, the one book my father thought was the best. I had heard him read it so much I didn't want to read it. I was still wearing half of my heart in adoration for my father and the other half in defiance.

Halloween, the Pagan Holiday

It had been six months since Carey had run away. We were living the new normal. Mom made her goat cheese, Dad cut wood, and Nye helped Dad with the horses more than usual—they became a team working side by side. I heard my father's loud voice less, it seemed. He played the guitar again. Rose and Jacinth strung green chilies on a line to let them dry, while sitting out behind the house on a pile of logs. It was October 31st, Halloween.

I knew very little of Halloween, as my father was completely against the idea of putting pure poisonous sugar into your body—that I was clear about. Fall was all about the harvest time, about prepping for winter and using the last bits of sunlight to best advantage. Along with harvest came piñon picking, one of our fruits on the land. Dad came around the corner to the pile of logs where we were stringing green chilies.

"I've invited some natives to come pick piñon on the property," he announced.

"Today?" Mom responded.

"Yes, today. Met some Navajo women last week when I was in town."

I was always excited for visitors, didn't matter who it was. Maybe they would bring with them some kids to play with. The women arrived in one large truck. They pulled into the drive and cut the engine.

"Kind day to you." my father greeted them. "The Lord has blessed us with a full crop this year."

The driver was a stout woman, with native clothes wrapped around her body in full length: deep reds and browns for the inside cloths and on the outside, leather wrapped tightly around her frame. Three other women stepped down from the truck and greeted my father. I ran out beside him and stared at them.

"This is Chloe," my father introduced me. Nye ran out after me and we waited for Dad to give us some instructions.

"Nye, help me gather some tarps for these women and we will help them gather piñons."

We walked from the house into the thick woods down below where the root cellar was, and there we laid out blue tarps under trees that had weighted branches full with piñons.

The women were quiet, walking gracefully in moccasins. The tribe leader was the only one who addressed my father, and he addressed her in return. "My son will climb the tree and shake on it to get most of fruit down," my father explained. "Then you can sort it and put it in buckets."

Up the tree Nye went, and down came the piñons. Piles and piles of the tiny brown nut lay upon blue tarps. We worked through the afternoon sunlight, the golden glow reaching down to us as we sifted the tiny brown nuts into white buckets. I worked right next to the tribe leader. I felt her heavy earthiness in her womanhood; she was a different kind of woman with a different kind of power. I liked her. After spending the afternoon together, she pulled a bag of orange-and-yellow striped candy from a satchel on her side.

"These are called corn candies." She showed me the bag, which my father caught a glimpse of from a few feet away.

"Oh, no ma'am, my children do not eat those." He walked toward her with a calm center in his stride.

"I'm sorry, Mr. Gallaway," the woman replied. "I didn't realize."

"Dad, a storm is coming in," Nye interrupted. The sky was dark when I looked up. My dad took notice of the sky and directed us to pull in all the tarps. We cleared the tree space and grabbed up buckets. The rain started and was a huge downpour within minutes. We hauled everything to the house. Dad invited the women to come inside. It was a torrential downpour. The *thump, thump, thump* sounded on our roof. We all gathered in the small living area. By nightfall, the rain had not let up and the roads were a washed-out muddy mess. The tribe leader looked nervous and explained she thought they should try to make a break for it and get on the road. My father stated he thought it was too rough out and that they should stay the night with us.

The rain kept coming. My mom made a pot of beans and a loaf of bread to accompany our cold hands into the night. All the vegetables were stored in the root cellar and we were unable to get to them. The Navajo women sat on the floor and ate in front of the potbellied, wood-burning stove. I listened to my father's cadence as he spoke to the women. I knew he wouldn't be letting go of his thoughts about that candy. All over the world, young children were dressing up in Halloween costumes, running around their neighborhoods to do a game called trick or treat. I had never played the game of trick or treat and did not fully understand its purpose. I listened to my dad's voice grow in the room.

"You know that Halloween is a pagan holiday," he spoke to the women looking at each of them now. "I don't particularly like the candy, but more than the candy is the whole 'if you don't give me the rotten sugar, I will pull a trick on you...' and this is what's wrong with the world," he continued. The tribe leader listened calmly. These women seemed to hear my father differently than some white women, and that strangely made me feel better. I still wanted the candy, though, and thought my dad was so extreme not to let me have any of it.

He went on venting his feelings about the world being full of ideas that were all about trick or treat. "I'll pull this trick and that trick if you don't give me my treat, a bunch of false promises and lying scoundrels running the world. Especially the government, men with little soul and even less heart." My father was getting wound up.

My mother gently patted him on the shoulder, "Why don't you play them a song, Mr. Gallaway," she politely inserted into the conversation. My father could not resist a song and out came the guitar. I was relieved that my mother had deflated the tension in the room, since the two younger native women were starting to look uncomfortable. The elder two must have had years of practice, listening to men go on and on about worldly things. No matter what, I wouldn't get to try that candy, leaving a longing in my mouth for sweetness, for truth about candy and the whole game of trick or treat.

Dark approached quickly and there was little room to spare in our cabin. My father took blankets and put them down on the floor for the women to sleep on. If anyone could handle sleeping on the floor, it was these women. The natives were the only families that lived similarly to us, right next to the earth, the dirt on their bare feet, the wind in their hair; they too got their medicine from nature. I knew this from stories my mother had told me. It helped me to understand how we lived in relation to others; there were no others like us, except the Native Tribes.

The rain continued and the roof started to leak. My father put out pots and pans under the small areas of the floor where the water started to drip from the ceiling. I went to bed. The kerosene lamp was turned off and somewhere in the dark, the rain slowed to a drizzle. I woke in the middle of the night to see the women in the moonlight all spread out across the living room floor, the sound of dripping water hitting the pots as each drop landed. My father sure had a lot against the world and at the same time he sure knew how to take care of people.

The Final Christmas

It was Christmas. The snow fell and covered over the land, and the root cellar was full of canned goods and fall's harvest. Carey did not come to visit. His visits were not easy with Dad not agreeing about his going to school. But they found a way to meet and be in each other's presence every now and then. Like a small channel of water making its way through a rock, it would eventually create a crevice in the rock and break through. Carey was determined to love my father, and eventually he would break though to my dad and continue on his path of going to school.

On Christmas Day, Dad went down to the mailbox and came back with a large box from Grandma Ogreta in Texas. She never forgot about us. The same fruitcake came every year inside a red, round tin. It smelled of all kinds of fruits, and the nuts crunched under my tongue. She sent a book, hats, and gloves. At the bottom of the box was a red bag wrapped tight, and inside there were ten perfect red and white candy canes.

My dad didn't believe in the Christmas tree or having candy of any kind. You were only supposed to cut down trees if you needed the wood for firewood or building. We were surrounded by Christmas trees but never did we put ornaments on them; they were already decorated with heavy branches of white snow and orange-chested robins. Mom snuck the candy canes away before he could see them. My mother had succumbed to a lot but deep inside of her she was still a rebel, always taking a risk to tell me something of the world or save us a treat from her mother. She gave us each one when he was not looking. I took mine, grabbed my sled with the wood frame and red trim, and headed out to the open field down from the house. Once out of sight,

I turned the corner where Dad could no longer see me. I loved these moments alone; it was pure joy to be alone in the woods.

I hauled the sled to the top of the field that was slanted and made a hill that ran for hundreds of yards out. The snow was up to my knees. It was late morning. The sun sparkled off the snow, a brilliant white. I was warm, with new gloves, a red hat, and my brown jacket. I stepped onto the edge of the field where the snow was packed hard. I didn't sink down. I jumped up and down to see that the snow was solid and did not give. I put down the sled, straddled a leg on each side, opened up my candy cane, and stuck it into my mouth. Peppermint, crisp air, and dazzling snow engulfed me. I laid down, the candy cane still in my mouth. I pointed the sled toward the bottom of the hill and pushed off, with the wind in my face, the candy cane cooling my mouth the whole two hundred yards. I was free.

I understood by now that my father lived in the woods to be free. He only seemed free about half of the time. The other half he was dealing with inner demons. There was a burning fire inside that needed cooling. He read the Bible, but that didn't seem to cool him too much; he had a point to prove after reading the Bible. At Christmas every year he would tell us again the story of Jesus, the savior who came to give us salvation. He didn't read the Bible for this; he had the story memorized; he recounted the Wise Men following the morning star to find the baby who was born in a manger. My father had walked with the morning star many a time in his life. The story of Jesus became mixed with his stories and he talked about the past and how Jesus had guided him to safety so many times. I felt strangely connected to this baby Jesus; I was almost born in a manger myself. I hoped that Jesus would help my father with his other half and set him free.

The Connection of
a Mother's Love

We waited outside the goat pen of the rectangular-shaped barn and fencing made of wire and post. It was winter, and the cold and dark came to us early at 5:30 p.m. *Why can't she have her babies in the daylight hours,* my mind questioned as I heard the mama goat moan and grunt in a rhythmic sound as the sun went down and the warmth of the earth was gone. Trees marked the path from the barn to the house. A lantern hung in the window; a yellow dim light shone through. I could feel the heat of the lantern, wishing it were burning into my cold fingers growing numb as I had forgotten my gloves. "The baby is coming, the baby is coming," I heard Nye yell from the corner of the bales of hay where he was down in the straw keeping Whitie company. I stayed back watching. I knew what birth was, the blood and liquid rushed from the body, the world, the earth broken down to one moment, one second, the lungs pink inside fighting for first breath.

"Come on Whitie, come on, girl," Nye said in a reassuring voice. The final moan rang the barn. My fingers were feeling frostbite; I shoved them in my mouth and ran straight to the bales of hay. The baby's head was pushing from the goat's rear, the sac a clear liquid of armor. Blue-purple legs tucked tight, a round ball broke through and onto the golden floor of straw.

"Nye, what do we do?" I shouted pulling my hands from my mouth.

"Nothing, we just wait." He sat calmly to the left of Whitie. *Mama goat, mama goat,* my heart reached out to her as blood rushed from her body, her belly breathing up and down. She gathered strength and twisted her head around to see the still wet, half-broken-open sac that held the baby. She pulled her body, dragging her front legs slowly round and round until she had reached the baby with her head. She licked her tongue up and down the baby's face, clearing away the sac. Her pink tongue licked into the night air, fierce, constant licking, her body worn thin, blood still spilling onto the straw floor. The baby goat whimpered and cried; the shield of armor broke off. *Ma ma ma* . . . echoes of new life sounded the barn. I sat next to Nye in the bales of hay, soft and cushioned behind our backs. The mother knew what to do, there was nothing to fix, nothing had been broken. The blood of life was upon us.

Was my birth much the same? Was my mother whole but seemed broken? Did she bleed and bleed into the night to bring me into this world? Was I covered with a sac of armor that kept me tight in a ball? I awaited my first breath like all the rest coming into the world. My birth was in the spring in the thaw of the land, just before the rushing waters would come to cleanse the earth. I was born late into the night, just after midnight, or so my father said with no clocks to tell the time—he had gone outside the stone-walled house to visit with the moon to gauge the time. I was his first daughter, after three sons, and was he in awe of my birth, not knowing how to hold a girl, not knowing how grace would get him through. He stayed outside with the moon for over thirty minutes. My mother held me naked, wrapped against her chest, a white cotton cloth covering the both of us. The kerosene lamp flickered light bouncing off the top of my delicate round head.

Those were our first hours together, Mother. The seamless wonder of creation, the thread of life that cannot be broken. The heart, the blood, the line between mother and daughter was seared into the tiny chest of an infant, into the bosom of a grown woman.

The Tree Can No Longer Bend in the Wind

It was early morning in January 1987. I was two months shy of turning twelve. I came in from the barn with the milk bucket in my hand. I heard yelling that rang through the cabin walls. I stepped up to the outside window. My dad's arms were flying about like the long tentacles of an octopus.

"God wants you to get this," he yelled at my mother, who stood across from him with a blank stare in her eyes, looking past him and past her own life.

I crouched down, holding my knees into my chest with my head tucked tight against them. I waited. My mother did not speak. Dad went on, his voice revved higher than a truck engine. I stood up to look again; no one else was in the room. His voice followed him as he danced in anger around my mother. I knelt back down in the snow wanting to pray but resenting God: how could God be in my father, if he acted like this? I heard a loud noise, a cracking of glass hitting the wall. I jumped to my feet peering into the window. I saw my mother on her knees on the floor trying to clean up glass. My dad stepped around her, his body shaking. He reached for his cowboy hat and swirled around. I could see his face was red, full with confusion; his eyes were on fire. I ducked down so he wouldn't see me in the window.

The front door slammed. He went toward the other side of the house, and called out to Nye and Jacinth. "Let's go, boys, we need to get wood."

I stood up and looked through the window. Mom was kneeling on the floor with her hair tossed over her face.

"Mama, get up, Mama!" I said through my tears.

I heard the truck pull away from the drive. I rushed into the house, knelt down next to my mother, and picked her up using both my hands. Tears streamed down her cheeks and over her lips. I lifted her to her feet. Rose came from the back room where she had been hiding under the bed.

"Let's go," I said, marching toward the back room to grab a bag.

Rose followed me and helped me load our clothes into the bag.

Mom now stood in the living room frozen, waiting for someone to force her out of her paralysis. She knelt back down to clean up the rest of the glass. I marched back to the living room. I was burning up with devout rage from my feet to my head. My father had been the one who taught me to stand up for what was right. He'd role-modeled for me that it didn't matter who you had to stand against when enough was enough.

"No," I said as I reached down and grabbed her arm. I lifted her to her feet. "Leave it, we are going."

She pulled her hair back from her wet face; her eyes were filled with stillness. She followed Rose and me to the door. We walked out past the driveway and toward the field. The snow was up to my knees. I hauled the cloth bag over my shoulder. Mom helped Rose get through the snow. We crossed the field, a wide-open space reaching out to the woods. I saw Juniper standing fifty yards in the distance. His white fur glistened, his head cocked to the side looking at us. He neighed three times.

"Bye, buddy," I said and kept looking ahead.

We scaled the cliffside, the deep snow bracing us, and we went down. The same trail where I had broken my leg that summer. The deep snow was now a safety net to hold our legs in place as we made our way from steep hillside to rock formations. We walked the forest in pure silence, the piñon branches hanging heavy with white limbs, the cold air brushing our faces. We made it to Mr. Bassett's. Joy got us water, and we sat for a few minutes. Her eyes were blue, and soft around the eyelids. She looked at us with worry.

"We just need to get to the bus station," I said.

She got a washcloth with warm water and wiped my mother's face. Mom held back her tears. Joy didn't ask what happened. She was a woman with thirteen kids, who had lived on the farm her whole life—she didn't need to ask what happened.

William Bassett was the calmest man I'd been around. I never saw him pick a fight and I was certain he was loving toward Joy, but somehow Joy still knew how hard life could be, how hard marriage could be.

Mr. Bassett drove us to the bus station in Cuba. The bus pulled around to the front of the station, and the engine idled. We stood outside the truck. Mr. Bassett wore his black cowboy hat, and the same overalls I'd always seen him in. He was a farmer, a tender of the land, reminding me of a shepherd from the Bible; he was a humble man. How he held the secrets of every person so close without judgment, I would never know. He would likely later help my father, after helping us, knowing all along each step was the right thing to do. He reached in his pocket and pulled out some waded up dollar bills. He handed them to my mother.

"Take this and go," he said.

The doors opened to the Greyhound bus, the driver looked down at us. He was an older gentleman with lines in his face, dark eyes, and black hair. We climbed on. Rose sat at the window, Mom on the aisle, and I in the middle. The doors closed and we drove away.

My mother had given up everything she knew, a life where she was admired for her beauty, her dancing, and her spirit. In 1968 when she met my father on the streets of San Francisco, he was the most beautiful man she had ever seen. He walked the crowd on Haight-Ashbury Street carrying his guitar. People reached out to touch him, tugging at his hand as he passed, calling out his name. "Jerry, Jerry, we want Jerry!"

My mom had gone to San Francisco to change her life with no idea how it would change. When my father climbed up on stage and slung his guitar over his shoulder, he sang, and the crowd went wild yelling out for him. It was in this place my mother had lost herself to the idea of my father. She couldn't see her future, nor could he, two souls rising toward the heavens meshed together as one pure force, out of which they would choose a different life and together have six children.

Rose looked out the window at the snow-covered hills as the bus rolled on. My mother and I both sat with her, our arms crossed on our laps. The heater warmed the bus from the floorboards and heat came into my feet; my body loosened from the weighted fear and the cold of life that had penetrated my heart.

My father could not escape his demons; they lived in him from generations past, all his ancestry running through his blood. He tried hard to escape his own fears and go toward the love he knew as a baby, but his fear caught up to him.

My mother could not escape my father. She followed him into the wilderness, ready for adventure. She gave me the best life she knew how, birthed six children on dirt floors, wood floors, sometimes alone, with no other woman, just my father, the man she had entrusted her life to. My mother told me how they had been friends once, walking hand and hand in the streets of San Francisco, dreamers with all of life ahead of them. The dark night of my parents' relationship had caught up to them.

Rose fell asleep next to me on the bus, her head leaning into my shoulder, and a heavy, dense weight of relief pushed into me. I reached my hand out and put my arm underneath Mom's. We sat arm in arm.

"I am never going back and you shouldn't either," I said.

We had to leave Nye and Jacinth behind. I could hardly bear the thought, and pushed it away. I laid my head back on the seat, and allowed myself to sleep.

I dreamed a dream, Dad. I saw your young boy face, round cheeks, pouted lips, brown eyes; you were the love you always wanted to be. We were a family. The cabin stood in the woods and we were all there. The smoke rose from the chimney; the horses and goats were in the front yard. We were whole. No one had died. No one had run away. Your darkness was gone, a light streamed from your head. All you had wished for your children was true. We ran in circles around the front porch, laughter was in the air as you played your guitar in the background. Mom was wearing a white dress and she danced in circles around you. I dreamed a dream, Dad, and it was you.

Our Ears Become Blocked When the Pain Is Too Deep

We stayed a week in New Mexico with Jane again, waiting for my grandmother to get us a flight to Houston. During the week we stayed in Albuquerque, I got an ear infection. By the time I got off the plane in Houston, my ear was about to burst with severe pain and pus oozing out. I embraced my grandmother, my spirit somewhere outside of my body. She hugged me and pulled back to look at my face.

"What's going on here?" she questioned my mother.

"Well, see it for yourself, she has an infection," my mother responded. My grandmother pulled me to the side and looked over my ear. "Let's go," she said and rushed us to the car. The frozen walls inside my chest started to thaw as I climbed inside the gray Honda Civic. It was evening and we drove straight to my grandmother's house. I was passed out in the backseat, my body limp from pain. I climbed the steps from the garage to the living area and lay down on the couch. I slept through the pain from sheer exhaustion. I awoke to hear my mother and grandmother in an argument.

"I'm taking her to the emergency room," my grandmother demanded.

"Our children don't see doctors," my mother spoke firmly.

"Well, I don't care what you've done in the past, this child is going to lose her hearing!" My grandmother's voice radiated throughout the large two-story house. She marched away, not giving my mother a chance to respond. I slept in the downstairs room with the radio playing all night to drown out my weeping into the late hours. Rose and my mom slept upstairs. By morning my ear was oozing green pus onto the pillow, even when as I was lying on my back. I cried out to God to make it go away, resisting the guilt that swelled in my back and inside my lungs. Maybe I got sick for defying my father. I pushed back the feelings. *He deserved it,* I thought. *I don't care if I do lose my hearing, I'm not going back to him.* My anger raged inside my small body, now overcome with warrior force. My grandmother came down the stairs, my mother in tow behind her; they were arguing again. My mother was trying to defend her beliefs, "All of my children's illnesses have been healed by God," she stated matter-of-factly.

"Oh really?" my grandmother turned to face her. "What about John? Did God save him?" she nearly shouted it out.

My mother was speechless. My grandmother grabbed me by the hand and pulled me out to the garage, the car doors slammed shut, and we drove away.

"It hurts, Grandma, it hurts, please help me," I pleaded. My grandmother never showed much emotion but in that moment I saw that she would do anything to save me. She put her hand on my knee. "You will be okay, you will be okay, I promise." She squeezed my leg hard.

The doctor's office had stale air and clean walls; it was cold and dimly lit with no life, no color. It was nothing like I'd dreamed it would be. I didn't care. I was dying of pain. I lay down on the medical table, my grandmother putting her hand on my shoulder as she waited for the doctor to enter. A man in a white lab coat entered the room. "What brings you in today?" he asked.

"My granddaughter has a severe ear infection." She prompted the doctor to examine me, already lying on the table.

He sat me up on the table and looked at my ear.

"This is severe. Why didn't you bring her in earlier?" he asked. "She could lose her hearing." The doctor was stern in his voice, but kept his eyes and hands on me.

"I can't explain it," my grandmother stated. "She hasn't been in my care till yesterday."

The doctor could not put his otoscope in my ear, couldn't fit a Q-tip in my ear. "We need to give her an antibiotic shot," he said.

"Whatever you can do," my grandmother responded.

My body shook from the coldness in the room, the stale walls now thin sheets of nothingness. My body was outside itself beyond where I had been with my broken leg, the pressure an explosive bomb inside my ear that was bursting my eardrum apart, and pushing my voice down inside my throat to where I could not speak. I lay on my right side with my pants pulled down so he could give me a shot in the glutes. I tried not to look at the needle; I had never taken a pill, or seen a needle in my life. I remembered my father setting my leg in place and took a deep breath before the needle went into my butt, sending a sharp stinging sensation through me. My ear was still throbbing in pain so it made no sense; why would I get the shot at all? He brought over a glass of water and gave me three pills he called pain pills. I took the pills and swallowed. I limped out of the doctor's office, my body and mind wrecked.

We drove the city streets, all the cars passing in the distance, my body floating away from itself, away from the pain. My ear had some relief from the bursting feeling, but the pressure was still there, pounding, pounding in my ear, my heartbeat sounding through my chest. When we arrived home, my mother was upstairs and she and my grandmother did not speak. I lay on my grandmother's couch for a week taking pain pills, eating very little, and forgetting who I was. One day the pain subsided and fluid in my ear broke loose like Elmer's glue slowly tearing off a wet page of paper; it seeped onto the pillow. Two weeks passed and the glue had dried up and started to crack apart from my ear. I could finally hear in my left ear. I woke every morning to a hot breakfast and Grandma waiting for me at the table to start my lessons. "You are with me now," she would say, "so let's get some schooling in." My grandmother had been a schoolteacher, a radiant force of strength and poise in her world. She was athletic and pretty, wore high heels with dresses and a classy two-piece suit on Saturdays. She was desperate to educate her grandkids every chance she got. When we lived on the mountain, she brought books every time she made a visit. Her visits were not frequent. To view my mother in that life so removed from anything she had been was too much, but she never spoke of it.

In the evenings we ate together, read books, and watched TV. I loved the TV shows, especially *Three's Company*. It was so funny and transported me from my current world, a world in which

I was separated from my brothers and a father that I loved, but could never return to in my mind. The sound of comedy had replaced nature; the healing of laughter from the TV and the kindness of my grandmother's cooking was enough to get me through. My heart was walled off like a thick piece of ice frozen over a lake in winter, but I could hear though both ears and life was full of possibilities. My mother and grandmother were dancing around each other much like my brothers had danced around my father, slow and steady steps finding a tiny open door to the heart, a space to connect.

My Mother, the Ballet Dancer

She is the twinkle in her daddy's eye, the soul in her mother's feet. The heavy maroon curtains are drawn to the side, bright lights beam the stage, the music of Tchaikovsky plays. My mother had heard the music over and over, it resounds in her body. She'd practiced the whole year now to embrace the stage and her audience.

She stands on the tips of her long, pink slippers and toes her way to the center of the floor, four young girls dancing around her. She dances across the floor, floating like a swan, her small frame suspended in the air, a delicate white dress waving along her body. My grandmother sits in the front row of the audience. She makes eye contact with my mom every time she makes a spin, circles and circles around, toes moving, arms out, forward and backwards, legs out and back.

From the moment my legs could carry me I wobbled barefoot on the dirt, balancing my way to a sturdy self. My core was strong, my vision clear with all of nature around me. I had grown to love animals as part of my family, as they lived with us on our everyday journey—goats, horses, chickens, and one great Donkey. By the time I'd turned five, I'd become aware of the great power of being on horseback. The smell of horse rose up to me as I put one foot into the stirrup and pulled myself up holding onto the horn of the saddle. I threw my right leg over and landed with each foot grooved into the stirrups. When I rode a horse I was free, my hands out to the sides catching slices of the wind as we moved. I felt weightless and guided by the sun overhead.

My mother had lived a completely different life. By age five she had started her first ballet class. It was my grandmother's joy to stand in the doorway of the stage and watch my mother get ready for rehearsal. My mother spoke of these moments fondly as she recounted the story of her most performed ballet, *Swan Lake*. She wore all white—white leggings, a white tutu, and a white bodice. Her auburn hair was so thick it had to be tied back with several white bows, pulling it away from her face, leaving only her blue eyes and white skin, with tiny freckles around her nose. She waited nervously for the maroon curtains to go up before she would move onto the stage. The stage was set with hardwood floors picking up every sound of tiny footsteps tap, tap, tapping across it with pink toe shoes. My mother took one look back at the stage door where my grandmother stood. She too wore a delicate white dress that flowed on her athletic, curvaceous body. *I will always remember this moment, Mama,* my mother thought to herself. No deep woods could bury these memories. Somewhere in there, my mother was herself, alive and free.

To Be a Girl

I was my mother's daughter but knew nothing of this life. At age five, I was straddling a horse and watching every move that my brothers and father made. To make it in the wild was to be wild. I never longed for girly things: dolls, pretty hair ribbons, or white dresses, until now, where there was a tugging at my heart, a long and distant tugging from beneath the wings of my birth where a little girl lived inside. I longed for my mother to be her feminine self as much as I longed for myself to embrace being a girl.

The Lost Sheep

My father had been calling for the past two months, speaking to my mother for hours, singing to her over the phone at times. He always asked for me and I always refused him. "No, I'm not talking to him." I'd shove off my mother's request when she beckoned me to the phone. My mother approached me on the couch one morning after breakfast and explained she had to go back.

"What, why?" I demanded a response.

She shook her head "There are things going on, I need to go back." And just like that, she was on a flight out of Houston. I held tight to my original plan of never going back, and slowly let my grip on my mother's life slip through my fingers. I was twelve now, big enough to make decisions, I thought.

It was late March and the humid Houston air was always heavy coming in the windows. I was adjusting to a new environment. My grandmother's green rotary phone hung on the wall outside the living area. It didn't ring often. My grandmother sat Rose and me down to discuss our future one afternoon. The afternoon sunlight stretched across the carpeted floor, like sparkles of gold meeting our feet.

"I can't keep you girls against your parents' will," she said. I looked long and hard into her face. My grandmother continued to explain her position on things, no tears, just the straight, hard facts of life.

"I just can't keep you, and we can try to find a way legally to work with your parents to allow you to stay longer, but for now you have to go back." The long aching of time pressed against my insides. *This was BULLSHIT,* I thought silently. The green phone rang and interrupted my being able to respond out loud to my grandmother.

She answered the phone. "Yes, this is Ogreta. Yes, the girls are here." She answered what seemed a slew of questions, her head bent down almost in submission. I couldn't see her face, but something was wrong. She hung up. She came back to the couch and sat next to Rose and me.

"That was the New Mexico Social Services Department. They have gone in and taken Nye and Jacinth." She held back her emotion. Whoa, how... I rubbed my hands on my forehead trying to grasp the moment. "That was a social worker on the phone, he has your brothers in custody."

I burst into tears.

"What does it mean, Grandma?" I whimpered through my cracked voice.

"It means that you are not going home."

"They have taken Carey too," she said. "All of the boys are together, and when you fly back they will meet you at the airport with the social worker. You will be going into foster care."

"But Carey was staying with a friend," I confirmed to her.

"I don't know how it all happened. You will find out more when you arrive in New Mexico," she said.

There was a moment of stillness wrapped in time: the golden flecks of light on the floor were gone; the stance I had taken against my father was not turning out as I had planned. I never thought about foster care, I never thought about how we might live away from my father, other than my mother and grandmother taking care of us. My grandmother explained what foster care was. She said she would call the New Mexico Social Services and find out as much as she could, but they advised her to put us on a plane in the morning. My grandmother had already purchased a plane ticket for Rose and me to fly back. I thought my biggest challenge was going to be flying on a plane by myself for the first time. I don't remember the flight back; it was a side note in comparison to the rest of my future. We landed in Albuquerque. Rose and I walked side by side until we could see my brothers standing at the gate. They waved us down with excitement. From that moment on, everything became a blur; there was no clarity from the woods, from a childhood I once knew; the world was spinning and I was spinning with it. My brothers had already been placed in a foster home with a teacher from the local high school, in Española, New Mexico. We grew up closer to border of Colorado, but were still in Rio Arriba County, which was New Mexico, so when my brothers got transported to the nearest Social Services department, it was Española, New Mexico.

A New Land, A New People

Española—the valley that never sleeps, the beauty that creeps from beneath the shadowed forest, the river that runs along the edge, the pathway to the tiny houses that sit on ridges and rocks and farmlands down below. Española was founded in 1880 as a railroad village and incorporated as a city forty-five years later. This was a valley founded by the Spanish and brought to life by the Spanish culture mixed in with the Native American culture. Mariachi music, New Mexican food, and pueblo pottery are all part of daily life in this seemingly serene valley, stretched alongside the Rio Grande River. Now the Spanish youth of the culture are taking over, the crowds of young folks roamed the streets, the night lights of the small northern town burned at all hours. From a distance, you could see low riders, cars with hydraulics lifting them up and down, cars touching the ground, and trucks that tower over the low riders, oversized wheels, and large cabs, with dark tinted windows. We see no face, know no name of who rides behind these wheels, touring the town late into the night. You can see through the back window of a low rider a man with an arm around his woman, she sitting right in the middle of the seat, she sitting with pride riding beside her man. You see *vatos*, and brothers fighting on the street, and bloodshot eyes from the wounded, drinking, battling, soldier who knows no other way to live; generation after generation he has been here in this little valley, the drugs and the family ties too strong to cut. This is the night, this is the darkness that looms.

But every town has its hopes and has its people that when seen face to face have a story. If you looked closely in the light, you would see brothers shaking hands, mothers and daughters holding hands while crossing streets, gentlemen opening doors, cowboys with hats being tilted down to greet young women. You would see grandmothers with gray hair proudly holding their grandbabies, mothers holding onto their young sixteen-year-old daughters because they would not be kicked out when they came home with child. You would see Christians and Catholics, and men with beards of all shades, all gathered in one circle of brotherhood. You would hear the elders speak in Spanish, "Come, *jita*, come and sit with me awhile." You would feel the backs of men breaking, the sweat running down their faces, their love of family pouring through their skin. You would see it all if you look closely. Española was a village with all the battles of inner city Chicago, and all the love shining from the top of the Empire State Building. The people had dreams, and morals, and working gloves that proved them to be men and women on the front lines of life, and yes, they drove low riders and monster trucks.

Life as the Outsider

When I say my world was spinning, it's the best description I can give. Things moved so quickly, with so many decisions and choices being made on my behalf, but I didn't feel a part of a single choice. My parents were not there, the woods were not there, the animals and all of life that had once given me a sense of direction were not there. I was in a strange town full of strange people and being placed in a foster home with some woman I didn't know. Throughout all of my story I remember even the faintest of moments: the sunset on every winter's eve, the warmth of a summer breeze, the feeling of horse fur between my fingers, the night sky a vivid friend in my mind's eye, but digging for the memories around this time . . . it's much like a black hole.

I don't remember going to my new foster home. I have little memory of being there. The woman had a daughter and a husband. Rose and I lived with this woman, her daughter and her husband for two months. One day I called Carey, crying.

"Carey, I hate it here," I sobbed. "She is mean to us. You have to help us get out of here." The communication between a brother and a sister was now being communicated on new lines created by the world, a phone.

Our pack was broken when John died, though there was still some formation there, tiny splinters on the ground were the markings of our pack split apart. I don't remember the call, but know it was what prompted Carey to go into the social worker's office and request that they find a place for all five of us. I would later learn from Carey that he had prompted the Social Services to go in and get my brothers, Nye and Jacinth. He had been battling his own inner demons since John had died. He was in school and finding a new path, but worried the rest of us would suffer the same fate as John. He was seventeen years old and God was asking him to make the decisions of a man. He loved my father deeply, but held strong to his instincts that we all had to live a new life. He had moved around from home to home living with different friends while trying to adapt to school, this being a struggle for him and bringing even more concern on how we would all make it. He went into his school counselor Louie Martinez's office one afternoon and confided in him his concerns. Louie was a friend of my brother's and together they agreed that a call should be made to have someone go in to get the rest of us. Carey had not been home and didn't know that I had left with my mom and sister.

Louie had known about my father and our lives for many years. He was torn with concern on what to do. He made the call to the Social Services. They had responded, saying that they could go out next week. Carey centered himself the way he did when he was in the woods, never lost, always calm, sensing his direction. "Call them back and let me talk to them," he requested. He pleaded his case to the woman on the phone that they needed to go today. They agreed and it was done.

Now here he was in front of our social worker, who was explaining to him that it was very unlikely that anyone would take five children.

"It just doesn't happen," the social worker explained.

Carey grounded himself again, this time deeper in the heart. "It may not have been done before," he stated to the social worker, "but if you can't help us I'll find a way to raise them myself."

The following week, Larry Wood, our social worker, took out an ad in the newspaper, with a picture of the five of us. "Five children looking for a good foster home," the post ran.

Uncertainty

A week had passed since our social worker placed the ad in the newspaper about five children looking for a home. I felt doubtful that anyone would respond, and if they did, would they be a decent person? The world was not turning out as I'd dreamed it to be. *Where were all the good people?* It was a Wednesday, late afternoon, when Larry Wood arrived with the news: we were being moved to a new home. I was twelve years old and Rose was nine.

I sat in the back of the white social worker car as it drove down a two-lane paved road. Outside on the door panel it read "State of New Mexico Social Services." I held a black and purple backpack tight between my feet on the floor. We rolled down a long stretch of poorly paved blacktop, the desolate hillside a blur in passing. Brown hills of dirt with small shrubs peeked up here and there, and the sky was a dim gray, casting an ominous light over the barren hills. I wished for rain. It was April but there were no signs of spring.

"Jesus, where is he taking us?" I thought.

My social worker was a middle-aged man, a bit on the stocky side with his hair pulled back in a ponytail. His brown eyes were deep set, and when he spoke, he said very little. He had come out the day before to visit my sister and me at our current foster home. He sat on the large green chair in the corner of the small double-wide trailer's living area. I watched his face closely looking for what might be an honest man.

"I found a permanent placement for you," he said.

"I didn't know this wasn't permanent," I rolled my eyes.

I caught a glimpse of the chubby, round-faced Hispanic woman I had been living with for the past two months; she was standing in the kitchen, and seemed indifferent to the words my social worker spoke. Relief passed over my shoulders at the thought of leaving. Remnants of her scolding me the day before while taking away my pack of gum still lingered in my mind. I had only one bag to pack, and did it quickly. Stepping slowly off the rotting wooden porch and the five measurable footsteps it took to get to the social worker's car could not have come fast enough.

My little sister sat next to me in the car, her blond curls falling loosely over her shoulders. She sat back all the way in the seat, her feet dangling off the edge, her eyes tilted down and focused on her hands as she fidgeted with the zipper on her baggy sweatshirt.

"You think our new place will be good, Chlo?" She looked up at me.

I questioned the God I once believed in, and was sure the human race was out for itself, but knew I had to lie to her.

"Things will be alright," I said, and gave her a reassuring look.

The car made a sudden jolt as we flew over a hillside, the road curving to a sharp left and back to right again. Rose flew forward; my arm automatically reached out to brace her. The road narrowed to one lane as we drove along a riverbank, the water rushing past us. Towering, broad-leafed cottonwood trees lined the banks of the river; a ray of sunlight etched its way through the green leaves that were free and twisting in the wind. Finally some green, a field of green grass with horses grazing, sparked hope in my bones.

We veered left onto a dirt road and drove toward a hillside covered by petroglyphs. The unpaved road was filled with ruts from a recent rain. Rose's head bobbled up and down; the car engine revved as we climbed a steep hill into a narrow driveway. At the top of the hill sat a two-story, brown stucco home, with a wooden wraparound deck.

As our social worker exited the car, a huge, black, furry dog greeted him wagging his tail. I clinched my knees tight together, and held my hands in a fist on my lap.

"Wait." I grabbed Rose by her hoodie as she tried to exit the car.

When the front door to the house opened, a woman with

short, dark gray hair stood in the doorway, the lines in her face telling of her age. She wore a simple orange blouse and light brown pants, no makeup, and no jewelry. Her thick glasses, set just above her nose, revealed ocean-blue eyes.

The social worker motioned for us to come.

"Let's go," I said, grabbing my backpack.

"Come in, come in," the woman greeted us.

We followed as she led us up a narrow stairway into a living area. Windows let in bright light all around the room, and you could see the fields of grass stretching across the land with tall trees blowing in the wind. The river we'd passed was just the other side of those trees. If I had a word in that moment, it would have been freedom. You could feel the freedom in the air. I hadn't felt free since we got the call at Grandma's; there was a knot in my chest that had been lodged there for months. My eyes started to tear up, but I shut them down quickly and focused back on the room. A light blue couch sat against the back wall, and a gray and white cat lay across the back, lazily soaking up the afternoon air. This was a place to rest.

The woman led us into the next room, a dining area with a chocolate-wooden table surrounded by chairs enough for eight people. A pitcher of lemonade was at the center of the table, and a plate of fresh baked cookies beside it. Yellow lemon slices floated around the pitcher. I was so thirsty.

The woman spoke. "Girls, I am Ida, and this is my home, and I want it to feel like your home as well."

My sister and I stared at the both of them.

Ida stood up from the table. "Let me show you your room," she said. She ushered us down the stairs. The floor turned from a mustard-colored carpet to a smooth, red brick floor. We entered a den-like room with one floor-to-ceiling window in the front. A piano was against the back wall, and bookshelves filled with books stood on each side of the piano.

"This will be your room," she said as she turned and opened a door. I reluctantly stepped forward, the light dim, and the air damp as I moved past the doorway.

I was comforted by the floor-to-ceiling wallpaper that depicted a blue sky with clouds floating about. I sat down on the bed rubbing my hands against the white, hand-stitched bedspread. It felt old but looked new.

"My grandmother made that quilt," Ida said.

Taken aback by her comment, I quickly moved my hands to my lap.

"That's a unicorn," my sister whispered in my ear. At the center of the bed was a gigantic stuffed unicorn with a yellow horn.

"I'll let you get situated," Ida said. She and the social worker exited the room to the den area. I listened with my ear pressed against the door.

"They are good kids," he remarked.

"Have there been any issues with drug use?" Ida asked.

"There are no known drug issues or behavioral issues."

"Okay," Ida responded.

"But, remember they have been living out in the mountains since birth, and they have had no formal schooling."

"I can work with that," Ida said.

"You will need to bring them down to the courthouse on Monday, so we can work on getting them birth certificates," he said, then his voice trailed off for a minute. "We have been working to get them birth certificates for the past month, and had several hang-ups." A few moments later they pushed through the door, and trying to mask my eavesdropping, I jumped on the bed with my sister who had been playing with the unicorn.

The social worker approached us. The lines in his forehead clinched just above his brow as he stood directly in front of me, a man with thoughts swirling in his head.

Great, what's he going to say now, I thought.

"Girls, Ida is going to take good care of you, and she has agreed to take your three brothers as well."

My sister leaped from the bed. "The boys are going to live with us!"

Since our separation, there had been no mention of the boys living with us. I didn't know that our social worker had placed the ad for all five of us. My brothers were the glue to my identity, my sense of strength. My idea of family had been shattered like a wall of glass, tiny pieces scattered about my world, too many to put back together.

I held my position on the bed, and dug my feet into the carpet. My instincts told me that Ida was one of the good ones, but my fear plunged into my core like a pungent knife, swiping away the tears that swelled in my eyes.

"When will the boys be coming?" I asked.

"I am picking them up tomorrow at noon," he said, and made his exit to the front door. I heard the door shut, then silence filled the room. Rose and I stood there side by side.

"How about we have some of those cookies I made?" Ida asked. She led us up the stairs. I reluctantly grabbed a cookie, my sister already on her second one.

"So, what is it you do?" I asked Ida.

"I am a kindergarten teacher." Her eyes lit up at this.

"Do you have children?"

"Four, but three of them are grown, and my last one is about to graduate high school."

"And your husband?" I pried further.

"No husband, he left years ago."

Silence fell around the table, the afternoon sky grew dark, and a faded purple land loomed outside the window. "I've got to make a few phone calls. Go ahead and look around, make yourselves at home." Ida said, as she excused herself from the table and went into her bedroom down the hall.

We sat, our butts frozen to our chairs; we didn't know how to make ourselves at home. Like children afraid of their own shadows we tiptoed around the house. The first bedroom had light-yellow walls, a bed, and a desk with a computer in the corner. Two more rooms with fluffy comforters, white walls with colorful paintings, and closets. *Who could have enough clothes they would need a closet for them*, my mind bugged at me. A bathroom at the end of the hall had a full bathtub, shower, and a white toilet. No more walking to the outhouse in a foot of snow, in the dark, in the mud, the rain. By night, our young bodies were worn thin, our minds overwrought with stimulation. We were ready for bed by eight.

"I made something very simple for dinner," Ida called us into the kitchen.

"Hot dogs," my sister and I both said.

We had only had hot dogs one other time in our lives; we jumped at the chance to eat them again. They were grilled to perfection, golden brown, with juices flowing from the sides. Adding a white flour bun with yellow mustard brought a smile to my sister's face. When Rose finished her fifth hot dog, Ida spoke.

"You may want to slow down on those…you could get an upset tummy."

"Okay," Rose said sheepishly.

My sister and I were both slumped over the table and rubbing our eyes by nine. Ida suggested we go to bed.

"Thank you for the hot dogs," we spoke simultaneously.

"I hope you can sleep. If you need anything, you can wake me at any time. I will see you both in the morning," she replied.

Without knowing where the light fixture was, we felt our way down the long dark hallway. I felt more fear not knowing my way around inside a house, than being lost in the woods. We entered our room and shut the door behind us. A space of our own, I was silenced, overwhelmed.

"Can we sleep with the unicorn?" Rose asked.

"Sure, but he has to go at the foot of the bed," I replied.

I pulled back the clean sheets and climbed in with my jeans on. I was still the same cowgirl who always slept in her jeans, and no one was going to change me. My sister lay back on the pillow, her breathing calm, her eyes weary as she looked at me. "I like it here," she said.

"Well, I don't know if anyone can be as nice as she seems. You better sleep with one eye open, 'cause she may try to kill us later." I looked at my sister half-jokingly and turned out the light.

Exhaustion wrapped around me like a warm blanket. My eyes started to drift shut when a sudden jolt shot through me. There in the darkness I could see my mother's face. By now the snow would be melting outside the cabin. Signs of spring would be popping up everywhere, yellow rabbit brush and purple-tinted sage gleaming in the moonlight. She would wander off into the woods to find solace. I wanted to tell her it would be okay, that we would be okay. Warm tears gave comfort as they melted down the sides of my cheeks; my eyes weary with worry, I let them close, and at last slept.

Later I awoke, startled by a strange sound.

"Rose?" I pulled the light switch next to the bed, and could see her, on her knees inside the closet, throwing up her hot dogs.

I ran up the stairs and called out to Ida for help.

"Rose is throwing up," I yelled to Ida as I approached her bedroom.

She quickly came, her pink nightgown flowing on her body. "It's okay," she assured me and started down the stairs.

She came to Rose and lifted her into her arms. Rose let her head fall over onto Ida's shoulders.

"Should I get a washcloth to clean this up?" I asked.

"No, I'll do it," Ida responded. She moved Rose over to the bed, laid her down on the pillow. I sat on the bed next to Rose. Ida came in with a warm cloth and cleaned Rose's face. "Is that better?" she asked.

Rose laid back and closed her eyes, still tired from little sleep and now depleted from throwing up.

"Why don't you lie down?" Ida advised me.

I wasn't sure how to respond. Ida truly was being a mother, taking care of all the mess and caring about my feelings at the same time. She cleaned up the closet floor. I watched until she was done.

"Go back to sleep," she said and closed the door behind her. I lay back down, the early morning light seeping through the curtain. My body finally let go. I slept till noon with Rose beside me.

Ida became a mother to me. My birth mother would always be my birth mother, my moon mother, my soul mother, but Ida became my world mother. The mother that would help me adjust to living in the world, and bring a new understanding of what it meant to walk in faith.

The Pack Was Back Together

The boys arrived at noon that next day. We hadn't seen them for a few weeks. I heard them piling in the door with loud footsteps. Carey's voice rang through the house and Jacinth came running down the hallway. He peeked in the door. "Hey, is this your room?" Then he bolted in and out. I crawled out of bed. Rose leaped up, too.

Wow, they are here. I rubbed my eyes and for the first time in months my body didn't want to wake up, but it was a new day, a new beginning. The day passed quickly with the boys helping us cook enchiladas. Carey was going on about stories of making friends in school and how he knew as much as anyone else in his class.

Jacinth ran in and out of the house, up and down the stairs. He was eight years old now, the kid in him still fully alive. Nye and Jacinth took one of the upstairs rooms and Carey took the room next to Rose and me downstairs. We all had a space, the house felt huge. Ida's youngest son, Eric, was still living at home and seemed annoyed by our presence. I understood him feeling annoyed; we were a loud noisy bunch of misfits in his home, but I thought he was selfish for not caring more. *If he only knew what we had been through*, I thought. I avoided him and he avoided us, until he moved out the following fall.

When he moved, I reflected on how he had given up his mother to five children, how he had given up his home to total strangers—and there inside thick-walled heart of a teenage girl was love for this foster-brother she hardly knew. The balancing scales had now tipped from the masculine to a softer feminine, living with Ida. The boys were wild and loud, but there was a place for all of us. Ida made it clear in her words, her actions, and her faith.

School Is Not About Book Learning

I got off the bus every morning dreading my walk to class, where girls called me *bitch* and *gringa*. I was learning that the insecure prey on others. I knew this somewhere deep inside, but in the lowly hours I wished them to up and vanish away. My father's voice would come to me in these moments and ask that I remember the mark of Jesus upon the soul, to remember that no man is without sin. I would shrug off his voice and hold my head up, tracing down the hallway. These girls were so immature and didn't know the meaning of respect. I couldn't believe this was what I got coming into the world. It was a disappointment for sure.

A few boys had asked me out. I didn't even know what going out meant, holding hands, kissing? I had seen some boys and girls holding hands and kissing after school and on lunch break, standing in the halls with hands upon butts, mouth upon mouth. *Ugh*, I didn't even want to kiss a boy, and if he dared put his hand upon my butt he would get a sure punch in the face.

I carried myself well after three months of school, and got used to the name-calling as I made it down the hallway. Ignorance was not for me. I just wanted to go to class, to understand everything in those books that had been waiting for me. Turns out all the lecture and review was so boring and hard to keep up with. I had learned everything experientially. I loved learning, but school was not the best place for learning, I was finding.

There came a point in which enough was enough of being bullied. It was 3:30 p.m., the school bell rang and out of class kids flew, arms spread wide, like birds trying to be free with backpacks strapped to their backs. I rushed to the halls like everyone else and came to the outside grounds where a girl waited for me. She had been name-calling and pushing at me for a few days now. Someone told me her boyfriend liked me and she was pissed. *Great*, I thought, *I don't even know who her boyfriend is. Can the both of them just get lost!*

She approached me on the school ground, a crowd of kids gathering around us. "Fight, fight, fight" the chanting began. The crowd narrowed in on us, with her getting closer until she reached out and grabbed my hair. I pulled my head back from her hand holding on tightly to my hair. "Is that the best you've got?" I shouted, and kicked her in the knee, then shot a right fist straight to her face. She let go and flew backwards, landing on her back on the ground. I jumped on top of her and punched her with right fist, left fist, right fist. Clock, clock, clock in the face. My adrenalin was pumping through me like I'd seen a mountain lion, until someone pulled me from her welling body. The crowd dispersed, and a teacher grabbed me from the back of my shirt. Panting and breathing heavily, I managed the words, "She started it!"

I was rushed to the principal's office, forced down into a chair. My breathing was still heavy as I pulled my hair back from my face. Mr. Hazz entered the room.

"Gallaway, why the fighting today?"

"Why don't you ask the other girl?" I responded.

"I will get to that," he said. "Now tell me, why the fighting today?"

"Why the fighting? Because there is pure ignorance around this place, girls are insecure and jealous, and all I want to do is go to class." My steel armor around my chest broke and I cupped my hands over my face to cry.

"Alright, alright. I understand this is a tough crowd," he responded. "But you can handle it."

"I did handle it," I spewed out.

"Well, there is no fighting in school, and if it keeps happening I will need to expel you," he said, his voice still holding a hint of compassion.

Get expelled, what a great idea, I thought, but knew better and did not speak. My insides forced me to see the hard, straight situation—school was necessary at this point. I had to learn no matter what the environment was.

"I will put in a call to Ida, and let her know what's going on."

That was fine by me. Ida would know before the phone even rang I was not the troublemaker in this situation. I stood up and shook the principal's hand, saying a quick "good day, sir." I walked out of his office. I saw the other girl being escorted from the nurse's office to the principal's. Her face was raw with a little blood showing on her lip.

I looked right at her. *Good*, I thought, *that'll teach you to keep messing with me.*

The school bus had left and most of the kids were gone. I sat down on a red steel bench outside the courtyard. A Hispanic girl, athletic in frame and very put together, with her hair in a braid, approached me and sat down. "Hi, I'm Laura," she said. "I saw what happened, and that girl's a bitch."

"Chloe," I stuck my hand out.

"I know you didn't start that fight."

"That's right," I said.

"A lot of these girls are like that, jealous," she stated.

A gray car pulled up.

"Hey, that's my mom, I gotta go." She swung her backpack over her shoulder. "You want to get together sometime?"

"Yeah," I said with some enthusiasm.

She drove off. I had made my first friend. Ida pulled into the parking lot, her eyes shining through her glasses, looking right at me.

I got in the truck.

"Hi, Ida." My head was sullen.

"I heard you had to beat someone up today." She tried to make light of it.

"Seems to be right," I said.

"Well, hopefully that will teach them to leave you alone. I know it's not your fault. I know who you are, Chlo." There was a hint of doubt in me about who I was and her affirmation of things rang solid in my gut.

I was at least glad for now that Ida knew who I was.

I finished out my seventh-grade year at the Española Middle school. I spent many afternoons playing over at Laura's house. She lived in Alcalde, which was only a few miles from Ida's house. She had one brother and her mom and dad were usually there, but sometimes I'd show up and she was the only one there. She would help me do my hair and nails, and we'd talk gossip about kids in school.

Laura was a studious person who got good grades in school, and always wanted things to be fair. I had turned thirteen and the following year we would start high school together. I didn't talk a lot about my past, though now and then a few things would come out and she would gasp in disbelief.

At the end of eighth grade, I had made another friend. Amanda Lujan was small in frame with more hair that I'd seen on anyone. She had perfect lips, and a tiny nose, making her look like a little princess. I wasn't into princesses. Never had a doll growing up, wouldn't know what to do with a doll if you gave it to me. But she was really nice, and after all the immaturity it was a relief to be around the heart-sounding truth of nice people.

Amanda had a tiny voice to match her stature, but she talked a lot and was full of ideas—man, she was going to run for president someday or something. She wasn't so much into fairness and equality like Laura was; she was more into dreaming, dreaming about boys and a life far beyond this little town. *I could get into that*, I thought. I had plenty of daydreams about leaving this little town.

I had no idea where I was going or how to get there, and felt intuitively that I still needed Ida. She had become my foundation, my rock. Ida was a Christian who prayed every night, but didn't preach about God. She was an angel in a human body sent to me from God. But on earth she was from Indiana. She seemed completely plain and normal and human as a person could be, but she was an angel.

I learned to sleep well at Ida's; the bedroom with the wallpaper made of sky and clouds was a sign of my place to be. I used to lie on the front porch at my parents and watch the sky and clouds for hours. *How was it that she knew I needed the sky and clouds floating all around me, long before I came to her?*

The Things We Push Away Come Back to Us

Ida made all five of us kids breakfast every morning—eggs, bacon, and pancakes. I liked the white-flour pancakes, and wasn't connected to my feelings around the food I ate, like I had been when I was young. I had forgotten that food was about nourishment. My feelings had been stored away, tight inside a box. *Don't bring them out*, I thought, *too much, too much, I must survive.*

Ida knew that being connected to our feelings was important when it came to our relationships, more than she knew it about food, and after first having us in April 1988, by November of that same year on Thanksgiving Day she packed the whole van with food and said, "We are going to have Thanksgiving with your parents."

My mother had been on a roller coaster ride of her own. When we were initially taken, she got a lawyer from Santa Fe, New Mexico. The lawyer advised her that she would have a chance at getting us back if she left my father. My father too came into town, the last place he wanted to be, and found himself in the office of a counselor provided to our family by the state. It was the foreground for much arguing between my father and Dr. Lang, the psychiatrist who was intelligent enough to keep up with my father in conversation, but not spiritual enough to meet him eye to eye. Mom told me I had planted my stake in the ground: "I am staying in the world." It was a whirlwind of emotion that I have little memory of, the breaking apart at the seams of a tightly stitched quilt, my father's painful grip, his fear of having to let go of his children. When asked, we all stated that we loved our parents but wanted to stay in the world. At this point, my mother gave up on her dream of moving to Santa Fe and getting us back. She went back to the woods with the man she had started it all with, and stayed by his side. It was a combination of loyalty to my father and not knowing how to find herself a place in the world after so many years of no place at all.

The battles were over as the decision was made for us to stay with Ida. Ida was following her heart in taking us back to my father, and our visits began on Thanksgiving Day. We drove the winding road through the red cliffs of Abiquiú, New Mexico, Georgia O'Keeffe land. The dwellings rose above the earth with a fire red and dull orange as the road wound up the side of the mountain; down below were far-stretched paths of green grass and fields of wheat. It was a calm and peaceful valley just north of Española. The road home to my father was even more peaceful up in the higher mountain ranges, with white sand dusted sporadically on red clay and finally thick green forest running on for miles. This was the land my parents had first come to in the early days of being refugees, places called the Mesa, and Gallina, New Mexico, the Northern Hispanic communities, set high above the cities, way out past the range of normal life, where fields and hawks meshed within the day's sunlight for hours on end.

Ida had met my father once in the courthouse and then in Dr. Lang's office, when we first went into foster care. She shook his hand, though they had told her that he was a tyrant. She saw his eyes and knew the truth within them; she had no fear, no judgment of the man. He was just a man, full with human expression, flaws and gifts, and most of all he needing healing. We all needed healing, and Ida knew it in her bones. She was the worker on the riverbanks you never took notice of, the quiet person in the rice fields of China, the Tibetan monk on the mountainside, never stirred by the cold. She knew her purpose and walked with it daily. She would bring healing to the collapsed souls, to the feet that needed to be scrubbed, and she would get right in there and do it herself.

We drove the last strip of rolling blacktop with vast clay colors whizzing beside us all the way to Lindrith. I had not been back since that day I hiked off the mountain with my mother. It was a crisp fall day and we were bringing a cooked turkey to my father.

The final push of the engine revved up the last hill and there it was, the cabin sitting in the woods. All the trees had waited for me, the same branches reaching out—

> Child of the woods
> We hold a place for you
> Know this to be true
> You belong
> You belong

After Ida cut the engine to the truck, my father came over from the cabin with his cowboy hat on, and a smile on his face.

"Glory Hallelujah," he marched right to Ida and put out his hand. "Jesus's name, God bless you, Father. I knew you were coming. I got the message this morning." A spiritual message he meant. My father always knew when we were coming. He would get a vision, a feeling, a sign, and that same day we would show up.

We all stepped down from the van. Jacinth was eight, Rose ten, I twelve, Nye fourteen, and Carey seventeen. Carey wore his heart and his bravery on his sleeve, being the first to greet my father, not holding back a big bear hug. "Papa, how's it going?"

The rest of us were more reluctant. I held my heart in my throat; boiling steam and fear rushing through my blood. My father cupped all of us under his chest and pulled us in close. I wasn't ready to show him love, it was buried, I'd have to do some digging to get it out.

Jacinth took off immediately into the backwoods; the woods were the soul of that little boy. He knew how to climb every tree, mark every piece of dirt—there was no fear in him, no waste of his mind to the little things of conversation, he and the woods were one.

My father helped Ida carry in food from the van. My mother came from the back room, greeting us with reluctance. She too had met Ida, in Dr. Lang's office, unsure of her feelings so she kept them buried—she too would need to do some digging to get them out. I hugged her, not hard to love. I felt she needed me so deeply that it didn't matter what she did, I was going to be there. I hugged her again, and she let her arms fall around me, no tears, for she never let them fall.

The eight of us gathered round the table that once seemed so large. It had gotten smaller, I had gotten bigger, life had gotten bigger. The turkey was in the middle and my father took a knife and cut straight through. We ate, silence around the table, until broken through with words. Carey was always one of the first to break through with words. "So, Dad, you seen any bucks this fall? I've been thinking about a hunting trip up this way."

"Uh yeah, there has been a few bucks off the north slope. I'd be glad to help you get one, if you feel inclined to come back up."

"Yup, yup," Carey spoke with food in his mouth.

Nye chimed into the conversation about deer and said that he might come too.

That was a sign, a break in the cracks of the earth, if Nye was going to come back and hunt with his father too. Nye was more sensitive than Carey. It took him longer to forgive, to forget. He too wore his heart on his sleeve, but he never wanted to get caught in the crossfire again.

I never liked hunting, and there was no bonding for me over it. I wanted animals to live, and was barely okay eating my turkey. I shoved handfuls of mashed potato into my mouth. Ida was a good cook. Not any better than my mother, just different. My mother sat in silence and ate only a few bites. Her eyes wore the depression of her soul. She got up and went to the back room. I followed her.

"Mom, are you doing okay?" I asked.

She shook her head. "Shhh, let's not talk about it here."

She had learned to keep quiet, to sit quietly, to read quietly, to knit quietly. "I need the outhouse," I said. "Let's go for a walk."

We up and walked a straight line through the forest, arm and arm. I felt the coldness in her blood. She was barely breathing, barely alive.

"Mom," I said.

"Well, your father has been a terror since you all were taken. He just can't be at peace. He rages over and over about the unfairness of it all."

I didn't know how to respond. I wanted to advise her to leave, *just go Mom, it's time to just go*, but my heart ached for my father being alone in the woods. Again I was caught in the crossfire, wishing so for their blood to be washed clean, peace upon their hearts whether together or apart; it had to come, let it come any way it can.

I sat in the outhouse and looked out at the clouds parting in the sky. I would always feel comfortable going to the bathroom outside in the middle of the woods.

Mom and I walked the distance back to the house in silence. Both of us knowing something had to give, something had to change. I was on her side, I would always be on her side. My father had God, the woods, but this was his dream—not hers.

We spent the afternoon playing in the front yard; Ida talked with my Mom sitting on the front steps of the porch. The sun moved toward the west as the five of us played freeze tag, stirring up the dirt as we ran from corner to corner of the yard. My father brought out his guitar to play. He sat in the sun, golden streams of light lit his brown eyes, singing with full heart, lips speaking the truth. The song was about Mother Earth and how she could not be harmed no matter the damage we brought upon her.

Was that about my mother? I wondered. I didn't believe it could be, my mother was surely broken. And my father was part of her brokenness. I couldn't stand him because of it.

Music filled the air. Crisp fall was here, but we were no longer here, and I was okay with that. I had made it out, and it's what my life needed. I pushed back my feelings of love for my father, and watched the sun sink through the tree line.

"We better get going," Ida spoke.

We loaded the van and backed slowly from the drive. My mother sat on the porch watching us go; my father walked beside the van telling Ida to come back, telling Ida that Jesus saves, heals, and brings new life. Ida shook her head in a yes motion till we pulled away from the drive. My father waited at the top of the hill and watched us drive out the long road. His shape was still there at the last curve we took.

Bye, Dad.

We drove the long way home in the dark, no red cliffs, no gleaming pine trees; small twinkling lights through small towns led the way. Like an apple falling from the tree, I felt bruised. I couldn't heal my parents, heal our lives, I could only keep living. Ida was building a bridge for us that would open the gates to wholeness one day, but for now I had to let it be. Rose and I fell asleep in the back seat leaning into each other.

Friends and Clothes
that Fit Us

In the eighth grade I made another friend, named Emma Pulido. She was a Filipino girl, dark chocolate skin, with thick lips, and an attitude to match. Emma was spunky, full of life, and she too was a transplant to the Valley. I felt connected to her because of our colored pasts and our fiery spirits. She was tough, witty, and ready to rebel against whatever she didn't agree with—she was a kindred spirit indeed.

She lived with her aunt and uncle right in town. I had to travel a ways from Ida's way out near the river. Ida would take me there on weekends. Her aunt was a sharp Filipino woman, and her uncle was as white as day. He was a jokester, and picked at me in a friendly manner. I felt welcomed coming in the door. I spent the summer hanging out with Emma. I had learned to swim in the public pool, and we often met up with Laura and Amanda. We would hit the local Baskin-Robbins to get ice cream. I had never had ice cream before the days of Ida. Vanilla and pecans and cream were a lift to my taste buds. I ate spoonfuls with no shame. We ate ice cream all summer and by August I was getting thicker around the middle. I was athletic when I left the mountain; I was a specimen of lean muscle with a few curves, I never thought about my weight.

Over the summer I started to look at boys differently, and noticed a lot of them looking at me. Laura, Amanda, and Emma picked out the boys they thought were the cutest, and we'd gossip about who would kiss who. I had never kissed a boy but knew when the time came I'd know how to handle it.

I was fourteen and the days of summer ended abruptly. The last sunset of summer crossed over the swimming pool, my body sleek and wet paddling through the water, my wet hair falling around my face. I said goodbye to a younger me as I watched the sun sink below the horizon; I was a young woman now.

It was time for school shopping, which meant new clothes. My insides beamed with excitement. All those years of wearing the same hand-me-down clothes felt distant. I had never been shopping to pick out something I really wanted then, and now I finally understood what it meant to want something. It was a double-edged sword to want, it presented a problem: you keep wanting, and you don't always get it. Ida got a voucher from our social worker to purchase us clothing.

We drove to the mall in Santa Fe. I coveted and eyed all the clothing stores as we rushed the mall. We had a small amount of money and Ida informed us we could only use the money at Sears and JCPenney. I found out quickly those were not the popular stores to shop, and it was clear why. I was going to be one of the most ridiculous-looking freshmen starting high school. The jeans looked like they were supposed to be worn by your grandma, too high on the waste, all washed out, and the blouses didn't fit the body. The girls of Española liked to wear their clothes real tight where everything showed, and if you didn't have anything to show then you were in trouble. You may as well stay home. I whined the whole shopping trip all the way through JCPenney.

Ida just kept picking out shirt after shirt. "How about this one?"

"Nope," I'd shake my head. "Next," I kept saying. Ida was consistent and patient. She never got mad, but finally she gave a look of despair. "Okay, I'll try it on," I said. A floral pattern blouse, yellow and white mixed throughout. *I can connect with the flowers*, I thought, drawing me back to nature, enough to get me in a piece of clothing. I looked into the mirror in the dressing room. I was a young woman. I had reached young womanhood without my mother around. I had breasts and curves, and shining eyes. *My mother would like this blouse*, I thought. She would be so happy to see me in new clothes. I held back my tears and headed out to meet Ida at the register. "It's a yes," I exclaimed.

We got back in the car and drove the hour and half toward Española. Ida was silent for ten minutes and then she spoke.

"Chlo, I want you to work real hard in school. If you do well in school, you will be able to go anywhere in life." I listened, not sure I believed her, with my father's idealism still in my head about school in the public form being a tight box to fit you in. But I listened, and knew her heart was in it.

"The other thing," she said, "is please, please, don't go falling in love." Her words were now pleading, earnest, strong.

"You are too young to know what love is about." Her eyes shifted from me back to the road.

Road Trips and Family Ties

That summer I turned fifteen, Ida took us on a road trip. All four of us kids piled into the van, with pillows and blankets stuffed in every corner, each of us with one small space to sit. Carey had left for college. The house felt different with him gone, but going to college meant he had made it in the world. I sat in the back of the van and watched the land change from brown to green as we drove from New Mexico to Texas. Our first stop was to visit my Grandmother Ogreta. We had kept in touch with her during our transition to Ida's, through letters. Letters were the heartstrings, the chords that kept our relationship alive. She was relieved that we were in school and living with Ida. I felt free, returning to her white, two-story home there on Tampa Street in Houston. The musky air was still the same but everything else had changed since my last visit, mostly I had changed. I was independent and, despite my insecurities, I knew that somehow I would make it in the world. My grandmother versed me in my multiplication cards that she had worked with me on two years earlier; to her shock I aced them all. Her smile lit up the room when, for the first time, I think she realized I was going to be okay too. The green couch I had sat on in the living area, when we got the call that the boys had gone into foster care, was just the same; but the terror I felt in that moment had completely lifted. We visited for a week. Ida and my grandmother, both being teachers, connected on many levels, conversing as we sat underneath a green umbrella on the shores of Galveston.

These were the waters of my past, my childhood solitude in the midst of a crowd. I longed for the smell of sea salt, the sound of sea gulls overhead, the sand between my toes, and my grandmothers' presence hovering over me while I sunbathed on my towel. Ida knew the importance of family, not creating a new family but keeping us intact with our original family. We continued on our road trip into Tennessee, where we visited my Dad's brother, my Uncle Craig, Aunt Deb and my cousins Ben, Chris, and Zack. Craig played the guitar like my father and taught theology at the college level. He was a scholarly, educated type, much like my Grandfather Ira. I had spent very little time with my aunt, uncle, and cousins, as they didn't visit us much during my years on the mountain, but they were a part of the streaming letters that came at Christmas.

My father had spoken often about his brothers and his sister. He had two brothers, Craig and Timothy Harold, and one sister, Cynthia. He would at times mourn the loss of his siblings and his mother and father in song and in story. He would go for months saying nothing and then out of nowhere would come a song about a brother who played music just as fine as he did, a brother who saw God in the flight of angels, a sister who flew to new lands to have her children on the banks of the sea. My Aunt Cyndi had lived in Hawaii for years with my two cousins Nick and Jessica. Cynthia looked like me in pictures that I saw. She had long, light-brown hair with golden tints and a wide smile that lit up the field of green where she was standing in the pictures. My father had come from somewhere, somewhere normal, but somehow he became something different.

Again Ida knew the importance of allowing me to find out who I was and how I was connected to a much larger whole in this world. We drove on from Tennessee east all the way to Maryland to visit my Uncle Victor. My uncle had just gotten married right around the time we were placed with Ida. He was torn at the time that he could not take us, and waited for some good news to come after we had been placed in foster care. He was teaching at a progressive independent middle school in Rockville, Maryland. Again, Ida was able to connect with my uncle around teaching. My uncle had married a woman named Susan Levi, who was from Houston. He could have married any number of women from foreign countries, yet he married a woman from his hometown. Perhaps it was serendipitous in my uncle's decision to settle down in his life and find a hometown himself. Susan had long, black hair and dark-chocolate eyes; she was original and as natural as a woman could be. She was every bit as sweet as I remember Victor's earlier girlfriend, Lorraine, but more motherly and like a good friend that you could always have tea with. She had a remarkable patience for listening and knew what questions to ask to make you think about your life.

My Uncle Victor was not too shocked by our wild uproar of chatter while making ourselves at home in his house. He'd seen with his own eyes the way we lived and knew somewhere inside what we had been through. He was still a walking education, now with pictures of his travels hanging on elegant walls, and exotic rugs decorating hardwood floors in his East Coast home.

We ate out in the backyard with green trees and plants everywhere. We had come a long way from eating hot dogs with him on the shores of a small northern New Mexico lake. My uncle had spent much of his life riding bikes for fitness and for the environment. We rode bikes down to the National Mall, thirty-six miles round trip. I had gotten accustomed to my lazy lifestyle at Ida's and felt a little strained by the ride.

We arrived in the middle of the city of politics. I had never really thought about the White House, and there it was, all white and taking up more space than an entire neighborhood. This was the place my father never wanted to be, right in the middle of politics. Though he had been voted most likely to become president of the free nation in his high school yearbook, he must have felt quite differently inside. His beliefs that formed around reading Emerson and Thoreau had had a profound effect on him.

Once we hopped off our bikes, my uncle gave me a new perspective of the world and on politics: there were some good and bad people involved in government, but most importantly we the people needed to use our voice. We needed to educate ourselves and be involved so that we could bring change to what matters in our lives. Standing in front of the White House, I tried to wrap my brain around the size of this place and the idea that here so many important decisions were made that affected our nation and the world. It made me want to run to the woods for a minute and then I saw my uncle riding his bike up ahead of me, fast legs pedaling, free as a bird. *There is a way to live in the world and be free as a bird*, I thought.

That summer my life was forever changed, by Ida taking me on this road trip, that brought about many realizations and strengthened my connections to family. I was someone. I had come from a great line of people. What I didn't realize at the time was that my full power would come when I honored the indescribable thing I was yet to remember—my connection to nature—along with my connection to family and others in the world.

The Mystery Boy

The Soul is deeper than the mind. It knows with full awareness the things of our birth, our family of origin, our purpose. There was still one piece of my family that had remained disconnected from us. My father's first-born son, Matthew. I found out in fragmented pieces about Matthew over the years. We knew about him, but he didn't know about us. How could the pieces of this puzzle ever be put together?

The son that we all knew of
The one that was left behind
The one that was held by his mother
Until there came a time
When he would find the truth
It was laid in his hand
There was no golden key
To help him understand
Somewhere inside he knew
He was born of another man
The one that was his father
Running all this time
Would be his bloodline

I can only tell this part of the story from the heart, because I only know bits and pieces of Matt's journey. When I turned sixteen and was living with Ida, a call came in one day letting us know that our half-brother wanted to meet us. My father's first-born son, whom he had left in California with his mother, had been told about his birth father, Jerry Gallaway. I don't know all the reasons that Jane kept my father's identity from Matt. She had remarried and my father was so far off the map, I'm not even sure she knew where he was. I tried to comprehend Matt not knowing about his biological father and the rest of us, all five of us. I was in my own whirlwind of life during that time, adapting to the world and finally working to get good grades in school. I couldn't put too much thought into it and wasn't sure how I could be helpful in a situation that a bunch of adults had chosen.

Matt grew up in California with his mother, half-brother and half-sister. I didn't know too much about his life, but thought it must have been easier than ours. He must have had the California coast as a sacred place. I had dreamed about the California coast my whole life; perhaps Matt had dreamed of a sacred place in the mountains, a tugging at his soul, telling him there was something he needed to know. I believe the soul works this way, letting us know who we are even if the world says something different.

Matt was told about my father when he was twenty-seven years old. He came with a friend to New Mexico and drove the land north to meet all of us up at my dad's. It was summer; the bright sun blazed its heat upon the clay earth underneath our feet as we waited in the drive knowing that Matt would come that day. The five of us kids, along with my mother and father. They arrived, the car stopped in the yard, the doors opened, two men got out of the car. I wasn't sure which one was my brother. Matt approached. He was tall like my father, with brown eyes like my father, strong hands, but gentle in their grasp. He fumbled for words as we stared at him and shook his hand. I wasn't sure if a hug was appropriate. How do you hug someone who shares your same blood but you know little of who they are?

My father went to Matt and hugged him, two grown men embracing. Matt was now older than my father was the last time he had seen him. It was too much to comprehend. Matt was brave indeed for taking the step to see this part of his life, to learn about this whole other family. He was no longer the mystery boy; he was real flesh and blood standing on the same soil we grew up on. My father was gleeful to have all his children there. He played his music and sang from his heart, never speaking of the past. All the while I wanted to ask Matt a thousand questions, but dared not make him answer anything on that day. I still wonder till this very moment what that day was like for Matt. We stayed in touch, by email and through family gatherings over the years. Matt invited us to his wedding in California. I got to see him happy on a sailboat, holding his dear Margot, the woman he loved for many years. I got to see him swim in the ocean and dance around the room with all the people who loved him. We loved him too, though it was hard to express, hard to fully understand. It was its own work of art, none of us had chosen it, but we could accept the gift in having another brother.

The Pendulum Has Swung the Other Way

L iving in the world was a bright light of spinning commercialism, the billboards on every corner, the night-lights of a flashing Walmart, a Circle K, the colors bright and noisy in themselves. Everywhere you went there was something to buy, something you felt you needed. The high infiltration of need stung at my insides. I had never known this need, need, need kind of feeling that bubbled up every time I walked through a store or restaurant. I need to eat that hamburger, with that Coke, with those fries, with the cheese piled on top.

I had been in the world before, when I visited my grandmother, but this was different. Now there was no going back, no ruler of a father sitting in the corner to govern my thoughts. I was free and I wanted to partake of most things worldly. Ida cooked with love, but not always from the garden. She didn't have a garden and we got most of our food from the Safeway grocery store in town. Occasionally we went into Santa Fe, and she bought food in bulk at Sam's Club. There was more food than I had ever seen at one time and to think you could get it right out of the refrigerator, no walking to the root cellar. The microwave was a profound spectacle of a box, into which you could throw food and in seconds it would be hot. This free-for-all feeling and space of living with food and convenience went on for a full year of my life before I noticed it.

After many meals we had dessert—ice cream, apple pie, pumpkin pie, pecan pie. I wasn't overeating according to the American standard. Ida was also big on salads and veggies, but it was certainly more food than I'd ever consumed in one sitting. I was fifteen now and the growing pressures of adolescence were upon me. School had gotten a little better, in that I had some friends and I was slowly understanding the teacher-student dynamic. I knew how to fill in the circle with answering a true or false question on a test. Whereas I used to fill in all the circles, because no one explained the test and so I picked everything. Being a teen was all about fitting in with both the boys and the girls. All the girls were striving for perfection and this is when I noticed I had gained some weight. I wanted to be my old athletic self; I was still that, but a little thicker, especially in the thighs and waist. I didn't like it. My entire world had always depended on my beauty and my strength.

Growing up in a masculine world, I had learned that strength and beauty did not come in a chubby body. All the convenience in life was like sitting on a big fluffy cushion, and if I had this cushion under my butt for too long, I would forget what it was like to sit on a solid wooden bench. The real wood underneath me would help me to hold my body upright, to keep my stomach in, to stay connected to how my body felt. I had also learned in nature about the need for balance: that everyone had enough, and that each season brought with it everything that was needed. No matter how harsh the winter was, the snow was needed to soak the land, and in spring it was always evident that this soaking of the land was what brought the plants to life. When I was young, I would sit on the edge of the cliff at the valley of the moon and listen as the snow melted and the water rushed through canyon walls, the sound of life passing through my ears. In the world, the snow of life melted very differently and it was difficult to remain connected to my intuition and my understanding of balance.

My ears heard too many car engines, too many voices from the TV, too many sounds from the electricity pouring through the walls, too many outside voices telling me what to do. The world didn't notice springtime in the same way, and because of this it was hard to notice the balance in things, in food, in love, in learning, in all of life. The intuitive feeling of what I needed was replaced with that feeling of need. When my mind first learned that I could have a toy, I immediately started to want more toys. Internally I was aware of this—my father's teachings were still in there—but there was a wall of pain over my past that kept me from connecting deeply enough to notice it.

Ida was my springtime, there to show me that I had everything I needed. It's true that Ida was of the world, but she had such strong faith and conviction in her human character that she had her own rhythm in the world. Ida's rhythm was love, and it was from this love that I would learn a new rhythm of how to be. It was from this rhythm that I would learn to visit my father again, the first steps in trying to understand who he was. Ida never placed judgment on my mother or my father. She always spoke with love and compassion toward the both of them. She didn't try to remove me from my past, with the idea of making me a new person. I would never be a new person; I could only be whole by coming to my past with clear eyes, forgiveness, and strength to gather up all the pieces of who I am.

I Was in the Game of Life

It was new grounds, a new place, new brick walls to be confined within. More life to explore, more mistakes to make, more lessons to learn, more trials to endure, and academia was in there somewhere, too.

I stepped down from the van and threw my backpack over my shoulders. "Bye, Ida," I yelled it out as I ran up the hilly lawn toward the school building. Ninth grade had arrived, it came at me like a slingshot and plunged me right into the heart of boys and girls rushing the halls, speeding through class, eyes opening wide, life moving, and now and then a moment of stillness. I found my classrooms, found my seat, found my place, and the words of the teachers had new meaning. Unlike middle school, I knew the format of the paperwork the program offered to me each day. *Drink it up child, this is your learning*. I paid attention when teachers spoke.

Mrs. Galbraith was my English teacher. She stood at the front of class, always standing, her gray hair making wavy circles around her round face. She reminded me of Mrs. Bassett, that strong, sturdy figure with wisdom in her eyes. I learned quickly that English was my favorite class. It was right before lunch break, and we got to write poems and study Dickinson. I sat close to the front, no longer in the back. Boys tried to get my attention, and I wouldn't look twice. I wrote and wrote, despite the fact that my grammar was a mess. Writing was freedom.

I got my first paper back from Mrs. Galbraith. Notes from teacher: "Chloe, your writing is insightful, and revealing, however. . ."

Here we go, I thought. "However, you must work on your grammar. Please review chapter six on sentence structure." At the top of my paper was a B. *Woo hoo*, I shouted to myself, *I got a B*. I had been getting C's straight through middle school. I ran out of class to find Emma at lunchtime. Emma was my biggest confidant; she knew my past, and how I felt it to be deeply wounded. She had a past, too, in which she was disconnected from her parents, and had moved to a new place out of San Francisco. Another connection we had. I'd remembered that my parents met in San Francisco, and I really wanted to go there.

Emma and I were two of a pair determined to find a fit. I showed her my B, and she yelped at my success. Emma was working hard to improve her grades, but cared more about hanging out and getting out of her aunt and uncle's house as much as possible. She took a job at the Baskin-Robbins ice cream shop right near her house. I would visit her after school and she would give me free samples of ice cream.

"Shh, don't tell the manager, I'm not supposed to give out samples like this." Emma's rebel side was becoming clear.

Ida dropped me off every morning at the curb just down the grassy knoll from the school building. I'd run up the hill and find my friends before class. It was the third week of high school. I climbed the hill in the morning air, all the students a blur before my eyes and upon my ascent. One day I caught a glimpse of a tall boy. He stood out in the crowd, being taller than most with a muscular build and thick, black hair. He stood alone looking out toward the parking lot. People rushed passed him. *He isn't a boy but a man*, I thought. My heart stretched across the lawn, I needed to meet him. He turned and went inside the school building. I went to class and could not stop thinking about him.

I paid less attention in class and found myself day dreaming about meeting the tall, handsome man on the school grounds. *He had to be older than me*, I thought, *better forget it*. I washed my memory clean of him and wrote a poem in Mrs. Galbraith's class. I kept writing poems and Ida found one of them loosely stuffed in my backpack. She approached me before dinner one night.

"Chlo, I'm little concerned," she said. "Are you feeling alright?"

"Yeah, why?"

"I found this poem." She handed me the paper. It had stars scribbled all around it.

Break me out of my chains
Break me out of my pain
Take me from here
Make it all clear
My blood is still
Frozen in my bones
I am alone

"Are you feeling depressed?" Ida inquired with concern.

"Well, yeah, pretty much. How could I not be depressed?" I answered. "My mother still lives in the woods with my dad, I never know if she is okay, or what's going to happen to them both. But I'm not suicidal if that's what you're asking. I'm not going to hurt myself, it's forbidden to do that, you know." I looked at her with all seriousness.

"Well, I think you should talk to a counselor," she said, giving me room to make the decision.

I had seen a counselor before when we first got to Ida's. *Ugh, I did not like that woman, so patronizing.* She would sit in front of me all glittered up with makeup and bright pink lipstick on her lips.

"How do you feel about leaving your parents?" she would ask.

"Hmm, how do you feel about lipstick that's too bright for your face?" I would respond.

How does she think I feel? I felt broken, torn to shreds, confused, alone, alone, alone. No one could understand how I felt, especially not her.

"Ida, I don't need counseling." I rejected her notions of my need to be fixed. "I don't need to see that stupid woman."

"I'm not saying you should see her again, but let's try a new person. I don't want you to feel like this. It gets in the way of life."

Lots of things had gotten in the way in my life. I was numb to the point.

"Alright," I conceded.

The following week I walked into Dr. Otais's office. He sat at his desk but pulled his chair around to the front of the desk to face me sitting in front of him on a couch. I sat back in the cushion absorbing my body weight. *Breathe, breathe*, I felt my lungs pull in air. "Mr. Otais, is that your name?"

"Yes 'm it is," he spoke with an accent. "It's a Greek name, and that's where I'm from."

"Greece as in the place with all the islands?" I asked.

"Well, of sorts, there is a lot of water," he said.

"Hmm, how did you get to these parts?" No one came from Greece to Española valley.

"Well, my wife is from Santa Fe." His beard reminded me of my father. White and gray mixed in, but his was trimmed. He had a bush of hair on his head, also white and gray. I immediately felt trust for him.

"So, Chloe, did you know that is a Greek name in origin?"

"I didn't know that," I responded. "I was given the name by my mother."

"Oh, have you seen your mother, lately?" He paused and looked down at my file he was holding in his lap.

I stared ahead, no words. "It's been awhile since I have seen her."

"Why don't you tell me about her," he requested.

I didn't know how to tell him about her. I never knew how to tell anyone about her.

"She's pretty, she has red hair, she is sad and has been since my brother died."

"Do you want to talk about your brother who died?"

"No."

"What would you like to talk about?" he leaned his chair in closer.

"I don't know, Ida wanted me to come here because I write sad poems."

"Writing poems is good. Do you want to talk about the poems?"

"They are sad, but it's just a feeling on paper. It doesn't mean I'm going to kill myself!"

"I understand," he nodded his head. "You are expressing something real, yes." His accent was very strong. I liked it.

"Of course it's real, but it's just how I'm feeling at the moment."

"And how is that?" he inquired.

"Sad, broken, alone. The world is not the place for me."

"Why is the world not the place for you?" He looked puzzled.

"I think I'm like my father, and he could never mix with the world."

"Very interesting." He looked at me closer. "Your father sounds like a very interesting man."

"Yes, I would say so." I nodded my head up and down.

He handed me a blank sheet of paper. "Why don't you write me a poem about your father," he requested with conviction.

I grabbed up the paper and wrote:

> Man in the woods
> Where do you run to?
> Man in the woods
> Why do you run?
> Man in the woods
> Why have you left me?
> Where have you gone?
> You believe in God the
> Father,
> but leave me
> To fend for myself
> You leave me
> You leave us all
> I cry for you
> Like a waterfall

I handed him the paper. He read through it, his eyes looking deeply into the paper. I felt him like I could sometimes feel my mother, his beating heart, his fear, his sorrow within the walls of his chest. I waited in silence.

"You are talented." He looked up from the paper. "And you have many questions for your father, I see."

I nodded my head.

"This is a good way for you to ask the questions. Keep writing and you will get to some answers. I truly believe this," he stated. "You know, Chloe, life will always come to you with many questions. You must sit in stillness sometimes for a while, and then, one day an answer will come."

He paused before he continued. "I can't give you the answers, they come from within, but I'd be glad to be a sounding board for your poems and your words at any time."

"I'd like that," I responded with sincerity.

He shook my hand, and we agreed on meeting the following week. I ran out to the van where Ida was waiting.

"How'd it go?" she asked.

I slammed the van door shut. "I liked him, he was really good."

Ida was happy. She drove us home talking about Indiana and her father growing the largest watermelon in the county where she grew up. You could tell she loved her father as she described his old body bent over the watermelon patch, his weathered hands picking at the dirt. I was happy that she had a childhood that was free of much suffering. Maybe it gave her a chance to be with those who suffered and wrap those chains around her own body to lift the load for us.

The next day I went to school feeling a lot lighter. I knew my poems had a purpose. They told the truth, and I didn't have to be ashamed of writing them. I sat through English class watching Mrs. Galbraith shine at her storytelling. I wanted to be a storyteller, too, someday.

A boy from my English class, the cutest boy in the class and at school—except for the tall handsome boy I saw earlier in the year, he was still somewhere in the back of my mind—was a boy asking me out. Carlos Ray was in my grade and on the junior varsity football team. He had deep brown eyes and thick lips. After class he approached me near the lockers in the hallway. He wasn't shy and came right up to me.

"Hey, what's ya doin', girl?" His beaming clear skin and perfect face were hard to miss.

"I'm just getting books," I responded, ashamed of my lack of witty charm.

"So, I really like your writing in English class." His voice got a little nervous.

"Oh, that's nice thing to say, thanks," I replied with more confidence.

The bell rang. We were late so I went to push past him, but he put his arm around my waist, and pulled me back to him, energy shooting through my body as I was bumped into him.

"Whoa," I said.

"Wanna go out with me?" He looked into my eyes.

I pulled his arm from holding me, and twirled out from under him, holding his hand as I moved. "Yes." I smiled a huge grin and ran off to class.

The rest of the day was a blur, all I thought about was his hand upon my waist. The bell rang and I had to dress for volleyball practice. I ran down the steps to the gym and geared up. Balls flew at my face, waking me from my trance. Focus, I told myself after Coach Jaramillo yelled at me, "Gallaway, what's going on over there?"

I pushed my thoughts out and dove for a ball on the floor, chin to the wood floor, head up, swooping up the ball. That was my best dive yet. I was in the game, the game of life, the game of boys, the game of high school.

I ate dinner that night and didn't mention the boy to Ida. I wasn't going to ever mention to Ida anything about boys. She had warned me and I hadn't forgotten, but she doesn't know what it's like to be a young girl these days. I pushed her ideas away.

The next day Carlos Ray was waiting for me next to my locker. I came in the door and saw him as I walked down the hall.

"Morning, girl," he said, quite chirpy.

"Morning," I replied, holding my smile and my breath. "How are you today?"

He put his hand over my locker.

"Excuse me, I need to get in there." I pushed his hand away.

"Well, I gotta get you to hold my hand somehow," he said with a chuckle.

The bell rang and we didn't move.

"Late again. You are good at making us late," I said.

The halls were cleared. Dim light lit the tile floor and marked our way down the hall.

"You're pretty, so pretty." He put his hand on my face, and leaned in for a kiss.

Our lips met, a soft, delicate sense of being, a few seconds of another life. I felt the wetness in his mouth just a little and we broke apart.

"I better get to class," I said, pulling away while holding onto his hand. He ran the other direction toward his biology class, and I ran to my geometry class. Not the class to miss as I was already behind. I slipped in the back while the teacher gave me an eye, "Gallaway." I was always getting in trouble lately.

Before lunch, I met Carlos Ray at the door to Mrs. Galbraith's class and we stepped inside like two new people. The rumors would start around the school soon. Everyone knew everyone's business, who kissed who, who liked who, there was no getting around it. By lunch everyone was asking me if we were going out. Well, I guess, he did ask me to go out with him. I was only fifteen and Ida had forbidden me to date until I was sixteen, so I couldn't go with him anywhere outside of school.

Nye was a year ahead of me in school. He played with the football team and they made it to the championships that year; he had gotten pretty popular with both boys and girls. He was making straight A's in school. I would sometimes see him at lunch, as he would occasionally check on me.

"How are things going? You staying out of trouble?"

"I sure am. What about you?"

I knew he had been to some late-night drinking parties with his friends, and would come stumbling in drunk to Ida's. I wasn't going to tell on him, and Ida was too innocent to handle the truth. I decided not to tell Nye I had kissed someone. I didn't know how he would respond. The one person I did tell was Rose. Rose was now going through middle school; she would be in high school when I was a senior. We hadn't been that close during that time; she was too young to understand what I was going through, or so I thought. She was beyond beautiful, with long, dark blond ringlets of hair that flowed past her face and neck. I didn't think she liked boys yet, but it was coming. I knew it was coming. I told her before bed about Carlos Ray.

"What did it feel like to kiss him?" she inquired.

"It was wet, and awesome."

Hmm, wet, she wasn't sure she would like that.

The next morning I expected to see Carlos Ray at my locker in the morning, but he wasn't there. *Hmm,* I was let down, my heart wondering. I went through all my classes thinking about him, and finally we arrived at English class. He sat in his seat not looking at me. *What the heck happened?* My mind bugged me. The bell rang and he waited outside of class for me. His face was changed.

"What's up?" I said a little defensively. *Don't blow me off,* I thought.

"I can't go out with you. I like you, but I can't go out with you," he said.

"What? That makes no sense. Is this because my mom won't let me date?" I inquired further.

"No, I just can't." He wouldn't give me a real answer and pulled away.

What the heck? He left me standing there in the hallway alone. Emma found me in the hall and said, "Dude, did you hear what your brother did to Carlos Ray?"

"What?" I was already annoyed.

"Dude, I guess Nye grabbed him in the hall and threw him up against the wall, told him to never kiss his sister again."

I hadn't learned yet to curse fully and spat out a "Jesus, what is wrong with him!" I went to volleyball practice and dug deep into the floor, diving for balls.

Why would he listen to Nye anyway? Nye was probably just messing with him. The sweat of practice was over and I ran up to the football field where Nye was practicing. I waited in the afternoon sunlight. They wrapped up practice and I grabbed Nye coming off the field.

"Nye, what the hell! Why did you shove Carlos against the wall?"

Nye laughed. "Who told you I did that?"

"Everyone knows."

"Well, I wasn't serious, I was just messing with him."

"Not funny," I said and shoved his football-padded shoulder.

"Well, if he can't handle a little rough and tumble, he shouldn't be dating you." He spoke a bit more seriously and walked off the field. I sat in the bleachers and watched the rest of the players exit the field. The last one to march off was the tall handsome boy. He looked even cuter in football gear. Deep eyes, olive skin, dark hair, lots of hair all spiked on his head, legs, and arms, but none on his chiseled face. I was taken aback, losing my thoughts over Nye and Carlos Ray. The tall, dark, handsome boy was going to be a senior and I was going into my sophomore year. *He won't even give me the time of day,* I thought. His name was Chance Williams. He didn't look Hispanic and he didn't look white. He just looked good.

Love Is Inevitable

We finished the year and Carlos Ray was out of my mind. I spent the summer riding around town with Emma, Laura, and Amanda. Emma borrowed her uncle's brown Buick and we cruised the streets into the late hours. Streetlights lit the bright pavement under us, dreams ahead of us. We drove up and down, up and down, turning into Sonic—never to order food, just to check out the scene.

Emma was chocolate from her toes to her head with perfect skin, no cellulite no lines, no imperfections. On our sleepovers together we would dress in sexy lingerie and take Polaroid pictures of each other. I didn't always like my white skin, and had on occasion tried to cover it up by putting on darker cover-up than was meant for me. The bullying I had experienced in middle school was mostly dormant in high school, with the exception of a few folks here and there who picked on me. But most people knew not to mess with me, or my brother. Nye was one of the toughest kids in school and everyone knew it.

I used Emma's eyeliner and lipstick to make myself up, and I'd snap a few photos. Emma and I were wild in our manner, free spirits, and didn't much care if people didn't understand us.

Laura had become a cheerleader, and she was still the same Laura, always doing good and wanting fairness for everyone. She made me feel there was a right and wrong in the world, and that could be a good thing if you paid attention to it.

Amanda was the opposite of Emma and me in so many ways. She was like a sweet southern girl who got dropped in the wrong place. She had manners and was kindhearted, speaking her truth through a sweet voice. She would curl her hair and primp her eyelashes to a perfect picture of beauty. She had been dating some guy down the street from her, and was quite in love.

I had yet to experience love, but felt I could handle it when it came my way. Chance was dating every girl in school. He went out mostly with juniors, seniors, pretty girls, most of them cheerleaders, all Hispanic girls with olive skin. I had gotten over my crush on him a little bit because I didn't like that he dated so many girls. In defiance, I told myself I didn't like him anymore. I had been asked out by a few boys but didn't feel like connecting to boys and still wasn't old enough to date.

My birthday would be coming later that spring. *I'll just wait till then*, I thought. I focused on my grades and my life with Ida.

Every one of us was doing well in school. Jacinth and Rose had been moved up a grade because they were too advanced in their classes. I saw Dr. Otais every week for six months. I wrote poems, and talked to him like he was a wise old wizard. I found answers to all my pain, but then the pain kept coming, and I had to block it to get through school. We visited my parents only a few times, and I wrote one or two letters to my Dad. There was still a hole in my heart, but life was putting something new in its place and I had to go with it.

Chance Williams's best friend, Johnny Valentine, had a lot of money, and together they drove around in a Camaro and went off campus for lunch. Johnny also went out with a lot of girls. I didn't like either of them at this point, and when Johnny asked me out, I reluctantly said I would go to lunch with him but not date him. We went out to lunch; I rode in the back of the Camaro, while he and Chance sat in the front. Then we went to Johnny's house. I don't remember having lunch; I just remember us in the den with Johnny grabbing me up and rolling around with me on the floor, and out of the corner of my eye I could see Chance sitting in the chair with all of his manhood prodding from within. We drove back to school. I left Johnny's car certain that my crush on Chance had returned.

It was a Friday night and the Española Sundevils were playing a basketball game against another local team. I stood on the side of the railing watching the players from down below. The red and yellow Sundevils ran up and down the court. Chance walked up and stood beside me, his frame making me a shadow next to him.

"So, who's going to win tonight?" he asked.

"Hmm, not sure" was my response.

"Well, I have an idea," he said. "How about if we win I take you to dinner, and if we lose you take me to dinner."

"Ha, well if you win the bet, I'm taking you to McDonalds, and if I win you are taking me to a nice restaurant."

"Agreed," he said and reached over to shake my hand. Our skin touched, and fire ran through me. The end of the night came quick, and the Sundevils won. It was time for my first date; the only issue was that I was three months shy of being sixteen, so Ida wasn't going to let me go. I couldn't say that to Chance. He said, "How about next Friday, a real date, I'll meet you after the social." They were called socials—the Friday-night parties that people threw could be in any place, someone's house, or out in a field. Kids knew how to get booze, and how to get drunk, and how to get laid. My connection to my past was the furthest thing from my mind. I hadn't had a session with Dr. Otais for weeks. I was ready to go to a social.

Friday came and I met Chance there. I had one beer while standing around a bonfire that was lit out near a cliff dwelling. I was cautious with my drinking as I witnessed its shadow beneath the drunken spirit. I watched the flickering light of the fire burn. Chance came over to me, took off his football letterman jacket, and put it on me. It was cold out and I felt tucked in and warm with it on. The fire and drinking and the voices faded. I had come with a girlfriend, and he asked if he could take me home. My heart pounded. *Home?*

We drove away from the gathering. There were houses all alongside the riverbanks of the Rio Grande, the temperature cool at night, the cottonwood tree branches dancing in the wind, the night air blowing against my skin.

We pulled up near a tree and parked the gray Audi. It was a nice car for an eighteen-year-old boy. Chance looked nothing like a boy; he was every bit the man I had seen almost two years earlier those first few weeks of school. Heat came up through the floorboards of the car, and more heat came through my body. He pushed my seat all the way back and climbed on top of me. I felt his body, his firm, stout legs and arms hovering over me. His lips met mine, wet and soft, deep kissing into the night. Steam formed on the windows; he cracked the window so we could breathe, and climbed back on top of me. His hands cupped my face and rubbed my neck, caressing me all the way down to my breast. I felt his hand and pushed it back; he stopped for a minute, and then we melted together with clothes on. I felt his hand reach down for my belt on my blue jeans; he took the buckle and unhooked it. I bolted up, pushing him off of me.

"What are you doing?" I snapped at him.

"Sorry, what? I thought, I thought you wanted this, too."

"Wanted to what? I'm not going to sleep with you. Don't even think of trying that again."

He climbed back over to his seat startled. "I'm so sorry, some girls—"

"Some girls what?" I said. "Well, I'm not some girl. Don't plan on going out with me if you just want to sleep with me."

"That's not all I want, I really like you," he said as he started the car. I was now embarrassed; I should have known better than to start making out with him. I wasn't sure where to set my boundaries, until it was almost too late. I'd have to work backwards now to make sure he understood what I wanted in a relationship.

He started the car and we drove away from the cottonwood trees, the dark riverbank behind us. I was already late. He walked me to the door.

"I really like you. Can we go out again?" he was very polite.

"Not sure," I said, opening the door and shutting it in his face. I had put my foot down, but knew it would be hard to do again. I quietly tiptoed to my room and crawled into bed without any lights.

Love is a burning flame
Love will find you
No matter your name
Love will come
At any hour
It won't matter
Your resistance
It won't matter
What you do
Love will come for you

I avoided Chance for the next three months, only because I couldn't date. He continued to ask me out, and I'd say, "Sure, I will meet you here or there" and then I wouldn't show up. He had girls coming to me asking me why I wouldn't go out with him—he was such a nice guy, everyone liked him, and he wanted to know why wouldn't I give him a chance.

I told them I didn't respect him because he went out with so many girls. He got word of that and met me alone in the hall one day.

"Hey, what's the deal? I really like you, I know you're not like other girls, and I really like you. Can you give me a chance?" His eyes melted into mine, his puppy dog look on such a handsome face, I couldn't say no any longer and my birthday was only a week away. "Pick me up next Saturday at 7 p.m."

"Dinner?" he said.

"Yes, dinner."

I had my first date with him on my sixteenth birthday. He picked me up in the gray Audi, which turned out was his mom's car. I found him to be charming in a quiet space; he said few words but when he spoke it meant everything. I liked more than just the way he looked; his heart was deep, buried inside of him from things that were not obvious. He was part Santa Clara Indian Tribe, and on the weekends he spent time working on pottery with his grandmother, who was his Native connection. *Wow*, knowing this I *really* liked him; there was more to him than his handsome face. Looking across the dinner table with the dim restaurant lighting, I fell into him. He got me home by midnight, my curfew time. He walked me to the door and kissed me softly, wet moisture, like another lifetime spanning across time.

I had completely ignored Ida's talk with me about love. It was buried somewhere in me, the same place my childhood was buried.

The days passed the fire between us, as it burned deeper and deeper. Months of summer were upon us; we were no longer in school and the night belonged to us: the riverbank, the night owls, the gathering of young people camping among forest trees, the sunlit days on paved streets, and bedroom talks with lava lamps flowing. Warm skin on skin, hand on hand, night after night. Ida sensed she was losing me and tried to have a talk with me one evening.

"I know you are following curfew, but Chlo, you have to think about your future. Please think about every decision you're making."

Ida could have said this to me a thousand times. There was no hearing it. I slipped under the spell that so many young people go through. We choose a partner based in feeling, sexual hormones, chemistry between our senses—love feels like it is wrapping you up inside a bubble and nothing else breaks through.

Young Love

I dated Chance for all of my high school years, and into my college years. I didn't want to date anyone else. He left high school two years before me, this making things a challenge. It took me away from my youth, away from my volleyball, and tennis, and other boys my age. It took me away and I didn't even notice. I held onto him the way any broken girl holds onto a man she loves. She wants it to be better, she dreams it to be better, and when there was a question that he was unfaithful to me, I still convinced myself it wasn't true. It got messy and black and purple like the wounds Nye had from his accident when we were young. I couldn't separate the colors of the good love, and the mistaken things I thought were love. I couldn't navigate the fissures, the cracks in the earth there were the molding of this young love.

I did everything I could to keep my grades up. Ida had hoped I would apply to college out of state. I wanted to go to Puget Sound in Washington State. I dreamed of that coastline, that air I had never felt. It called out to me, and I was sure I would make it. Chance and I had broken up once or twice. He went away a few hours' driving distance to a local college, and there was more talk of his being unfaithful. When it came time for me to get serious about my college of choice, we were talking again, and seeing him made things impossible. When I embraced him it was like coming home. Since I had been lost from home for so long, this feeling was even stronger. He'd wrap me up in his large arms, my body then nuzzled into his chest; I could feel his heartbeat coming through his body and wanted to be inside the walls of love. I decided last minute to go to school in state. We would both go to The University of New Mexico, a few hours away in Albuquerque.

The last summer with Ida flew by, like a blue jay from my childhood, flying overhead. It was August and we loaded all of my belongings into the van. We drove the stretch of blacktop away from Ida's home near the riverbank. The same stretch of blacktop I had driven on a few years before, a tiny hint of hope inside my broken chest, as my social worker took my sister and me to our new home. I saw the desert bushes sticking up from brown hillsides and now knew the land like the back of my hand. I had become a young woman on these roads, had found myself in the world, and wanted to find my new life moving beyond everything I knew.

We cruised through the town of Española. I'd had a love-hate relationship with this town, much like I did my teen years, desire and longing mixed with growing and letting go, a bittersweet taste of life forever imprinted on my tongue. Tiny brown stucco houses on small streets said their goodbyes. The people were the heart of this place, the center of the blood pumping through the cold, dark nights of loss. I would miss the people. Large Hispanic families, small stores, little authentic New Mexican restaurants. There was no place like it, but I was ready for a new beginning.

Ida's love had given me wings to soar, but soaring meant to rise above the noise of the world, all of the judgment of who I should be, the thick coat of youth weighing heavy on me. Boys wanted me to be beautiful, strong, sexy, and smart. Girls wanted me to be beautiful, strong, sexy, smart, and a good listener. With all that everyone else wanted from me, I couldn't see my own self. Self-worth was not taught in school.

I had stopped seeing Dr. Otais my junior year after he moved his practice back to Santa Fe. He was making a path with me, a path that would lead me to self-worth, but the path was dim, and with all the pressures of youth it was hard to keep my sense of direction without the support of someone else holding up the lantern for me to see my way. Chance was a deep well with his emotions; he rarely let them be completely exposed. He too needed someone to hold a lantern for him to find a new way. I tried to be that lantern for him and he held on tightly, but it didn't work, because we needed to grow separately to grow up.

On the Way to Independence

Ida drove me the two hours to the University of New Mexico. It was the fall of 1994. I thought about my dream, which had been to attend the University of Puget Sound, a small liberal arts school set on ninety-seven acres in Washington State. It was just the kind of place my soul dreamed of. I had made several inquiries to go, but gave up on my acceptance, because I was still talking with Chance and thought that he and I might get back together. I believed it was his fault that I didn't follow my dream, but the truth I would learn later was that it was my own fear, my own pieces of the little girl locked inside. Without knowing it, I deeply wanted to be closer to my mom and dad. They were still living in the same cabin in the woods, and it was only a few hours away.

Ida pulled into the parking lot of the Coronado residence hall, where I had been placed by Admissions. We unloaded the van; all my belongings fit into just two boxes. We carried them up the steps of the dorm where I would soon be on my own. I sat in the van with Ida before she left. She hugged me tight. I now knew that hugging Ida was coming home, and this gave me some perspective on my feelings for Chance.

"Chlo, you've made it this far," she said, her voice cracking a bit. "I'm so proud of you. You started where you did and there is no telling where an education can take you." The light outside the van was musty, a bit of wind was blowing through the opened windows. I felt the presence of nature coming back to me. It always came back to me in the most important moments.

Ida measured life by the quality of truth in each moment. She knew this was a big moment for me and she wanted to ensure me that I was someone, that I was really important, and that I could do anything with my life. On my outer shell, I appeared quite confident and in fact may have been in comparison to many eighteen-year-olds, but deep inside my little girl self was quite shaky.

"Thank you, Ida. I can never thank you enough."

I got the words out. I had a hard time telling Ida how I felt. I feared that if I let out all my feelings, I'd never be able to pull them back in. Ida had saved my life. She was my intervention, my turning point toward wholeness. How could anything I say at eighteen affirm that to her?

When I returned to the dorm room, my roommate was unpacking her bags. It was on the second floor of a towering tan building with hundreds of dorm rooms. One small room with two beds, the size of the room I spent most of my early years sleeping beside my sister. I would now sleep next to a complete stranger. This would be interesting. I felt excitement more than anything else; after all, making it to college was one of my big markers for making it in the world.

"Hi, I'm Lindsay," she reached out her hand.

I shook it firm, like my father had taught me to do. We sized each other up while making nice conversation. She had shoulder-length blond hair that was messy, and green eyes. *She's playing the hippie part*, I thought. I was the real hippie, but was wearing a tight-fitted dress that showed all my curves. My hair was neatly combed and I had on a pair of shoes with a slight heel. Lindsay was in shorts, a tie-dye tee and sandals.

We had been placed in the dorms together based on a survey we had answered on our likes and dislikes. I wasn't sure at the moment if we would fit, but by evening it was clear that Lindsay was my other piece to the puzzle. We talked for hours about our excitement over college. I learned that Lindsay came from a broken past too. Her parents were divorced and she had been transplanted from her beloved California to New Mexico with her mother. Our biggest thing in common was that we both had a first love that we felt had destroyed our insides in one form or another. We loved and hated boys, loved and struggled over our parents, and couldn't wait to be free of it all. The nights rolled into days and we were halfway through our first semester.

It was a time of youth, a time to fly, and time to stay up late with no reason why. The collage of colors from night to day, from classroom to dorm room, was a fun and fast time. I was now in my own revolution, years later after the counterculture movement; music was the heart of life. Lindsay introduced me to Tom Petty and the Heartbreakers. We drove the night streets listening to "Wildflowers." I was aware there were lots of drugs and drinking at every party and my long journey to where I'd come heeded warning. I'd reached the college age that both my mother and father experimented with drugs. My father once told me he had done something called an eight ball in which he shot heroin and took cocaine at the same time. It had a seething trickery of a soul within itself, and it would take your life either slowly or quickly—it had no conscience about it, he said. He never tried it again. He was friends with Janis Joplin and some of the others rising to fame at that time. He watched as their talents grew and their minds became lost. Marijuana was the only drug he didn't feel was dangerous. Even with that, I didn't want to try it. I stayed clear of any drugs all together, with the exception of drinking beer, wine, and some shots of tequila. It all knocked me on my butt. The lights would spin at parties, boys and girls faces all fading till morning, no room for logic, all room for letting go. I had plenty to let go of, but letting go of my body or my morals was not going to help. I partied with Lindsay and many others but kept myself tucked in tight on who I thought I was. A country girl at heart, a girl who wanted to be deeply in love with my life and with the man in my life, a young girl who wore her heart on her sleeve in the search of life's meaning.

Lindsay was fun and free, making her own choices. I watched her be a girl, a woman, a child, a seeker, and lover of life and a crying mess at times, as we both were. One of the biggest things I learned from her without her speaking of it was that you can make God complicated or you can make God simple. She wasn't raised in a religious home and wasn't sure if there was a God or a Jesus. The simplicity of it was that God was all in the good and kindness of love, the realness of humanity. There was a right and wrong and it was all formed around how we treated each other. The complicated was a million other things, like war and all the rules of the world, that if you didn't follow them, they made you a bad person. She reminded me a little bit of my childhood friend Sage, except it was clear that she had not been raised in the woods. Girls who were raised in the woods had a firm handshake that took you by surprise. They might arm wrestle every girl in their class, even some of the guys, and never be defeated. Not sure if Sage did any arm wrestling, but if she had I'm sure she would be a champion at it like me.

I was okay beating Lindsay at arm wrestling, but when it came to her not believing in a God I believed in, I wasn't sure how I felt. I wanted her to feel the grace I had often felt in my spiritual connection, the comfort that came in my darkest hours, the hand of Jesus that led me while climbing the cliff with a broken leg. However, her differences gave me room to question things, and that felt good. I had felt at a loss for many years by not being as connected to nature. The sounds of the city, the rolling cars, the billboards, and the constant noise were all distractions from feeling and being. When I hurt inside, the woods were not there to hold me. It was subtle but big, and my heart knew it. Lindsay became my tree branches in the world. She was the human connection that I had longed for at ten years old. There was something very powerful about living in the world and it was this human connection.

The Big Lesson

We spent late nights talking, Lindsay and I. We watched the lava lamp in our room bubble up and down until the quiet stillness of morning. Something about being young keeps you up all night. You are either questioning everything until the wee hours, or out living the experience to get the questions answered, until the wee hours. Lindsay and I did both, yet we could never seem to get any real answers on love. Our conclusion was that it was one big lesson and we were tired of the learning.

We recounted our stories on love and life to make sense of them all. In these moments things became very clear. I recalled a few months into dating Chance, he'd had this great idea to go night sledding. He picked me up around 7:00 p.m. It was dark out and hard to see the white packed snow on the hills near Ida's house. We drove to the top of the highest ridge. He brought with him some big, round inner tubes, for sledding. I could feel my breath in the cold night, my hands warm inside gloves, the stars packed in the sky, the snow packed on the earth.

Chance jumped on first and rode his body down the side of a cliff for about fifty yards. I looked up at the sky, there was my old friend the moon; I hardly looked for her anymore since being in the city, but love had taken me back to loving the moon. I watched the moon and listened as Chance yelled at me from down below. "Hey, are you coming? It's a smooth ride."

I threw my body on the inner tube and glided into the night air. Pure exhilaration flying into the open air in darkness, a hint of the white snow beneath me, until I flew off the path and slammed face first into a rock! The numbing severe pain cracked though my entire face.

"Awe!" I screamed out. Chance came to me quickly and carried me up the hill. We got into the truck.

"Oh my God, don't touch it, it's so bad." I tried to breathe through blood gushing down from my mouth and onto my shirt. My shirt was soaked in blood.

Chance looked at me in the light. "Oh, you cut open your whole lip. You may need to get stitches."

I took my scarf off and held it over my mouth, fighting back tears. We drove to Ida's, then to the ER. Six stitches later, my top lip just under my nose was stitched back together. This would be my relationship with Chance. Pure exhilaration until faced with the brokenness.

I was forced at such a young age to let go of so many things that I didn't want to let go of. They included Chance, even though I knew there was a healthier love somewhere in the world. In him was the young mystery of a boy, that deep, soul-seated handsome fella that could never reveal to me his true self. I thought my commitment to our love would get us through anything. But confusing commitment with old loss is asking the sun to change its pattern of rotation that's gone on for millions of years.

My lungs burned and heaved with fire, a fire of letting go of someone that I'd loved, of a dream that I had dreamed. At the bottom of the bucket when all had been emptied out, there was my childhood, my mother and father still waiting for me to heal them.

Come now, Chlo
Let us take you back
Let us tell you what
It's really about
Lets us show you
The door
Get up off the floor
Dear child
It's not about the man
Before you
Or any man that shall come
After

I was surely broken, but the only path to healing starts with acknowledging the broken heart. I did get up off the floor, I climbed stairs and mountains, stayed connected to Ida, and crawled my way back to God. And somewhere in those moments, in those years, I crawled my way back to my mother and my father. It was a slow crawling with many wet tears on my face.

I wrote my father many letters. I asked him questions about why he chose the life he had chosen. I blamed him for not being there for me for the years of my youth, blamed him for my broken heart, and blamed him for my mother's broken heart. Blame, blame, blame as the ink poured onto the page, the white page covered from corner to corner. I was on fire when I wrote and when it came time to send it, I would re-read the letters and tear them up. At the same time, I also saw his sorrow, felt his sadness, and wanted nothing more than for him to be healed, to no longer be alone, to find his greatness and be with us in the world.

I would get a poem in my heart and sing it out loud.

This old man
He is love
This old man he
Lives with doves
This old man he is alone
This old man has a broken
Past
For this old man
My love will last

My father had enough pain. He had buried a son who was only fifteen, and lost all of his other children a few years later. He suffered alone in his journey on the mountain. Clearly he deserved love, and blaming him would bring me no answers. I still saw his little boy face lit with grace, and wished for his salvation. I believed him about the world. I had lived in the world long enough now, and saw the truth of what my father saw: a wounded nation of indoctrinated minds; too many followers and not enough leaders. Not enough connected to the heart, and too much stuff, too many choices. Nothing was real and it was all for sale. My father wanted everything about my childhood to be real—the pain of it, the joy of it, the wind, rain, and sunshine of it. It was all real, and deep down I knew it, but I wasn't ready to go back to him and say it. I needed more letters written so I could tear them up.

Forgiveness: The First Step in Letting Go

Along my path to forgiving my father, on which I was far from the completing the journey, I worked on forgiving Chance. I always thought he should have known better, done better, understood love better. Though he loved me at times, at other times he buried me deep in a casket of hurt. One night sitting alone in my apartment, no man to distract me, I realized how young Chance was during our time together. I knew that he had gone on to be with a woman he had started dating during our final breaking up.

I had met his girlfriend once while working out at a Gold's Gym. She was a cute, thin, curly haired brunette. She wasn't particularly athletic, but worked at the desk at the gym. There was a question for both of us: if Chance had stopped dating me before he started dating her. I didn't care much for her, though I knew nothing of her besides what she looked like. One evening she came into the bathroom at the gym and stopped me before I exited the locker room.

"Can I talk to you for a minute?" her sweet voice bounced off the lockers.

My heart sank inside of my chest. I must have glared at her. *She was a brave one*, I thought. I had just started taking kickboxing classes, where I was doing full-on fighting with both boys and girls. I was pretty ready to kick someone's butt.

"Sure," I replied.

The room spun for about five to ten minutes. I felt my insides twisting and turning as the dim overhead light shone down on us. She was kind, decent, and respectful as she showed me a doorway to knowing the truth. I don't remember her exact words, but she wanted me to be clear about her intentions, and to know how she and Chance had gotten involved. She had known that I had been with Chance for the last four years, and she had known how much he adored me, how he couldn't bear to let me go, nor could he tell me all of who he was. He needed me to see him the way I saw him, a young knight who was brave and worthy of my love. The minutes passed and the light came into me like a stream of morning light from my childhood. Jamie, I learned was her name, wanted truth and she wanted love, just as I did.

It was a summer evening and we both felt the breeze on our skin as she walked me to my car. She hugged me, and gave me reassurance of my place in the heart of the man that she might end up with. It was a moment I became free. There was still much healing, but that was the doorway to my letting go.

When I later learned that she and Chance had a son, I wasn't the least bit jealous. There was no bitterness toward the other woman. Over the years she briefly kept in touch with me, always assuring me of my beauty and grace as a human being. I got to see how Chance was never the best match for me, how he was young and sometimes foolish in his ways, and that he was human like so many men in the world. There are golden angels on the earth; there are healers and lovers of goodness at every crossroads in life, if you are open to letting them in. Jamie was just that for me.

What It Means to Be Family

I was living in an apartment with a good friend of mine, Tenille Otero. Tenille was a beautiful Hispanic girl I'd met my freshman year of college. We were destined to meet, she and I. I walked one afternoon from the dining hall at the university, the concrete beneath my feet, a hard ground I had grown accustomed to after years of being away from the soft dirt of the land. Tenille was passing me on the sidewalk and we both stopped out of nowhere and started chatting. I don't even know if we exchanged names, it was like an old familiar friend had stepped back into my life.

She came from a large family, and by large I mean her father came from a family of nine siblings, four boys and five girls. I couldn't keep count of all the aunts, uncles, and cousins, but there was something similar in their faces, their walk, their loud, joyful voices that rang the air. They had lots of social gatherings at the Oteros' house, in which Tenille's mom, a classic beauty with luminous hair and graceful style, was the center of the party. She glided across the room, putting her touch on everything and everyone; her hands made the food that fed the soul and her smile gave way to grace. Her dad, Ray, was a jovial fella with huge muscles protruding from his arms, legs and chest; a solidness of heart rang the room when he spoke. And her brother Joseph, a younger version of his father, was quiet but strong inside. Going to Tenille's was an adventure in family. The affection in that house poured like a good class of wine. If you listened closely you would hear not just the party in them, but the struggle as well. I learned from the Oteros that families are not perfect, they are not without brokenness; they may suffer with illness, doubt, all the struggles of humanity, but the thing that keeps them a family is love. The thing that keeps them strong is love. My notion on family had been pretty wrecked, but there was something in the idea of family as love that gave me acceptance for my past and hope for my siblings and parents to still be considered a family.

Now, Tenille and I were living in an apartment together, finishing up our college degrees and living the good life of the early twenties. I had just turned twenty-one.

I hadn't seen my mother for some months now, though I often thought of her, and hoped she would find the courage to leave my father. It was a Saturday when she showed up on my doorstep with Carey. I was in shock when I opened the door and Carey stepped inside with her.

"I brought Mom down for a visit," he said.

He left her with me for a few hours. We sat in my room and talked. It was harder to feel her heartbeat, like I had heard in the past. She was even more distant, the blood in her body more still, the look in her eyes more frozen. She was aging.

"Mom, why don't you leave?" I said, feeling like this was the thousandth time I had asked her that, and once again she would go back up the mountain to him. As a husband he was a different man, and when I spoke of him as a husband he was no longer my father; I saw through the eyes of a woman now and not the eyes of a daughter. I had felt the sting of love, but only a small fringe of what my mother felt, for she had followed her dream of a man into the woods. She sacrificed her whole life to be with him, to give every breath to him. She had loved him through and through. She felt his heartbeat inside his chest before she felt her own, and that was the problem. *I'll never do that for a man,* I thought. *I will never lose track of my own heart, I don't care who the guy is.*

She couldn't even cry, for God's sake, she couldn't even feel her insides anymore. *Enough was enough, she needed to feel again. Let him die in the woods, it's his dream to live there anyway.* I didn't even have to speak all the words to my mother; she felt me from across the room. I told her about my breakup with Chance. It was over, and it needed to be over—it didn't matter how much I loved him.

We sat on my bed. Her face looked like I had gotten through to her, but when Carey showed up to get her she headed out the door with him to go back.

"Bye, Mom," I said, closing the door to the sunlight that came in from the west. The door shut, and I stood in silence. I didn't know when I would see her again. I went back to my room and saw my mom's purse sitting on the bed.

The doorbell rang. I opened the door and there she and Carey stood.

"She forgot her purse," he said. I motioned for her to come in. She walked into my bedroom, the evening light brilliant on my flower-covered bedspread. She sat down on the bed.

"I'm not going back," she said, her head bowed to the floor. "I'm not going back."

I didn't know if I could believe it, but I would damn sure try. My mind raced with what she would do, *where would she live, how would she make it?* She had been living for twenty-five years out in the woods. She didn't know how to use a phone, or drive a car, or do anything in the world, but that didn't matter, she wasn't going back.

I told Carey and he came in and hugged her. He let tears run down his cheeks as he wrapped his arms around her. "Mama, it's gonna be okay, Mama." He stood up and left us for the night. I asked her what she wanted to do.

"Well, I'll stay with you," she replied.

My mind went to Tenille and my great apartment and my life that I had gotten together so well. I had no boyfriend but lots of choices, I was in great shape, a sophomore in college paying my own way, hanging out on Friday nights at the country bar where I loved to dance with cowboys who tilted their hats down for me. But that didn't matter. She wasn't going back.

I went upstairs to talk with Tenille about what was going on. We whispered back in forth in the kitchen.

"Chlo, she can't live with us, I'm sorry."

"I know," I said. "I will have to move so I can help her. I have no choice, I have to help her."

Tenille agreed and said that she would move out and that my mom and I could stay in the apartment together.

The woman in battle
She rages she rages
She turns the pages
Of her life
She holds her hands to
God,
She breaks though the
Rod
That held her bound
No freedom found
She rages, she rages
She turns the pages of
Her life
Until there is none left unturned

My mother's battle was much bigger than mine. She had years of living in the wilderness and a deep mix of love and rage for my father. Her battle scars were deep and no soldier could carry her out of this war, no father or mother could save her. Her life was hers to look on at the bottom of the bucket. It was hard for me to understand this, to let go of this, to let go of thinking I had to save her. I did everything I could to help her regain a life. I sheltered her for some time and put myself through college. She was a wounded bird that would find her way. It was too much for me to bear.

I met with her over coffee and explained that we could not live together. She would have to find a way to live on her own. She denounced me as her daughter, her own loss raging beyond any logic. I could barely see straight but my heart knew the truth. I buried my face in pillows and cried it out. She had to find her way, her energy was stuck inside of me like a bullet shot from a gun. It was there from birth and from years held against her chest; it took away my childhood, and took away my girl self, and it made me into a woman before I wanted to be a woman. I had to cut the cord from this energy. Healing was deathly hard when you had so much trauma, but Dr. Otais's words rang out again and again, from my earlier times with him. "You must sit in the silence, sometimes it can take months, even years, and the answers will come." I knew I could only save myself, I could not save my mother, I could not save my father, and I didn't want to be in the crossfire any longer.

It was six long months of separation between my mother and I; her blue eyes were piercing my memory as I tried to feel normal. She left in a little red Nissan that I had helped her practice driving in only a few months earlier. I feared for her life. How would she make it? Where would she go? It was summer, I was out of school and the burning heat of the city concrete under my feet left me feeling empty. The phone rang.

"Chlo, it's Mom."

I was so relieved to hear her voice. "Mom, where are you?"

"Can you meet me for coffee?" she requested.

I drove to Central Avenue, the cars on all sides of me just shapes in the distance. What's my mother going to say? I was a bit guarded, ready for anything, but glad she was okay. I walked into the coffee house, spotting her in a seat way in the back, noticing she had cut her hair and dyed it a brilliant red, the color of her youth. She looked younger and I could see her blue eyes. I ordered coffee and went to sit down.

"You look good, Mom." I sat across from her, making eye contact.

"I owe you an apology," she said. "I never should have spoken to you like I did, and I'll never do it again." She was a grown woman coming to terms with her life. My insides wanted to spit up the tears, but I held it in.

"Thank you," I said. "I know it's going to be okay, Mom."

We all have days in which we change, maybe it's a cold day, maybe it's a warm day, maybe it's a day you can't remember because you've blocked it out, but the day is there, the moment when God pulls you from the rubble of life, the dark circles under your eyes become clear, and the rest of the world feels and sees you.

My mother was on her way. She signed up to take college classes in my last year of school. She had dropped out of the University of Texas when she was a sophomore. She took philosophy, English, and creative writing. We sat in creative writing class together. She didn't want to tell anyone that she was my mother, and I was fine with that. We wrote about life, about old life, and new life, and life on the mountain. Now and then the teacher would look over at us, after we had both read a piece from living on the mountain, the expression on his face was, "How do you two know each other?"

One day after class he approached us and asked, "Are you related?"

"I'm her mother," my mom blurted out. I guess she was finally okay with it. We sat over coffee in cafés writing our papers, reading to each other, and talking about men and life. My mother knew a lot about men and life, and I accepted her friendship as the past moved further behind us. I had always wanted my mother to simply be herself. She was an amazing woman with such knowledge and insight.

One Day You'll Be Safe

I graduated college thinking of my father. He had been a scholar with a full ride to Yale. What would his life have been like? I asked this question often, what would his life have been like? A great sorrow would come over me and I would daydream about how his life could still be something, about how he could make a life as an artist, a musician, anything he wanted, even "the animal whisperer." My dad could do so many things, so why be disconnected from the rest of the world? My anger at the situation would rage, but at least my mother had made it back to the world and made a life for herself. I had her, and when she was next to me she made sense.

She was still a bit of an oddball, always saying things from out of left field, but she was with me. To be with my father, I had to drive all the way back up the mountain, sit in the middle of the woods, let him talk about his relationship to God, to the trees, and to the animals. I liked it for about four hours, but I could never stay the night. The sun would start to set and I would jump up in the middle of him playing a song.

"I gotta go, Dad, gotta get back before it's dark."

Sadness would stream his face and eyes. He had become the wounded soul seeking forgiveness for so many years, from so many, from all his children. He had given me an official apology for the way he treated my mother. Looked me right in the eyes and told me it was not right. I still could not let it go. I had dated several men and stayed in three long-term relationships after my breakup with Chance, but there was always an upheaval of doubt, fear, and distrust deep inside of me. It would take some digging to get it out. I didn't always like the digging, and one day I realized it was not about the digging—it was about the allowing. Allowing things to come to surface so I could let them go. But only through mistakes could I learn this, only through the experience of life, of wearing my heart on my sleeve, of conversations with men, arguments, another face walking out the door of my life.

I would remember those words, *"It's never about the guy before you,"* the wisdom God had offered me years before when he told me to pick myself up off the floor, after my breakup with Chance. Many a time I landed on the floor again, needing to be close to the earth, not some tile floor. Needing to be close to the woods, and close to my father. For years I made the trip to my father's, taking him food, staying as long as I could, and driving away at sunset. He would follow me out to the car, I'd push the brake off and start to roll backwards out of the yard with my car window down, and he would walk beside the car as I backed up. "Hallelujah, daughter, you came. God bless you, heavenly Father, for your forgiveness. Keep his name upon your lips, daughter. He will help you through."

One time he added, "I'm getting old, not much help to anyone from here."

"It's alright, Dad," I said while rolling in reverse out the yard slowly. "It's alright, Dad," I assured him as he reached inside the car window and hugged me one last time.

Every time I pulled out of the drive, I'd watch him stand at the top of the hill as I drove the winding stretch of road out of the property. I'd keep looking back, his tall frame getting smaller as he stood at the top of the hill watching me go. While driving, I was tucked inside a protected shell with the woods on all sides of me. I'd let my tears fall in this sacred space as I watched the deer jumping through the pine forest with the evening light resting on tree branches and doves landing for the evening. Somehow I had to accept my father and let it all go.

The Animal Whisperer

The concrete jungle was no place for a beating heart to feel. I walked these streets by day and night. Now a part of the world, I drove my SUV in high traffic with the constant motion and sound of civilization booming. It was the opposite of the blooming plants of my youth that took their time to grow freely in the sun as they reached for the sky; here everything moved quickly and you felt the need to keep up with it.

I was stopped at a red light, the crisp winter air wanting to get in through my window. I rolled down the window to breathe in the air and heard the loud pounding of someone's rap music jarring my ears. I rolled the window back up and cut my own radio off that was playing, Willie Nelson's, "Blue Eyes Crying in the Rain." *Blue eyes crying in the rain*, I thought about it. In the world people were so sheltered, they rarely felt the rain; they had umbrellas to keep them dry, coats and hats to protect the skin; they rode around in cars and trucks tucked into their own bunker of protection, cutting off connection from the air, the earth, and one another.

I thought of my father and how he'd now spent thirty-five years alone in the woods. He had always been very close with the animals, but now they were all he had. He and Juniper were the best of friends. *Remember that a horse can live to be forty, if well cared for.* Red lights where I'd wait in my car gave me time to reflect and often in these moments I'd think of my father and Juniper riding through the backcountry with no red lights. But on this day my heart was broken. I had seen my father that weekend. Making one of my visits before the last bits of fall, we sat in the living area with the old familiar sound of his voice and guitar playing. He got through one song and cried. He placed the guitar down beside his chair.

"I had to shoot Juniper," he said.

"What!" I reacted. "What do you mean?"

Juniper had gotten off the property and was chasing a group of mare horses a few miles away. My father tracked him down and when he found him, Juniper was lying down on a patch of ice with his leg bleeding from a severe cut. There was a snowplow blade that had been left in the field and it had blood on it. Somehow Juniper had cut his leg open on the blade and then fell on ice near the plow.

"Dad…" my voice cracked, I couldn't believe it.

"I tried to get him up, I tried, daughter, but I couldn't save him.

I had to help him from his suffering. His red blood poured out onto the icy ground from his head when I shot him. I never saw an animal bleed like that," he said.

I shrugged my shoulders, the lump in my throat a gigantic knot wanting to burst. *How could my dad shoot him?* I knew the answer to this; I was taught young that once an animal is severely injured, they couldn't make it in the wild. It was our job as the human caretaker to take their life in order that they not suffer.

"I shot him right in the temple, the best place to end it quickly," my father said.

My father was always teaching me a lesson. He gave me specific details so that I'd feel the experience and so that I'd understand all things real about life. Sometimes to end someone else's suffering we had to take on our own. My father was a tough man who could handle the blood of life, but I knew for certain he was crushed in losing his friend.

By spring my father had made a new friend. This time a bear, a female that had made her way onto the property. My father always felt an animal's energy and could tell if they had a good or bad intention in them. This bear was soft in the heart and my father greeted her one afternoon on the front steps of the cabin.

Animals need to feel our energy too, and as I learned from him, it is important that we align with our highest truth when speaking to them. Fear is a chaotic energy that startles them. You have to be completely in tune with yourself and your courage to approach a wild animal.

"Hello, girl," he spoke candidly.

She stood up on her back legs, making a low growl to greet him, bear to human, then landed back on all four paws and waited.

"What brings you this way?" my father asked her. He waited in silence, and then let her know she could stay around for a while, if she followed the rules.

The rules: she could eat from the compost in front of the goat pen, there were no goats at this time. She could not come inside the house, but could sleep on the porch.

They continued in a harmonious relationship for three weeks, until one evening after my father laid down to rest, he heard her tipping over all the buckets on the front porch and pushing against the front door.

It was late at night and my father stood inside, behind the heavy cedar door to the cabin.

"I told you that you must sleep outside." He spoke clearly though the closed door. Feeling the bear's energy a bit temperamental at that moment, he felt it was best to stay behind the door.

She banged on the door rapidly.

"I know you need more food. I don't have anything else for you, you better keep moving to take care of it," he stated.

She had stopped fussing while he waited in silence and then said, "I'm lying back down, good night, girl."

In the morning when he woke, she was gone.

I was impacted by my father's relationship with animals. There was no one like him in the world. I started to accept how different he was and see the gift in it. It gave me comfort that he was never really alone and he made me consider that animals were easier to get along with than people. It was a fair question indeed, as I'd now had several relationships with young men that I adored, but could never seem to get the relationship right. I had tried my best at this game of love. This game of give and take seemed to need a lot more give than anything else. I was twenty-seven years old and wasn't sure if I would get married and have kids, as I'd planned since I was sixteen.

The Heart of Two Men

Christian was a rugby player from Paraguay, South America. I was twenty-seven and not dating anyone for the first time in a long while. I watched him run the rugby ball down the long hundred yards of grassy field, the afternoon sun shining through his golden brown hair. He was one tough, athletic specimen of a man, with solid muscle and the heart of a lion. I felt his heart when he spoke, when he ran, walked, or smiled. He was funny, charming, and unusual. I had always felt I was unusual too, so for me it worked. We were both out of college, working, playing, running the nights with our friends, drinking wine—there wasn't too much to worry about.

And there it all began. I was captivated by so much of him and felt he was pretty much the opposite of my father in the way he was worldly. He had grown up in Paraguay, and had attended a private school in which he learned a dual curriculum for South and North America. He was bilingual and played the guitar. He grew up with money, but money was not at the core of his heart. He knew how to dance and would spin me in circles any time we were out. I was used to men who didn't know how to dance and stayed on the sidelines of life. Christian was full of personality and never on the sidelines. When I took him to visit my father in the woods, I didn't get the usual shocking response of "why would anyone choose this life?"

My father still spoke a bit of Spanish and greeted Christian in his first language, then later played him a song in Spanish. Christian was right there with him as the two men tapped their feet on the wood floors of my childhood. Christian was fiery like my father, and had deep connections to his past and country.

Paraguayans are a nice people, kind-spirited and rebel-like, with doors open to people from all walks of life. They are no strangers to the struggles of humanity, having survived many wars, including the War of the Triple Alliance, in which Argentina, Brazil, and Uruguay fought against them to bring down what was once a wealthy country in South America. During the War of the Triple Alliance, most of the men in the population were killed, leaving the country to be far outnumbered with women till this day. If you listen closely to a Paraguayan speak, you can hear the beating heart of loss, and love of country. Christian carried this beat inside his chest; he loved his country, and his family. Though he grew up with his monetary needs met, he was no stranger to the suffering and poverty of life, and in this place he could meet my father heart to heart. For some time in his twenties, my father had lived in Guadalajara, Mexico, where he learned the Spanish language. He then spoke Spanish to the natives at the Mesa in northern New Mexico. The two men, my father and Christian, would gather in the small cabin and play their guitars. My father played songs in Spanish and English, songs he wrote himself, while Christian played cover songs from music of the late '60s, Led Zeppelin, being one of his favorites. I thought that Christian was so different than my father, being that he used the currency of money for living life. I would learn they had quite a few similarities. Where my father was a young man in the sixties, following the counterculture movement and rebelling against the establishment, all through the pounding background of a new music, Christian would later spend much of his young years seeking the same music. The sixties music of The Beatles, The Doors, Jimi Hendrix, Janis Joplin, Bob Dylan, and the Rolling Stones were all a part of Christian's music vocabulary and rebel sense of being.

There were more serendipitous connections to the boy who was raised on the other side of the world from me. We could not have grown up more different, me on dirt floors in the middle of the woods and he on tile floors of a large hacienda where cooks and maids were a part of the daily living.

When Christian was sixteen years old, he got into a car accident in which he nearly died. It took him four years of dating to tell me about it, but one night there we were with him shedding light on his past. Like many of the youngsters of Paraguay, he had been out very late on New Year's Eve. It was five o'clock in the morning and he and a good friend of his were returning from San Bernardino, a small village outside of the much larger capital city of Asunción. Christian's friend was driving while Christian was in the passenger seat of the SUV. Christian checked with Rafael to see if he was good to drive.

Raf assured him that he was fine.

"I'm going to lie down in the back seat till we get home," Christian replied. At 5:00 a.m., he was finally worn out.

During the hour-long drive somewhere along the red dirt road, the SUV swerved out of control and flipped three times. Christian awoke to his body being bounced from seat to ceiling as the SUV rolled over and over, finally hitting a tree. The tree split and crashed right through the passenger-side window, where Christian had been sitting earlier. Christian was thrown from the vehicle and onto the dirt. He was unconscious and by the time he came to, a circle of women had gathered around his body. They stood over him with rosaries praying. He had faded in and out, not sure if he was dreaming or dead. A few minutes later, he was loaded onto the back of a little truck that was used for hauling bricks. They drove him to Asunción, where he was taken to the ER. He had a collapsed lung, broken ribs, and internal bleeding. Had he stayed in the front seat where he was sitting, it would have been certain death.

Christian shared the same birthday as my brother, John— June 21st. I didn't have full understanding of why my brother had to die young, but was certain it was a gift that Christian had lived. I would celebrate Christian's birthday every year and silently wish John a blessing.

My father said he would not go anywhere he could not take his pocket knife, so that meant no plane rides. When Christian and I got married in 2007 in Asunción, Paraguay, my father did not attend. The rest of my family, including my mother, made the trip. It was three days before Christmas, and the hot sticky streets of Paraguay were far more humid that I remember it being at my grandmother's in Houston. I would have been snowed in and huddled by the fire at Christmas back home, but it was the middle of summer in Paraguay. I loved the green hills and towering trees that popped right up in the middle of the city. The winding, broken streets filled with cars, motorcycles, and buses brought new meaning to a chaotic world. South America was buzzing with life, the rich, the poor, and few in between. The city was a hard place for me to feel comfortable, but I was captivated by all the nuances and courtesy of the people. You were constantly greeted formally with respect, and the service was impeccable, something Christian missed while living in the United States.

One of Christian's favorite places was outside the city, this the same place he had his accident when he was sixteen, San Bernadino. The small town of "Sanber" was a summer town located on the Ypacarai Lake. Red brick streets echoed the walls of Spanish villas, little houses dotted every corner, and right in the center of town was a little Catholic church with wooden benches and wooden windows that opened to the rows of green trees meshed against the rustic yellow of the church. This was the church where Christian and I would say our vows. In front of several hundred people, of which only a few I knew, it was a dream for him to be married there, in the country that held his heart, and it was a dream of mine to hold his heart. After our wedding we returned to the States and began our life, returning to Paraguay a few times a year for visitation. I had always wanted my children to understand different cultures, to travel, and to have a broad sense of the world at large. This was good, but there were many struggles.

Turns out holding someone's heart can be a long journey to which each person is required to grow, sometimes in ways they don't yet know how. Our relationship split apart like a seed that had been planted in too shallow a dirt. We lacked the foundation for making it through the rocking storms; the seed got picked up by the wind and carried across the land. Our marriage would never become a full-grown tree.

The Dark Night of Relationships

The dark night comes when you are sleeping, when you are awake; it brushes past your shoulder and allows itself into the body. Somewhere in the good of all things, in the powerful connection of two young people, in the splitting moment of a kiss, the problems of a marriage creep up. The lack of communication around all your differences, the tired nights, the long hours of work induced by a suffering world—it all catches up to the beating heart. If you don't have a similar past and similar ways of dealing with stress, tiredness, fear, worry, daily life, and the emotional evolution of becoming whole, then you may not make it.

Christian and I divorced in March of 2014. We had two beautiful children together. Jonah Oliver (Little Dove) and Sofia Azalea (Little Wisdom).

Christian loved babies. He was that guy at the grocery store that would ask to hold your baby while you were going through the checkout line. He was that guy at parties who would dance with the young children, flipping them into the air while teaching them about rock and roll. He had many layers, just as my father did.

I had watched my parents go through a lifetime of struggle. I had watched them learn a new way to love. My mother always gave me the best side of the story when speaking about my father; she told me why she had loved him, why she had followed him, and why he was a great father to me. In turn, my father sang songs about my mother, whenever I visited. He told me how she held me when I was a young child, and how she had labored in love for all of us. I drank red wine and broke bread with my father while he apologized for his temper, his sins, his life unspoken. Somewhere in those hours, my father was giving me the acceptance in my own story.

I knew that my true path to healing would come from within, and from drawing awareness from all the life I had lived. The lessons were clear. It took me three years post our divorce to realize that our love would become a full-grown tree, through Sofia and Jonah—their roots were grounded deep in the soil of love and their branches were all that beauty could be.

I would find a new way to love Christian.

Writing would be my doorway to awareness, my path to solitude within the walls of my own heart. Sometime after we divorced, I realized that I had prepared for the storm, I had been through enough trauma to know how to survive a divorce, but I had not prepared for a joyful, long-lasting relationship. No one had prepared me for that, no one had prepared my parents for that. In this culture we prepare for school, a career, long work hours, sports events, marathons, competition, getting ahead, taxes. We prepare for everything but having a good marriage and raising a family, and so when the dark night of a relationship arrives we almost don't know what hit us and then it's too late.

It's never too late, however, to get the lesson and do better next time. Watching my daughter, Sofia, holding hands with my father, walking that same dirt road I walked as a child was my grace. I stood in the distance watching them go, every year a new sunset, a new chance to let go. We would visit and they would walk, the tiny little strawberry blond toddler, one, then two, then three, four, and finally five.

At five, she raced to him, running a hundred yards of the yellow dirt road, and he lifted her into his arms. The years of forgiveness came with the birth of my children. I now had Jonah, who was almost two years old. Jonah was a bubbly little guy with a stout gait, glowing brown eyes and a grin that would sing to your heart. Sofia looked like my Grandmother Sally, with huge round blue eyes, soft white skin and strawberry blond hair, wild like mine when I was young. Both Jonah and Sofia loved my father; he wasn't awkward to them in any way. He looked like someone you might encounter climbing the side of a mountain in Nepal, his old ragged clothes, and hats, everything all meshed together with a purpose. For them it was a big adventure to visit the old man in the woods. Small children see the truth, and mine showed me that my father had made his path to forgiveness. He had done his work, he had been on bended knee before God a thousand times, and now God's grace shined upon the back of his head as he walked the road hand and hand with the two little ones. They were me inside, they were him inside, they were truth inside—the road had never changed, but my father was born again in my eyes.

Mother's Day

It's Mother's Day, 2009. Every year I take my mother for coffee and buy her flowers. Sometimes I buy cut flowers and sometimes a plant to hang in her window. Usually it's a geranium plant like the one that hung in our window when I was young. The flowers breathe life into our past and hope into our future.

We have come a long way, Mama and I. She has lived in the world for almost twenty years now. We have had our battles, our slow, mourning moments of trying to be a mother and a daughter. We have landed in a soft place that I would call an interesting friendship.

My mother is not like other mothers; that means so many things. Today I meet her outside the Co-op natural grocery store that's in her quaint neighborhood known as Nob Hill in Albuquerque, New Mexico. It's May 12th and the sky is a piercing blue, the air a just-right temperature to sit on a steel patio chair with the glistening sun burning down on us. Today I bring her cut flowers, a mix of deep reds and purples, from the Co-op, and we both sip decaf coffee, as we stopped drinking heavy caffeine years ago.

My mother is thin, and her henna-dyed, deep-red hair glistens against the blue sky. She has retained her beauty all these years, a sophisticated older-looking woman with blue eyes, a short curly bob, and a few freckles spotted about her face. She laughs and talks like a normal person whose life has been majestic. But I know and can see the scars of life riddled across her face, in her eyes. I hear it in her tone as she speaks. I'm five months pregnant with my first child. All of a sudden my mother and I have much more in common. I already know the aches and worries of a mother, the weighted feeling of a round belly resting on my pubic bone. My mother did this six times, I can't imagine.

We get to talking about John, who comes up often enough in conversation. Today we are at his burial, the cold snowflakes floating down onto me through the hot sun, as she speaks. I never saw my mother at John's burial. She was missing, but today she is telling me she was there, she was standing right there when we put him in the ground. She described the scene, the cold earth that would now hold her son, the deep woods that would cradle her loss, they were all right there inside of her chest, bursting through her blood as her heart pumped and her voice told her story.

I watched her eyes as she spoke. They were full of color and then turned gray as she said, "I realized that when we buried John, I had loved him too much."

I felt my round belly want to sink. *My baby must have felt that,* I thought. I kept my senses about me and responded, "Mom, you didn't love John too much, that's just how much it hurt to lose him. It's normal, Mom. Everything you felt was what you should have felt."

The conversation stops for a minute. My head is spinning with thought, then a moment of calm comes. I think of Ida and how much love she poured into me. She wasn't my mother, but she gave everything a mother could. I realize this, and in that moment I let go of any resentment I had over my mother not being able to love me fully. My baby swam in circles inside of me, my mother's eyes swelled with tears, but she couldn't speak. I pulled all the love I could up through my veins and out into my hands, and placed it on her. "You did everything you could, Mom. It's all okay, we are all okay."

My mother had made a life for herself in town; she lives alone in an apartment. She has become a Christian Buddhist. Jesus has always lived in my mother's heart and she has found her own path in being a Christian, but she also practices Buddhism. Buddhists were the only people who accepted my mother's Christianity. She tried traditional churches all around town and could not find a place for her spiritual expression and beliefs. The Buddhist Zen center was right in her neighborhood and she recalled going to the Zen center in her younger years in San Francisco, so there she found herself one day in sitting position, listening to the sound of her own breath. The Buddhists were open and kind, and loved the earth—all these things resonated with my mother. She would take Jesus with her into the Zen room and together it would all flow.

My mother's second practice outside of the spiritual work is reading. She likes stories from Russian author Joseph Roth about what happens to people under oppressive governments, war, and loss. He and my mother came from a similar heritage, western and northern Russia. He started out in the backwoods of Ukraine and made his way to becoming an educated man, a journalist and later a writer. My mother's father, Oscar, had emigrated to the U.S. from Latvia in 1904. My mother read a lot of books from Russian authors like Tolstoy and Dostoevsky. I imagine that she missed her father deeply and wanted to know who she was; through each word she read, her life was being revealed to her. These readings also gave her perspective on how hard life could be, helping her to heal from what seemed a very long journey of her own.

Through my mother's eyes I could see the world, just as my mother was my connection to the world when I was a child. She has read books on spirituality, Thich Nhat Han and many Tibetan study books. Historical nonfiction, memoirs, dietary books on juicing, and herb books on longevity and keeping all illness at bay are all on her shelf in her apartment. She often re-reads them as a form of caring for her aging body. My mother says she won't touch fiction because she doesn't want to even be breathed on by any non-truths. She never watches television and sometimes listens to political discussions on the radio. She once told me that if she had lived in the world she would have chosen the career of a choreographer, or a book critic. When it comes to my own writing, my mother has simultaneously become my biggest critic and my biggest fan.

On this Mother's Day, for the first time in many years I'm seeing my mother's heart, I'm feeling her life as it's unfolded like the pages of a book slowly peeling back each one. I'm in those pages with her and know it's been a work of art to have survived it and learned from it all. There are more pages to be written, more healing to seep into our bones, but for now the flowers and the coffee on this Mother's Day will mark the path to the rest of our journey.

Forgiveness Is the Path to Spiritual Connection

The more I was able to have compassion for my father, for my mother, for all the mistakes I thought they had made, the more I was able to feel. To feel meant to be alive and connected to all the parts of myself. The distraction of the world had pulled me away from nature, but avoiding my own pain had pulled me away from myself. I began to see and feel nature right in the midst of the chaos. A mulberry tree branch on my street reached out to me, the evening sun of my childhood was still there, lighting up my face. I learned to be still in the midst of the noise. It wasn't the same as being in the woods; it was something different, but it was there.

My intuition also grew stronger the more I was able to face my own pain, and this came most profoundly through writing. I was simultaneously writing, healing, and connecting to all the parts of myself that had been buried. My brother's death had always been a momentous thing for me, the feelings of grief never completely gone. The more I connected back to nature, the more I felt at peace with him.

In the softness of love comes an opened door. I felt John's presence for the first time while driving over a hillside with tall pine trees glowing in the evening light. It scared me at first, and I stopped the car and cried while looking at the tall pines. It was like he appeared out of nowhere, not physically, but it was him all around me. As the years moved on, I felt him in the same way. I got used to it and welcomed his boy-like presence into my space. I started to communicate with him as if he were there.

While writing the scenes of his death, I broke down. I had waited a long time to write these scenes, hoping that when I arrived as a writer, when I could truly write, then I'd be able to write these scenes. It didn't matter how many scenes I had written or how many books I'd read on writing—when the scenes arrived, I broke down. I was lying in my bed, tucked safely under a white down comforter, sobbing. The curtains pulled in the middle of the afternoon. I was awake with my eyes opening and closing, tears streaming my cheeks. The image of my brother strapped to a hospital bed with his head swollen and his legs broken kept coming to me. I saw blood all over his face and his broken body convulsing on the bed.

I was paralyzed with grief and could not move from this moment, when John's presence appeared to me on the right side of my body. I felt him hovering over me like a gentle guide, a shepherd boy coming with a message.

"Hey, come with me," he said. "Chlo, I'm not over there." He motioned his hand in the air for me to follow him away from my thoughts of him dying. "I'm not there anymore. I'm over here." He motioned again for me to come out of my paralysis. I kept sobbing and listened. I couldn't do it, I couldn't move. It was then out of thin air that he packed a snowball and walked over to me with it.

"Here, take this and throw it at me as hard as you can." He placed the snowball in my right hand and backed away, waiting for me to throw it. A game we played together when we were young. I grabbed up the snowball. Holding it tightly, I could almost feel how cold it was, even though it wasn't real. I was having a full on spiritual experience. John motioned for me to throw it at him. I launched it as hard as I could and it socked him right in the chest, to which we both burst out laughing. I was awakened from my paralysis of grief. I lay in the bed having this surreal experience; I had forgotten where I was. I then felt John needing to go and I started to get sad again. "No, don't leave yet," I started to cry as my heart spoke. He approached me one last time and whispered near my right ear.

"I have something for you" he said. I reached out my hand and he placed a book in it. The book was turned to the back cover, so I couldn't yet tell what it was. I grasped at the book, tightly holding on as John's presence faded. I was now alone and turned it over to the front cover. The front of the book was the picture of me at three years old, with the title, *The Soulful Child*.

A Man with Many Friends
Is Not a Hermit

My father spent his life building friendships. He was an introvert who loved people, who also loved to socialize, now and then. Clearly from his early days at the Hill School in Pottstown, Pennsylvania, all the way into Native American land and south of the border in Mexico, he made friends, played his music, and spoke from his heart. People would never forget him, that Jerry Gallaway, the man who left a handprint wherever he went. Where he was the outsider in his mind, the others wanted him to fit right in. They saw his strength, courage, and flare for life. After our leaving the small town of Lindrith, my father continued to have many friendships with his distant neighbors. Kevin Macpherson was one of my father's best friends. Kevin was like the old man of the sea, no stranger to the suffering of humanity; his worn and tattered body was still moving, his white hair a whisper in the wind. Kevin's daughters as well as a few other young folk in that backwoods community showed up with love to embrace my father, leaving me with an eternally grateful heart. There were so many interesting things about my father, and the walks of life that encountered him continued to show presence.

His two high school roommates at the Hill School were Peter Bassett and Fred Bingham, who had come from wealthy, established families that had long been alumni of the Hill School; these two fellas never knew what happened to their friend. He had been voted Most Likely to Be President of the United States in his senior yearbook, but that couldn't be—they would have noticed that. Fred, who had gone on to work on Wall Street, living in New York and all over the East Coast, was married and had raised his children in a most traditional way. Pete had become an oral surgeon and was living a good life in Phoenix, Arizona. The two men came together just before they turned seventy and decided to track down their old friend, Jerry Gallaway. It took some research, as they found little information about him online, but they came across Jerry's father, Ira Gallaway. He was all over the Internet, for books he had written, and ministries and tours he had led all over the world. Ira had made a name for himself.

Fred picked up the phone and called Ira. Ira remembered the young Fred from a dinner he had come to in their home when the boys were in their teen years, and Ira greeted him with surprise. His heart then sunk inside his chest when they wanted to know how they might find Jerry. Fred learned from Ira that my father had abandoned society all together many years earlier. Blown away by this finding, he congratulated Ira on all his success and reminded him of how much they loved Jerry. "He certainly was one special fella." Ira took the heartfelt expression and pulled it in close to his chest, allowing himself to feel some admiration for his son. The men hung up the phone, and immediately Fred called Pete to let him know.

"Pete, you're never gonna believe what's happened to our old buddy, Gallaway."

"Oh yeah? What's the story?" Pete said.

"He left the world all together and has been living out on a mountain range in northern New Mexico for nearly forty years! Pete was in shock as well, and after gathering themselves, the two men devised a plan for a road trip to track Jerry down. Fred would fly into Albuquerque from Florida and Pete would fly in from Arizona; then they would rent a car and drive north to find their friend.

Carey had spent years going back to my father. He had made his peace with him and was now helping my father in his old age. Bags of food, supplies, wine, conversation, he took to my father everything he could. He got him a cell phone. My father had lived for thirty-five years with no phone. The digital age was now in boom, cell phones were common, and when my father got his little flip phone, it was like a toddler seeing the world for the first time. My father made calls to all his family, to his brothers and sister, and to me. I spoke to him a few times a month, the calls becoming more and more frequent as he aged. I was already writing the book and would call him up to ask questions. It was sometimes hard to get an answer, but now and then he was clear as day and came out with the truth.

I was coming out of the grocery store on a hot summer day here in town. My cell phone rang and I saw it was my dad. I sat in the car with the window down while we spoke. He told me how hard his life had been and that he wouldn't wish it on anyone. I asked him if it was what he had wanted. He said when he was in his early twenties, he had dreamed of having a cabin in northern New Mexico. He was at the time working on his grandfather's ranch in Clovis, New Mexico, far to the south, near the border of Texas. This is where he dreamed. This is where he dreamed of going north, working with wild horses, and having his cabin.

"I just didn't know it would be a full-time life," he explained, "I thought I'd just come here to take a break from the world. Turns out I couldn't live in the world at all." There was silence on the line for a moment and then I spoke.

"You know you've done a lot of great things with your life, Dad. I have learned so much about all things real in life." I affirmed to him. He was getting another call on the other line. I couldn't believe it, the hermit in the woods was a socialite on his phone. "I'll call you back later," I said and hung up.

That evening I called my father back. He answered and he sounded like he was having a party. He was almost always alone, so this caught me by surprise. He was full of excitement, going on like a young man about to find his treasure map and strike out on adventure.

"Fred and Pete found me," he said.

"What, Fred and Pete, who?" I questioned.

"You remember my roommates that I've always talked about, from the Hill School? Fred, I called him Bing, and Pete."

"Wow," I did remember. "Really?" I couldn't believe it either.

"They drove up today," he said, all excited.

"Let me give the phone to Fred, he wants to talk to you." I wasn't sure if they had been drinking or what; they were all so excited as I could hear the conversation going on in the background. Fred got on the phone.

"Chloe, this is Fred Bingham, your father calls me Bing."
Pete and I tracked down your father, and to our shock found
out how he had been living out here all these years. "We are just
blown away. I want you to know what a great man your father
is… he was some kind of fella back in the day and still is."

"Wow, thank you, Fred." I responded in shock myself at the
reunion.

"Chloe, your father tells me you're writing a book?"

"Yes, that's right, working my way through it right now," I said.

"Well, that's just great, it's an incredible story and I've only
heard bits and pieces of it. I'd like to connect you with my wife,
Barbara, who is an editor," he stated.

I took the serendipitous moment and realized the power in
all things. Here I had been a kid growing up in the middle of
nowhere with no connections and my father had connections to
every kind of person in the world.

"Sure, that would be great. Thank you, Fred." I felt both
tearful and giddy with my father's joy over his friends finding
him. "I'll be back in town and would love to meet you in person,"
Fred stated and he gave the phone back to my father.

I was speechless, full of emotion for my father, as I told him
goodnight.

I sat in my backyard looking for the stars that were harder
to see in the city. My father had left the world; he had made
every attempt to let go of all things worldly, but this connection
to others was so big, so real, so full of heart that nothing could
separate him.

God Whispers Many Things

It was my father's birthday, May 23. Spring was everywhere, gathering up the smells of poppies in the yards of my neighbor, the juniper berry full, and the mulberry spreading its wide leaves in the summer air. I had promised my father I would come up to see him. I had made that promise before, and sometimes didn't make it. Guilt rang at my insides with this. But today I was going to make it. I hadn't slept the night before because both my children were up. I called up a good friend of mine, Jeni McCormick. She was supposed to make the trip with me. She was an unusual girl from the backwoods of Texas; she would of course understand my father.

I had met Jeni while working at a call center as a health educator. I would be fired from that job, the only job I ever got fired from, after going out of scope of practice they said. I was supposed to do routine health checkups on clients all over the East Coast, by phone call. I went off the script too many times while helping a woman who'd found her husband was a cross dresser after twenty years of marriage. She didn't care about her blood pressure medication, because she would now have to die with this huge secret inside of her; she couldn't tell her children about their father. Of course I met her right in the heart of the matter and addressed her depression and anxiety over this. She later wrote me a letter that thanked me for saving her life, but I still got fired for going off script. It was a huge blessing to be fired from a place that cared about rules more than people, a place I never should have been to begin with, except for meeting Jeni.

I've always felt most at home with people who are unusual when viewed through the lens of typical American culture. Jeni was just that and over the years she became a second sister to me, connecting with me around the love of nature, spirit, goats, pigs, and anything wild and random. She liked visiting my father and met him right at the heart of the matter every visit. Jeni's mother and my father shared the same birthday, one of the many uncanny similarities in our lives.

The morning I was to leave for my dad's, I called her up, but she explained she was feeling sick and couldn't go.

I sat down on the chair, no one to help me drive or help with the kids if I went up, but *No*, a voice shouted at me, *you are not canceling on him*. I loaded the kids in the car, along with all the food I had prepared to take him. With tired eyes, I pushed back from the driveway. We made the drive and Jonah and Sofia slept for half of it.

"Hallelujah, daughter, you made it." His words were always affirming. His smile gleeful, his arms ready to scoop up Jonah and Sofia. His beard and his wide, sunken cheek-bones didn't seem to bother either of them. He was seventy-one today.

"Happy birthday, Dad," I said.

"Okay," he said. "You know, daughter, the Bible says if a man makes it to 70, he's lived a full life. Anything after that is an added blessing."

I moved quickly in gathering up the food from the back of the SUV, listening with one ear to what he was saying. The wind was blowing fiercely that day, making it hard to hear and lulling my heart back to childhood.

"Not sure how much longer God's going to keep me here."

I ignored this part of his words, feeling a pain inside when he said it. "Well, we still need you here," I said carrying a bag full of groceries inside the cabin. "We still need you here, Dad." Besides, my father had been struck by lightning three times in his life. *This old man always talked about death*, I thought, and *yet death never came for him*. I pushed aside any feelings over his talk of it being his time to go.

That afternoon we played in the sun on the front porch. Jonah walked the steps up and down, up and down, two-year-old little body with chubby legs carried him up the wooden steps I had played on all my childhood. Sofia ran in and out of the cabin door, the wind picking up and blowing her hair, her blue eyes still in the chaos of wind that rose around us. The sun beat down from a blue sky; the red clay beneath our feet was brilliant. Jonah put his hands in the dirt and I saw John's spirit of the past in his hands, in his eyes, while he lifted the dirt up and let it run through his fingers. *We are alive, we are alive, we are alive,* I thought.

We walked from the house to the well house where I used to play as a kid, running up and down the hillside, the fresh water freezing to the bone. We stopped at the well where my father now had an old bear-claw bathtub sitting out in the open, porcelain white, the sun shining brightly on it. He turned on the well and freezing water ran from the hose. Jonah and Sofia came to him and stuck their hands in the water, then their mouths. One at a time they came to drink, spilling water all over their clothes and bursting out in laughter. My father stood above them holding the hose.

We had talked about building a cabin for me and the kids right there in that very spot. My dad had spoken with a fella up in that area who sold pieces to build your own log cabin. We had talked about it for weeks. It would cost five thousand dollars to buy the pieces. If I could come up with the money, my father would help me build it. It was a dream—I would finally return home and bring my children into the woods of my childhood. Not full time, but on weekends and whenever we wanted to stay. I felt tears knotted in my throat and told my dad I needed to walk in the woods alone for a bit.

I walked down from the well house and through a thicket of trees. At the bottom of the hill there was a dried-out pond basin. It was filled with white yarrow flowers. I sat down in the patch of white-tipped flowers spread out all around me. The blue-green forest caved in on all sides of me, and blue-tinted sagebrush dotted the forest line. I looked out at the mass of land, the Mother Earth that had held me for so many years. I remembered Dad's story about the yarrow plant.

My father called yarrow *plumajia*, the plant that saves lives. When John was a boy, he twice had gotten a really high fever, so high his boyish body burned obviously; you could tell by just looking at him, red hot skin against blue eyes. My father knew he was going to die. After cold baths and washed clothes, he ran to the field of yarrow, picking the white flower as fast as he could. Then he ran home and boiled the flower, the whole time praying that God save the life of his son. John lay in the back room silent, breathing in and out slow breaths, Mom holding a washcloth to his forehead, the cloth burning up in her hands. Dad came in and held John's lips up to the tea, saying, "Drink, son, drink, son." He drank, and within minutes the whole cup was empty. The sun set and Mom held her hand upon her son's head, still the heat coming forth, so she prayed a silent prayer.

Dear God,
keep my son,
my first born,
hold him now,
make him whole,
don't take him
heaven has no place
for such a young soul

She lay next to him all night, silently praying between her wake and her sleep. When the morning light streamed through the forest, it revealed John's skin, and she saw in his face that the fever was gone.

I sat there in the field of yarrow, tears running down my face. *How is it, God, that he died anyway?* He lived to fifteen. I guess Heaven did have a place for such a young soul.

I felt God speak to me in spirit, saying, "Everyone has their time, dear child. You are allowed to mourn when their time has come, but you must give allowance for their transition."

I wiped my face and sat up from the dirt, dusting off my pant legs. I didn't want to hear God's message about letting those we love go. I walked back up the hill to my father. We stood in a circle amidst the trees, the piñon needles gathering around us. Jonah and Sofia stood looking at each other and broke out in song, a humming song that lasted five minutes. They held a tune and belted it from their lungs, strong and mighty from a two-year-old and a five-year-old. My father stood in awe, his right hand upon his wooden walking stick, tears streaming his old man face. Finally the two broke their song and looked up at him.

"It's an affirmation of faith, it's a true affirmation of faith, bless Jesus," he spoke out in glee, smiling from ear to ear.

"Happy Birthday, Dad," I whispered to myself.

That afternoon, we sat in coolness inside the cabin. Dad had a cell and with his new connection to the world he had been calling all his siblings and his father every Sunday. It was a Sunday afternoon and the phone rang. It was my grandfather Ira. I listened to the two of them speak, kind words flowing.

"How are you feeling today, Dad?" my father asked. The conversation went on for about ten minutes, to which I heard my father mention the cabin we were going to build, the kids and our visit. Then I caught the last bits of the conversation in which my father said to his father, "I don't know who will go first, you or me. I don't know how much longer I will make it, Dad," then came "I love you."

They were two very different men who had disagreed on much in their lives, but somewhere in the hours of grace they finally met each other, father to son and heart to heart. My father hung up the phone and sat down to play a new rendition of his song called Tres Palomas, *The Three Doves*. I watched his face as he played and lost track of the words, until one part of the song jumped out at me, "love is stronger than death." He sang it with a gleeful heart and then came the tears. Jonah and Sofia ran circles around him while he played; they were in the dance of life in the woods. The sun started to set as I loaded everyone into the car, I pushed back from the driveway as I had so many times, my father hanging onto the driver side while I backed up. I sat in acceptance of my father's words, in his blessing of Jesus on our lives, letting the car roll slowly backwards. Jonah and Sofia yelled out to him from the backseat, "Bye, Grandpa, bye Grandpa."

The Strongest Man in the Woods Has Fallen

I pulled into the driveway, the long, two-and-a-half hour drive settling in behind me, my hands still holding tight to the steering wheel of the car. Carey sat in the car next to me, his face wet and red from crying. As I pried my fingers from the wheel, my heart rose up from my chest and into my throat. I opened the car door, slid my left foot from the driver's seat, and pushed myself off the leather of the new Volvo SUV. My feet touched down on the ground; my mother, my father, the earth beneath me. My childhood home stood before me, tilted to the side from years of wear and tear. The little hunting cabin covered with deer antlers, the horse hitching post, and the water barrel collecting rain under the right side of the pitched roof. Behind the little hunting cabin, the larger, two-room cabin my father had built when I was four years old. Over the years it had accumulated many layers of hand-me-down pieces of red tin roofing, glass windows, pine vigas set in place to hold together the awkward, makeshift glass pieces strung together as a front porch on the cabin.

Evening was upon us. The sun was settling through the thicket of trees, three hundred and twenty acres of them stretched across the land, the wind blowing through silence. My heart remained in my throat as I made my way in front of the car. Carey stepped down from the SUV at the same time I did, meeting me at the front of the car, and we clasped hands. We slowly took steps toward the front door of the cabin, our bodies aligned, backs straight, both of us gathering strength.

Four hours earlier, I'd had plans. I was getting ready for my high school reunion. After weeks of deciding to go, then not to go, I finally had made up my mind. I would go, and blow them away with my slightly aged face, my slightly aged body, with my insides that had been broken apart by divorce, life, growth, change, love, and two children—but no one was going to see my insides. I'd keep them protected well by wearing a fitted white dress with orange flowers scattered about, paired with a pair of cowboy boots to represent my past and the present, to show nothing gets this girl down. I had it covered. I would march in there with a "life is good" smile on my face. It had been four weeks since that last visit to my father's on his birthday.

I drove down the two-lane stretch of highway in Santa Fe, the brilliant New Mexico sky above me, the cars, the air, the streetlights all aligned to my needs making it a smooth drive. My cell phone rang. I picked it up, Carey's voice on the end of the line. The transmission was clear, but he stumbled through loud sobs to speak.

"I am sorry to call you like this, Chlo. I am sorry—

"Dad died."

I clutched the steering wheel and held the phone to my ear. My chest welled, my body rose with heat all over, my mind searched for the meaning in his words.

"What? What? What do you mean, he died?"

"Someone hiked up to the property and found his body. Some young kid from the farm down below."

I drove through traffic without any awareness of driving the car, tears poured through my heavy breath, my chest wheezing in and out, in and out.

"Well, did they check him, did they check his body? How do they know he is dead?"

"Yes, Chloe, the kid saw him face down. Looks like he fell."

I weaved through traffic with my body now floating in pain, confusion, and disbelief.

My brother cleared his throat. "Todd is on his way up there now to check on the scene." His voice now steady, he said he would call me back and hung up.

I pulled the car to the right lane, the traffic zooming past me, a dizzy spinning motion inside and outside. Holding the phone in my right hand, I managed to call my childhood friend, Sage. We had reconnected some years back while both living in

Albuquerque. She was now a doctor and the most familiar place I could go with my grief. She answered. I wept into the phone trying to speak. Sage was always calm and I think that's why I called her. "My Dad, died." "My Dad, died." I repeated the words to her. There was a short pause and then she asked me where I was. I'm driving down the street in Santa Fe. "Chlo, you need to get off the road right now." "Look for a place to pull the car over," she repeated, as if it were her only task at the moment. I searched for a parking lot to pull into and made a right turn, the sun blaring through the back window onto my head. I stopped and cut the engine.

I let Sage know that I had parked, and then started to weep. She kept her composure and asked me a few questions. I couldn't hear her words, everything was a blur around me. She probably said, *I'm sorry*. She probably said, *it's going to be okay*. She probably asked what I knew. She probably said, *I'll call my dad right now and see if he can go up there and check on your dad*. The five minutes of the call evaporated into thin air while I tried to get breath into my lungs.

"Dad. Dad."

I wept, my body convulsing as I leaned over into the steering wheel. My hands fell to my side, I breathed through my tears.

"Dad. Oh, Dad."

I saw his old-man face, his gray beard, the wrinkles under his brown eyes, his swollen feet, and then his young-man face, chiseled high cheek bones, brown hair, brown eyes. I felt his heart pumping blood through his body, as my heart pumped blood through my body. I felt the earth and all that he was upon the earth: strong, brave, troubled, complex, dark, light, fearful, and joyful. I saw his guitar in the corner near his chair where he played every evening. I pulled my head back from the steering wheel, wiped my wet face, and thought about what I should do.

It was around four o'clock on a summer's evening in New Mexico. Three hours till sunset. *I would drive straight to the mountain and check his body*, my mind flashed. There was no other choice.

The phone rang. Carey spoke on the other end and this time he was more centered.

"I think we need to go there, Chlo. I think we need to go to his body and figure out what to do." He had no burial plans, other than he had told Carey he wanted to be buried next to John there on the property.

Pruning Knife – Peace Maker

Pruning Knife – Peace Maker is the name my father had
given himself years back when he left the civilized world.
He had been on the mountain for forty years, no plan for his
death, and no plans for his life.

"God willing," he would say if he was to head into town
for a visit. "God willing, I will see you, daughter."

He was a warrior, a hunter, a protector of spiritual law.
Living half in this life and half in the next. He wanted to be
something different, something beyond his time. One evening,
he walked along a cliff ridge, watching the colors of the land
fade into darkness below. A bow and arrow was slung over
his shoulder. They had called him straight arrow since the day
of his birth. He had the straightest shot in the village, never
missed his mark. His father thought he would be one of the
greats of his time. He never missed a day of hunting, the fresh
kill, the cold body in stillness, the soul retreated, it was a part
of life. But always he had one hand in this life and one in
the next.

Deep inside he wanted to be a peaceful man. He wanted to
lay down his bow and arrow. Thoughts of this would come and
go, swept out by the wind, always pressing on and knowing that
few would understand what he truly wanted. To lie peacefully
in a field of green grass with arms stretched opened to the
heavens, the soul in one piece, for once. He wanted to lie next
to the deer, wrap his arms around it, and feel its heartbeat, *ba
boom, ba boom, ba boom.* He would rather be alone than take
one more life. He'd given up on anger and rage; he'd stopped
battling the world around him many years ago. He called to

his God, the one he wanted others to know, and laid down his bow and arrow once and for all.

Too much of the time I was too busy with my life to visit my father on the mountain, busy being a student in college, busy being a twenty-year old running around trying to figure out who I was, busy letting go of my past and trying to hold onto a future.

On moonlit nights, I could feel my father praying for me. I could feel his faith piercing through the night air, reaching down to me in my broken state, cupping large hands around my heart, trying to make it better the only way he knew how.

The first time I had seen myself completing my book, I had a vision of him sitting beside me at a reading, with me mouthing the words of my past and him playing his guitar. I could feel his smiling from beneath his soul as he sang, and I knew that someday we would stand together united in this world with a message, to make the world a better place by being who we truly were.

That dream is over, my mind flashed as I sat stuck to my car seat in the heated parking lot in Santa Fe, New Mexico. My numb insides pried at me to make a decision. It was time to go back on the mountain one last time. The strength of the little girl who rode a horse at five, who saddled and ran through the woods day or night, that little girl was going to get her father.

Now I was on the mountain, this was happening, and my mind refused to reconcile the truth. I thought I would open the cabin door and scoop my father up into my arms. Carey approached the house with me trailing my big brother by two steps. The porch door was slightly cracked open. Carey's hand reached for the door to pull it open.

"Oh, man, looks like it's been a few days." His words caught me at the same time as my eyes caught a glimpse of my father's leg. It was purple and swollen.

"Oh, Dad," Carey repeated to himself. Dad, Dad, Dad…" Carey's voice trailed in the wind.

I couldn't speak any words, standing beside Carey as I viewed my father's whole body, from feet to head, his arms tucked tight under his chest. *His heart*, my mind raced, *it was his heart*. My body heaved, shaking, sweat on my fingers and hands. *It's just the body*, I repeated in my head, but my stomach had been punched so hard, the punch hitting all the way back up my spine, carving me out to emptiness. I looked my father over one time, stopping at his head where a pool of blood circled around him. He was face down, his left cheek against the cement porch floor, his baseball cap just a few inches from his head, his feet stretched out long behind him. *It's just the body, it's just the body*, I repeated and stepped away. *That was enough*, I told myself, there was no reason to look any closer. My feet dragged me away from the scene, heavy, beaten pulsing inside my shoes, the child within not knowing what to do next.

I went around the other side of the house, the opposite side of where his body lay. I sat on the camel saddle that was there on the front porch. He had ridden a camel in Egypt at twelve years old on this saddle. I sat there looking across at his body, working with all my being to communicate to him.

"You did good, Dad. You did good. I got all the lessons."

"I got it. We love you. We always loved you. You did good."

I felt the weight of a thousand years lifted from my father's body. I felt him weightless for the first time ever. I sobbed and sobbed. I listened while Carey walked in and out of the door, tracing what would have been my father's last steps. Carey was a warrior, the boy inside crushed, but the man in physical form looking for the cause of death. He traced my father's steps where he found a screwdriver dropped just outside of the door. One of my father's sandals had come off his foot while the other was still on. There was no sign of struggle; it looked like he had fallen straight to the ground while clasping at his chest. Carey stood over his body, able to look past the blood and discoloration right into the heart of death. I couldn't stomach the heart of death. I had to go to nature with it and listen for the inner voice of guidance.

It was 8:30 p.m., minutes before sunset. The summer night air cooled the back of my neck, as I walked back behind the house. I stood alone in the thicket of piñon trees. I let my arms fall to the side and let myself fall into the late sinking sun, keeping my eyes fixed on the horizon. I wept, wept, and wept, years of sorrow pulling blood from my body. *I'm alive, I'm alive, I'm alive, and you are not*, Daddy. All the years I had missed my father came up through my body in that moment. The last line of the evening sun was fading away, the green tree branches cradled me. I felt something moving in around me, the presence of my father and God all wrapped like a woven blanket. A stillness like none I have ever felt came over me, my tears stopped, and a voice sounded in my body, and through the air.

"It's only my body, daughter, I'm right here, you have to let go of my body." I listened, a small child heading the words of truth.

"Okay, Dad," I mumbled back. My mind flashed on my memoir that I was hoping to finish this summer. How will I ever finish this book with you gone, Dad? I asked this question in silence. The sun was now gone, the silhouette of the trees barely visible. I felt my father's final embrace, the blanket wrapped even tighter around me and the words,

You and I are the message, daughter.

Then the blanket holding me unraveled and up it went into the night sky.

The Soulful Child didn't die. She didn't crumble beneath the loss of the cold and sometimes frozen ground. She looked and looked for the red berries no matter where she went in life. She looked toward the sun, even on the darkest of days. When she couldn't feel her own heartbeat, she kept her eye upon the blood of Christ, the red blood of the cross. She was guided, led, and transformed. When the broken pieces inside of her were brought back to life, she took the pieces to her mom and dad, and said, "Here, I forgive you," and "I understand you." I have felt your loss, your sorrow, and your burden. I have also felt the gift you planted inside of me. Know this, Mama and Papa, I will take my gift and share it with the world.

Epilogue

I did not make it here by chance, I learned the dance of life from so many. My journey has brought me to the other side of the mountain where I stand in awe at the miracle of it all.

The Pack All Grown Up

My brothers are much like my father in that they are independent thinkers, strong and expressive; you know right off if they like or don't like something.

Carey went to college. He studied environmental science initially and then found the bitter taste of all that was happening to the earth, through and by the destruction of man. His heart could not follow that path and he changed his major to wildlife and forestry; this was close enough to his heart and yet he could make a living in the world. He never took a job working for someone else. He decided to become a landscaper, to run his own business, putting plants into the ground and making people's lives more beautiful by bringing nature to them. It was fitting, I thought. Carey needed to be his own boss and he needed to touch the earth everyday. He was a boy born with bare feet in the dirt, living among the woods and counting every bird, listening like a wolf with sharp ears for every sound. Wearing his heart on his sleeve, he has made a place in the world.

Nye has always been physically strong, outspoken, and independent. Something inside of Nye was more sensitive, though. A deep well of truths boiled from his roots and as he worked to bring them to the surface, sometimes they would come boiling over. He played rugby like a lion and ran all the steam out of him. He was trying to make amends with his past and fully embrace himself. After many injuries, and a full-blown knee surgery, he looked to food and yoga to heal his body. No more yelling down the field; he had to go inward to heal his body and mind. He carried my father's torch of wanting the people of the world to be free of ignorance, eat real food, put real medicine in their minds, and stand against worldly greed and destruction. The whole pack was looking for a way to balance our connection to nature while living in the world. Nye found it in food, in growing and cooking his own. He produced his own nutrition bar, called a Nye Bar. Now You're Energized. It's a truly balanced superfood bar that will revolutionize the world of unhealthy eating and obesity. Nye is always designing ways to bring a healthy truth to people's mouths and hearts.

Rose. My sister has grown into one of the strongest women I know. She studied biology and anthropology in college, was a college athlete and at the top of her class. Rose has walked her own path to wholeness, finding her connection in travel and nature. Out of college she lived in South Korea and traveled all around Nepal and Cambodia, a young woman alone with her backpack. For eighteen days, she trekked the Annapurna Circuit in the Himalayas of central Nepal, with a guide. The highest point crosses a pass (Thorung La) at 17,769 feet. On the trail she passed grown men who had to stop when out of breath. Her lungs had been developed at high altitude and her will was a sharpened ax when it came to challenge. She later lived in the south of Spain for two years. I traveled to see her and together we drove all over the olive grove hillsides into the flat seabeds of southern Spain and down into Portugal. We watched the sunset from the other side of the world. We had never forgotten the story of Flicka, Ricka, and Dicka and now we knew the power of being a girl—we lived it every day. When Rose returned to the States, her courageous heart and fire for life led her to become a commercially certified pilot. The young girl with porcelain hands, who spoke little, who sat and observed life, had grown up to fly.

There was not one of us who found it harder to be on earth than Jacinth. The youngest of us, he loved the woods. He was much like my father in his wild nature and spirit—you couldn't tell that boy what to do! Jacinth struggled living with Ida, the last of our pack to leave her, and upon his final high school years he moved to Albuquerque to live with Carey and Nye. A kind, generous spirit, always reading books and swaying in a hammock, he wasn't much for the world and seemed to have one foot here and one foot in the spiritual world. He fell in love and experimented with drugs, much like my father did at his age, early twenties. Somewhere on his ride of learning to let go, learning to be free, learning to greet every man as equal, because that he was good at, he lost himself. His world is one of its own, one I will not put any worldly labels upon. As I lean into spirit for understanding his life, he is a brother dear, no matter where he goes. Someday I hope he will tell his story. It's a story needing to be heard in this culture, in this land in which we lack insight into the full capacities of the human mind.

I majored in psychology in college to figure myself out and fix anything that might be broken. I had a dream of fixing others too. I worked with kids as an experiential educator, leading them on high ropes courses and into the woods to face their problems. I wrote poetry and brought my soul back to life. I did plenty of running from my past, but kept the door to my heart cracked opened. I adored my father and longed to mend our brokenness for many years. My true calling was to write and once I broke though my fear of not being a good enough writer, writing became the song of my life.

In 2013, I started a writing business with the intention of changing lives though the power of story. My father had come into town for a rare visit and was standing in my kitchen one evening, the two of us enjoying a late-night talk. He reminded me of my earth name, Flowing Springs River, and said it was no surprise I had become such a good writer, the words flowed from me like water. The summer evening air breezed through the open window while he told me a story of an event just after my birth. He had a vision of me squatting beside the banks of a golden river, a toddler with my hands in the wet dirt, my hair blowing wildly, the golden river split into wings up ahead of me. "Your pen name is the Winged River Writer," he said. I felt his words deep like any and all of his truths. The name of my business would become the Winged River Writer.

My siblings each have walked their own path. I witnessed the love and warrior-like cause in each of them to find a way to live in the world and find their honest place with my parents. I saw Nye give bear hugs to my father, like only a lion and a bear could do if they had become best friends. Carey more than any of us became a friend to my father; they both laid down their bow and arrow to be on the same team in life. My pilgrimage of forgiveness came through the telling of my story and sharing my journey with my father. Rose's connection to Ida and her past has helped her to become a strong role-model for women. Teaching us that we are strong and wise beyond gender identities. I hope that, much like it has been for me, the birth of her children has brought her home to some of the gifts she was given by her life experience. Jacinth is wise and has always had a connection to my father, one that cannot be explained. He rides the wild horse in his mind and Dad rides right along with him.

My mother has become a source of knowledge and under-standing over the years. She spent many years unraveling her past while I was building my future. I held the intimate moments of time in my hand when my mother told me stories of herself and my father. She was my main source and support in the writing of this book. She finally came into herself, finding a place in the world. She plays her music in coffee shops under stage name of Holly Hock and has proven that at any age you can be unstoppable.

My father spent the later part of his years letting us go. Learning to love without control, learning to send prayer as the only line of communication. While he was letting each of us go, we in turn were working like miners to unearth the lessons we had learned. I can't give the exact story for my siblings. I did the best I could to tell my story and bring light to all of our lives. They each had their own journey, including Matt, who grew up so differently, but with no less of a struggle, just a different one.

Then there are "my three teachers." My grandmother, Ogreta, my uncle, Victor, and my foster mother, Ida, were all teachers. They dedicated their lives to developing and enriching young minds and hearts. They were each a thread of hope, inspiration, and knowledge-seeking for me. When I graduated from college, my Grandma Ogreta was still alive, but she had lost most of her memory. I wanted to run to her and tell her that I had made it in the "real" world, but her frailness was evident, and the look in her eyes was distant. I sat across from her in a final visit, telling her of who I had become, and she stared back at me with no words. I held on to her hand, wishing for every vibration of my body to remind her of our journey together. Victor continues to play an important role in my life, supporting my goals and aspirations in my search. He is still a classroom teacher in a progressive school in the East, while keeping up with all of us out West.

Ida, my second mother who brought grace to me in the most unexpected way at the most unpredictable time, has been a part of my life in every way since the first day that I came to her home with Rose. She remains as close to me as a phone call away, a prayer in the night, a gentle soul with complete acceptance of who I am. Ida has taught me the greatest of lessons: love and compassion will heal the brokenness of the world.

Much of my journey has been graced with my extended family who became more and more a part of my life after we left the woods. I got to know my grandmother, Sally, the one I begged not to drive away on the day we buried my brother. She was a pillar of strength and grace, planting her flowerbeds in spring. Her silver hair had become white, her eyes still a piercing blue as she gave me her poems and showed me another world. My grandparents Ira and Sally moved first to Pagosa Springs, Colorado, where they had a beautiful ranch with horses. Their home was everything of perfection, the high ceilings with pine vigas and a stone wall fireplace where the light that danced from floor to ceiling gave new meaning to the idea of home. Every tablecloth, cup, saucer, and piece of furniture was delicately placed in their home, making it a sacred space to walk on bare feet. My grandmother cooked and wore a red apron that made the world seem pure and lovely. My grandfather was strong and devout in his beliefs. I had many questions for them about their relationship with my father, but never asked. Some questions cannot be answered.

The more I observed my family the more I realized we were

all asking the questions, about my father's choices and about our own lives. I was getting an education every time I saw them. I somehow understood that perfection wasn't perfect and inside of their love for me I saw everything that mattered most. They later moved to Albuquerque, New Mexico, to be closer to me and my siblings. Knowing my grandparents helped me to see a wider picture of my family and of the world at large.

My Aunt Cynthia, my dad's sister, also moved to Albuquerque, and brought with her my two cousins, Nicholas and Jessica. I was certain we were all related; it was hard to get a word in edgewise, with all of us in one room. The voices of family rose and fell around the beautifully set table every Thanksgiving we shared at my aunt's house. She was clearly her mother's daughter, as the saucers, plates, and tablecloths were all matching and placed delicately to reflect a home that had fineness and style. It was like nothing I had grown up with and so again I was getting an education. My biggest education of all was that families come in all shapes and sizes. Ours was not perfect but it was LOVE that made us a family.

We were still family if we had never met. Later in life I connected with two of my cousins I had never spent time with, my uncle Timothy Harold's kids, Genevieve and Adam. Gen was my age and oh, the life she had lived. I had a few rare moments to feel her past, her beating heart upon the page; she too was a writer and told me story through her writing. I learned that we were all broken at times, but okay in the deep depths of sorrow that had visited us over the years, we on the mountain and them in the world. There was a connective tissue running through each of us, the longing for connection and answers was widespread in this family. I hope that some of my answers will bring meaning to my family.

I am certain that John is a part of our pack and has always been. Across the great divide of spiritual planes, he has visited me, comforted me, guided me, and led me to a truth beyond the seeing and hearing in this life. I'm still gathering the lessons from both John and my father, the two of them now in the same place. With each insight the song that is life gets more and more clear, "death is not the final chorus."

Acknowledgments

Where do I begin when thinking of how this book came to life? It all began when my daughter, Sofia (Little Wisdom), was born. Somehow her birth and life, gave me the courage to find out what my childhood had been about. Next came my son, Jonah (Little Dove). Along this journey he kept reminding me that we each have a soulful child inside and it is within the precious moments of life that we are molded to being human. I want to thank Christian, Sofia and Jonah's father, for giving me the most treasured gift, the two of them, as well as for lending his support of my being a writer. In the early stages of my writing, Christian helped me to see that I could be in the big leagues among any of the famous actors, writers, and artists of our time.

Writing a memoir requires much on a soul level, combined with the craft of writing, and I want to thank Connie Josefs and Jennifer Lauck, both of whom led me down the path to telling great story by understanding the mechanics of the writing process. Jennifer Lauck gave me hope on the coast of Oregon, where my dreams began to unfold. I too could write a bestseller, it was becoming clear in the midst of Oregon fog. Tom Bird, the Book Whisperer, held space and guidance for me in both his Sedona and Santa Fe retreats, connecting me deeply to the soulful child within.

Heloise Jones is an author, writer, and insightful writing coach that I connected with many years ago at the beginning of my writing journey. I was fortunate in that, years later, she returned to Santa Fe, where we collided in still moments, in the beautiful corridors of a large rustic casita with a Zen garden to envelop my heart while I wrote. She helped me to seek the hidden potential in my story and bring it home.

Mother Nature was my truest teacher in all forms. I want to thank the trees that held me, the wind that caressed over my shaken body when I wrote my most challenging scenes for this story, the soil beneath my feet, the land that I grew up on. The sacred land of my childhood embraced every part of me as I embraced my being a writer while sitting in the middle of the woods.

I'm grateful in the most unfamiliar ways to my writers who are currently on the path to voicing their truth, while allowing me to guide them in telling their stories. Every one of you has made an impact on me. To my trio of writers, Bonnie Bassan, Kevin Scott Day, and Helene Brongniart Rojas: you have changed my life, becoming a part of my wholeness as we rode the evening skies with pens in our hands. Together we formed stories, created magic, and told truths that someday the world will hear.

To my dearest longtime friends who have supported my becoming a writer, Marlene Gallegos, Lindsay Worth, Jeni McCormick, and Tenille Otero. Thank you for hearing my stories over and over and helping me to make sense of them all.

My deepest heartfelt thanks to each of Ida's children, Sug, Tim, Steph, and Eric, for sharing your mother with us. Perhaps it didn't feel like much of a choice, because Ida is Ida and extends herself beyond measure to help others. Know that I have thought of each of you and live in gratitude that we got to experience the rhythm of love through your mother.

To my publisher and editor, Penelope Love, from Citrine Publishing, there are no accidents. We were brought together by fate, love, and faith, and our friend Beverley Golden. You and I have crossed the bridge of literacy together, forming meaning and power around this book, around the voice of the soulful child. I graciously thank you, for being you, for standing in your intuition combined with your knowledge and understanding of the industry to bring forward the best in all story.

To Steve Thurson, you have been a guiding light, a force of love that wrapped around me in the ups and downs of birthing this book. Your love was the one true constant that was there every morning. For every teardrop that fell, you held it all together, reminding me of who I am at the core. There is no greater gift than the love you have given me in these past few years.

My life has been a dream unfolding and along the way I have met many who are part of the dream. Barbra Zuckerman Portzline, the newest member in my unfolding dream, has led me to a wonderful group of women. I want to thank my Polka Dot Powerhouse sisters for bringing me into their club of women supporting women to become fully empowered in business and in life. I have felt truly at home with you. I'm grateful for your connection to my story and your support in passing the torch of its inner wisdom.

For all my pre-readers, I can't name all of you, but know that I am deeply connected to each of you. I'm entirely grateful for your connection this book. I know it would not be the same without you. You are the ones helping me bring this book into the world, helping me to see its release through in a most profound and connected way, giving rise to this story straight from the heart.

And finally, this book would not have been possible without the support of my mother and my older brother, Carey. Carey helped me to sort through so many memories and events, bringing me back to vitally important ideas and moments around this book. I thank you for your big heart and desire to bring the truth through in this story. My mother was by my side in both the literary sense and as a champion of making sense of the pieces of our lives that were torn at the seams. She helped me sew them back together in my heart and with words. Thank you, Mama.

The Pack

From left to right:
Nye, Rose, Carey, Chloe, John, and Jacinth, 1983

Photo by Victor Stekoll

About the Author

Author and intuitive writing coach Chloe Rachel Gallaway is the founder of The Winged River Writer and author of *The Soulful Child: Twelve Years in the Wilderness*, a memoir of her childhood through age twelve in the wilderness of Northern New Mexico. Chloe's unusual life of growing up deeply connected to nature and spirit has led her to a unique process of intuitively connecting to writing. The writing of this memoir became the foundation for her business and empowered her to become a warrior for helping others to find the truth in their story. A big believer in the power of owning our voice, Chloe is leading the VOICES book series™ movement, helping people become writers who show up with their heart-centered message in the world.

As a mentor and facilitator of the writing process, Chloe is unlike anyone in the industry. She combines her experience of growing up in the wilderness with her training in mindfulness tools and literary writing techniques to deliver a powerful process of self-transformation and empowerment through writing. She helps her people move from fear to courage, and from doubt to confidence, in mastering the dance between craft and intuition. For detailed information about her programs and retreats, visit ChloeRachelGallaway.com and VoicesMovement.org.

Thank you for reading *The Soulful Child*. Please pass the torch of connection by helping other readers find this book. Here are some suggestions for your consideration:

- Write an online customer review wherever books are sold

- Gift this book to family and friends

- Share a photo of yourself with the book on social media and tag #ChloeRachelGallaway and #TheSoulfulChild

- Bring in Chloe as a speaker for your club or organization

- Suggest *The Soulful Child* to your local book club, and download the *Book Club Discussion Questions* from www.CitrinePublishing.com/bookclubs

- For group orders of ten books or more, contact Citrine Publishing at (828) 585-7030 or Publisher@CitrinePublishing.com

- Connect with Chloe Rachel Gallaway online by visiting ChloeRachelGallaway.com and VoicesMovement.org

Printed in Great Britain
by Amazon

46493179R00196